D1256015

The Midrash

The Midrash:
An Introduction

JACOB NEUSNER

Jason Aronson Inc.
Northvale, New Jersey
London

The **Library of Classical Judaism** is a series of five volumes by Dr. Jacob Neusner.

The Mishnah: An Introduction
The Midrash: An Introduction
The Yerushalmi—The Talmud of the Land of Israel:
                 An Introduction
The Babylonian Talmud: An Introduction
The Tosefta: An Introduction

Copyright © 1990 by Jacob Neusner

10 9 8 7 6 5 4 3 2 1

All rights reserved. Printed in the United States of America. No part of this book may be used or reproduced in any manner whatsoever without written permission from Jason Aronson Inc. except in the case of brief quotations in reviews for inclusion in a magazine, newspaper, or broadcast.

Library of Congress Cataloging-in-Publication Data

Neusner, Jacob, 1932-
    The Midrash : an introduction / Jacob Neusner.
      p. cm.
    Includes bibliographical references.
    ISBN: 0-87668-740-0 (series)
    ISBN 0-87668-814-8
    1. Halakhic Midrashim—Introductions. 2. Midrash rabbah. Genesis—Introductions. 3. Midrash rabbah. Ruth—Introductions. 4. Midrash rabbah. Song of Solomon—Introductions. I. Title.
BM514.N482 1990
296.1′41—dc20
                                         89-18274
                                           CIP

Manufactured in the United States of America. Jason Aronson Inc. offers books and cassettes. For information and catalog write to Jason Aronson Inc., 230 Livingston Street, Northvale, New Jersey 07647.

For
Étienne and Ann Trocmé
Strasbourg, France

A token of thanks
to dear and cherished friends and colleagues
for hospitality beyond all imagining
on a splendid day in Paris
February 13, 1990

Contents

PART II

THE FOURTH- AND FIFTH-CENTURY COMPILATIONS

The Earlier Rabbah Midrashim

PART III

THE SIXTH- AND SEVENTH-CENTURY COMPILATIONS

The Later Rabbah Midrashim

Preface

When people refer to "the Midrash," they generally refer to a collection of interpretations of a scriptural passage. So "the Midrash says" means, "this is what the Torah means in this particular verse." The word "Midrash," which uses the root DaRaSH and hence means "search" in Hebrew, speaks of the same thing that the word "interpretation" or "exegesis" does in English. "Midrash" also stands for a compilation of such interpretations, as in the title of a collection of such documents called Midrash Rabbah, which covers Midrash-compilations for the Pentateuch and the Five Scrolls (Ruth, Esther, Lamentations, Song of Songs, Kohelet/Ecclesiastes), biblical books read in the synagogue liturgy. And, finally, "Midrash" may speak of the particular approach to interpretation, or exegesis, taken by Judaic sages.

All of these equally valid meanings attached to the word Midrash treat the various interpretations by sages of Judaism as pretty much uniform in time and place of origin; all of the documents as interchangeable in their approach and message; all of the specific interpretations of verses as essentially saying the same thing, only about a different verse or subject; hence, "the Midrash says." Along these lines, people may say, "it's a Midrash," to imply, "it's a fanciful meaning imputed to a simple verse," or to just refer to a story (for which, in Hebrew, the word is *aggadah*). Given the variety of meanings imputed to the word Midrash, a whole range of questions may arise. In this book, I promise to accomplish only one of many valid tasks in introducing "the Midrash." It is to set forth the Midrash-compilations that reached closure and conclusion in the formative age of Judaism, that is, the first seven centuries of the Common Era, the time in which the Mishnah (c. 200), Talmud of the Land of Israel (c. 400), and Talmud of Babylonia (c. 600) were written. I have translated (or retranslated) all of these compilations of Midrash-exegeses of Scripture. In these pages I mean to make it possible for readers to recognize one such compilation from another and so to begin studying on their own.

The bibliography covers my translations and studies of the Midrash. It includes other introductions I have written to these same writings, each serving its own purpose of exposition on a given thesis and problem, none repeating the others in any material way. Introductions, of course, may accomplish diverse purposes for various readerships; I intend this introduction to serve as the first step in the approach to one of the most important kinds of holy books of Judaism. When readers have completed the account of each document and sizable sample offered here, they should be able to explore on their own the writings of our sages of blessed memory, who taught us how to read the Hebrew Scriptures as the written part of the Torah.

For the sages wrote *with* Scripture, by which I mean that the received Scriptures formed an instrumentality for the expression of a writing bearing its own integrity and cogency, appealing to its own conventions of intelligibility, and, above all, making its own points. Any notion that the authorships (those who collected and compiled the materials now formed into a document), of Judaism proposed a systematic exegesis of Scripture conducted in terms of the original or historical program of Scripture, or appealed to Scripture for validation or vindication of doctrine or practice perceived as independent of Scripture, distorts the character of the discourse of Judaism. Scripture formed part of the Torah. The authorships of Judaism, particularly in late antiquity, also participated in the discourse and statement of the Torah. They did not write *about* Scripture, they wrote *with* Scripture, for Scripture supplied the syntax and grammar of their thought, hence, "writing with Scripture."

In this context, we understand, Scripture served as testimony and testament. It accomplished important purposes in the formation and expression of a larger, wholly cogent statement. But it constituted a subordinated and merely instrumental entity; not the court of last appeal and final judgment, not the ultimate source of truth and validation, except—of course—after the fact. The fact found expression in the figure of the sage, in the model of Moses, our rabbi. People commonly suppose that when Judaic or Christian authorships turned to Israelite Scripture, it was in search of proof-texts. The relationship was "exegetical" (getting meaning out of the text) or "eisegetical" (reading meaning into the text). But when our sages of blessed memory proposed to compose their statements, and while they, of course, appealed to Scripture, it was an appeal to serve a purpose defined not by Scripture but by a faith under construction and subject to articulation. Scripture formed a dictionary, providing a vast range of permissible usages of intelligible words. Scripture did not dictate the sentences that would be composed through the words found in that (limited) dictionary. Much as painters paint with a palette of colors, authorships wrote with Scripture. The paint is not the picture. In terms of this book, "the Midrash" is a vast painting, begun in the age in which the Judaism of the dual Torah took shape, continued from then to now. But the painting is made up of a large number of completed paintings, a collage of perfect compositions. In these pages we examine the earliest parts of the vast composite, the Midrash.

We do so through the simple device of introductions to the various books, covering subject matter and general points of interest, and then sizable abstracts from each of the Midrash-compilations. The introductions deal with the traits of the documents before us, but not with questions such as origin, authorship, context, and history, as they are anonymous, and reach us through a long process of copying and recopying, the evidences of which we do not now possess. All we know are the traits of the writings in their final condition, and these are the traits to which I mean to call attention. If we know for sure that the named authorities to whom sayings are attributed really said what they are alleged to have said and did what they are supposed to have done, then of course we should possess considerably more information than we do about these writings and the age that produced them. What we cannot show we do not know; we cannot demonstrate the validity of attributions or the veracity of narratives, and hence in these pages we focus upon the things we do know. I maintain that, given the fundamentally religious program of the Midrash-compilations, their plan of setting forth, through Scripture, the Torah revealed by God to Moses, our rabbi, at Sinai, we learn from what we know that which we should want to find out. That concerns how our sages of blessed memory understood Scripture, for the documents as we have them provide ample and perfectly reliable evidence about the faith of our sages of blessed memory—their faith and how that faith taught them to read Scripture as testimony to the Torah.

The program of the book is very simple. In the prologue I show why it is important to read each document on its own and not as part of a single undifferentiated literature, "the Midrash." Then in the eleven chapters that follow, I present introductions and selections for each of the principal compilations of the formative age of Judaism. The bibliography lists other writings of mine on these topics, and each of those books contains ample reference to studies other than mine, of the same literature and their problems.

It remains to explain the notation system that I have invented for the representation of the rabbinic literature. In ancient times punctuation as we know it was unknown. We supply punctuation to make the ancient texts accessible to ourselves. Originally, there was no indication of sentences or paragraphs or chapter-headings. Until now, modern translations have presented chapters and paragraphs and sentences, but have not indicated, through a notation system, how we may conveniently refer to them. I mark what we should call a chapter with a Roman numeral, which always corresponds to the enumeration system of the texts as printed in Hebrew. I then use an Arabic numeral to mark a paragraph, and a lettter to mark an individual sentence. In this way I not only make ready reference possible, I also indicate what I conceive to be the smallest whole units of thought, which we call sentences; these are sets of words that hold together to make a single coherent statement, that is, a statement of fact; any further division within those sets of words will not yield a coherent statement at all, hence the lettered components of a composition. These groups of sentences ordinarily form coherent statements, which we should call paragraphs. The composites of lettered sentences then are marked with an Arabic numeral, which indicates that, in my judgment, the components form a cogent whole. Then the groups of such composites form a still larger one, and that is, as I said, the one marked by a Roman numeral. These notations therefore allow us to immediately perceive how a given composite is made up of its individual parts and how they relate to each other. No other translations of the rabbinic literature in any language provide notation system, which means that analysis of the translated document (all the more so the original Hebrew) is not possible. The advantages of my system are self-evident.

My thanks go to Arthur Kurzweil, editor at Jason Aronson Inc., with whom I have enjoyed working on this and other books. The advantage of his thoughtful criticism is evident on every page.

Prologue

Should we read "the Midrash" all together, without paying attention to the different Midrash-compilations and their interests, or should we study "the Midrash-compilations," one by one? In these pages I mean to lead you through the compilations one by one. Why do I think that is the right way to study Midrash? The reason is that, when we see how two compilations treat the same passage, we discover that they have nothing in common. The two authorships go their respective ways, with little to say to one another. They may be characterized as different people talking about different things to different people. That is because the approach of each set of exegetes to the base verse derives from a clearly defined program of inquiry, one that imposes its issues on the base verse but responds only to the verse's provision of exemplary detail. Accordingly, neither of the documents we shall see here merely assembles things people happen to have said. In the case of each document we can answer the question: Why this, not that? They are not compilations but compositions; seen as a group, therefore, they are not the same, lacking all viewpoint, serving a single undifferentiated task of collecting and arranging whatever was at hand. And that is why the only right way of studying these documents is to study them individually.

To show what is at stake in the approach taken here, we look at the documents one by one. We simply select a verse of Scripture—Numbers 7:1—and read it as two different compilations. The upshot is simple. We shall see that joining these very different readings obscures what was important to the two distinct authorships. We miss the distinctive message of each, and that means we really do not grasp what our sages of blessed memory wished to say to us. To homogenize is to miss the point. Let me make that proposition stick.

1

NUMBERS 7:1
SIFRÉ TO NUMBERS
PESIQTA DERAV KAHANA

In the present modest exercise, we compare the treatment of precisely the same verse by exegetes within the same religious world, that of the sages of the Judaism of the dual Torah, written and oral, who flourished between the third and sixth centuries C.E. In their shared reading of Numbers 7:1, "On the day when Moses had finished setting up the tabernacle . . . ," we see strikingly different approaches to what is important in the verse. The group of exegetes behind Sifré to Numbers, a close reading of selected passages of the book of Numbers possibly concluded c. 200–300, asks one set of questions, while the authorship of Pesiqta deRav Kahana (possibly, c. 450–500), finds a different point of interest in the same verse. As we shall see, it is difficult to relate the message of one to the other. This is a surprising result, since we have every reason to expect people who read Scripture within the same framework to seek in the same passage similar points of stress. If the theory was that the sages of the dual Torah differed profoundly on what required stress and what did not, the following comparison of exegeses—comparative midrash—would provide solid evidence. How to sort out the amazing differences in approach, emphasis, and inquiry between the authorship of Sifré to Numbers and of Pesiqta deRav Kahana remains a puzzle. I intend at this point only to raise the question of how both documents belong within the same canon and how we define canon, when the authoritative writings relate so slightly. The translations in both cases are my own.

I
Sifré to Numbers 44

The text we follow is *Sifré debe Rab. Sifré al sefer Bammidbar veSifré Zuta,* ed. by Haim Shaul Horovitz (Leipzig 1917) [series title: *Schriften, herausgegeben von der Gesellschaft zur Foerderung der Wissenschaft des Judentums. Corpus Tannaiticum. Sectio Tertia: Continens Veterum Doctorum ad Pentateuchum Interpretationes Halachicas. Pars Tertia. Siphre d'Be Rab. Fasciculus primus: Siphre ad Numeros adjecto Siphre Zutta. Cum variis lectionibus et adnotationibus. Edidit* H. S. Horovitz]. There is no complete English translation of the document prior to mine.[1] We do

---

[1]Jacob Neusner and William Scott Green, *Sifré to Numbers. An American Translation* (Atlanta: Scholars Press for Brown Judaic Studies, 1986), I–III. I and II are now in print, covering Pisqaot 1-116.

not know when the document came to closure. All the named authorities
belong to the age of the Mishnah, but we have no way of identifying the
authentic from the pseudepigraphic attributions. In the model of the
Tosefta,[2]—a demonstrably Amoraic document, a large portion of which
cites verbatim and comments on the Mishnah and so is post-mishnaic—we
may hardly assign the present composition to a period before the end of the
fourth century.[3] Sifré to Numbers makes use of two basic approaches; first,
the syllogistic composition, which rests on the premise that Scripture
supplies hard facts that generate syllogisms when properly classified. By
collecting and classifying facts of Scripture, therefore, we may produce
firm laws of history, society, and Israel's everyday life. The second maintains the fallibility of reason unguided by scriptural exegesis. Scripture
alone supplies reliable basis for speculation; laws cannot be generated
solely by reason or logic. That is the recurrent polemic of the document—a
point of interest completely outside of the imagination of the framers of
Pesiqta deRav Kahana, as we shall see. They are arguing about different
things, presumably with different people. Nothing in the program of
questions addressed to the Book of Numbers draws one group into alignment with the other: they simply do not raise the same questions or
produce congruent answers. Whether or not the exegetical–eisegetical
results can be harmonized is a separate question.[4]

XLIV:I

1. A. "On the day when Moses had finished setting up the tabernacle [and had anointed and consecrated it with all its furnishings and had anointed and consecrated the altar with all its

---

[2]I have demonstrated that fact in the systematic comparison of the Tosefta to the
Mishnah in my *History of the Mishnaic Law* (Leiden: E. J. Brill, 1974–1986), I–
XLIII, and in my *Tosefta. Translated from the Hebrew* (New York: Ktav, 1977–
1986), I–VI.

[3]Moses David Heer, *"Midrash,"* *Encyclopaedia Judaica* (Jerusalem: Keter Publishing Co., 1971). I have found no more authoritative statement on the present
view of the dates of all midrash–compilations than Heer's. It is a question that in
the future will have to be reopened.

[4]This question demands attention in a far wider context than the present one. It
is the issue that will require us to ask what we mean by the canon, and, more
important, what meanings inhere within the canon as a whole but not in some
one of its parts: what holds the whole together that is not stated in any one
component? I have no doubt whatsoever that the Judaism behind the systems of
the several components of the canon of the dual Torah awaits systematic and
rigorous definition, but at this writing I am uncertain how to proceed.

utensils, the leaders of Israel, heads of their fathers' houses, the leaders of the tribes, who were over those who were numbered, offered and brought their offerings before the Lord, six covered wagons and twelve oxen, a wagon for every two of the leaders, and for each one an ox, they offered them before the tabernacle. Then the Lord said to Moses, 'Accept these from them, that they may be used in doing the service of the tent of meeting, and give them to the Levites, to each man according to his service.' So Moses took the wagons and the oxen and gave them to the Levites]" (Numbers 7:1-6).

B. Scripture indicates that for each of the seven days of conse-crating the tabernacle, Moses set up the tabernacle, and every morning he would anoint it and dismantle it. But on that day he set it up and anointed it, but he did not dismantle it.

C. R. Yose b. R. Judah: "Also on the eighth day he set it up and dismantled it, for it is said, 'And in the first month in the second year on the first day of the month the tabernacle was erected' (Exodus 30:17). On the basis of that verse we learn that on the twenty-third day of Adar, Aaron and his sons, the tabernacle and the utensils were anointed."

This is the focus of interest: the meaning of the word KLH, that is, "completed," and the same point will be made in Pesiqta deRav Kahana. But here it is the main point, since the exegete proposes to say what he thinks the simplest sense of the verse is. The second compilation of exegeses, by contrast, treats the matter in a much richer and more imaginative way.

XLV:I

2. A. On the first day of the month the tabernacle was set up, on the second the red cow was burned [for the purification rite required in Numbers 19], on the third day water was sprinkled from it in lieu of the second act of sprinkling, and the Levites were shaved.

B. On that same day the Presence of God rested in the taberna-cle, as it is said, 'Then the cloud covered the tent of meeting, and the glory of the Lord filled the tabernacle, and Moses was not able to enter the tent of meeting, because the cloud abode upon it' (Exodus 40:34).

C. On that same day the heads offered their offerings, as it is said, "He who offered his offering the first day . . ." (Numbers 7:12). Scripture uses the word "first" only in a setting when "first" introduces all of the days of the year.

D. On that day fire came down from heaven and consumed the offerings, as it is said, "And fire came forth from before the Lord and consumed the burnt offering and the fat upon the altar" (Leviticus 9:24).

E. On that day the sons of Aaron offered strange fire, as it is said, "Now Nadab and Abihu, the sons of Aaron, each took his censer and put fire in it . . . and offered unholy fire before the Lord, such as he had not commanded them" (Leviticus 10:1).

F. "And they died before the Lord . . ." (Leviticus 10:2): they died before the Lord, but they fell outside [of the tabernacle, not imparting corpse uncleanness to it].

G. How so? They were on their way out.

H. R. Yose says, "An angel sustained them, as they died, until they got out, and they fell in the courtyard, as it is said, 'And Moses called Mishael and Elzaphan, the sons of Uzziel the uncle of Aaron, and said to them, "Draw near, carry your brethren from before the sanctuary out of the camp" (Leviticus 10:4). What is stated is not, "From before the Lord," but, "from before the sanctuary.'"

I. R. Ishmael says, "The context indicates the true state of affairs, as it is said, 'And they died before the Lord,' meaning, they died inside and fell outside. How did they get out? People dragged them with iron ropes."

The exegete draws together a broad range of events which, in his view, all took place on one day. But what is interesting—as the contrast will show in a moment—is what he does not say. He does not introduce the issue of Israel and Israel's redemption. Rather, he focuses upon the here and the now of what happened long ago. There is a perceived difference between the one-time historical event of the setting up of the tabernacle and the eternal and paradigmatic character of the event: its continuing meaning, not its one-time character. The tabernacle is not the paradigm of the natural world, and Israel's salvation simply plays no role in the passage. Now to the matter at hand.

The expansion and amplification of the base verse runs through I.1. From that point, I.2, we deal with the other events of that same day, surveying the several distinct narratives which deal with the same thing, Exodus 40, Leviticus 9–10, and so on. This produces the effect of unifying the diverse scriptural accounts into one tale, an important and powerful exegetical result. One of the persistent contributions of our exegetes is to collect and harmonize a diversity of verses taken to refer to the same day, event, or rule.

XLIV:II

1. A. ". . . and had anointed and consecrated it with all its furnishings and had anointed and consecrated the altar with all its utensils":
   B. Might I infer that as each utensil was anointed, it was sanctified?
   C. Scripture says, ". . . and had anointed and consecrated it with all its furnishings and had anointed and consecrated the altar with all its utensils," meaning that not one of them was sanctified until all of them had been anointed. [The process proceeded by stages.]

Once more we shall see that the second exegesis—that of Pesiqta deRav Kahana—makes precisely this point. But it is swallowed up in a much different range of interest. The later document covers nearly everything in the earlier one, but makes nothing of what is constitutive of the received writing.

XLIV:II

2. A. ". . . [And] had anointed and consecrated it with all its furnishings and had anointed and consecrated the altar with all its utensils":
   B. The anointing was done both inside and outside [of the utensil].
   C. R. Josiah says, "Utensils meant to hold liquids were anointed inside and outside, but utensils meant to hold dry stuffs were anointed on the inside but not anointed on the outside."
   D. R. Jonathan says, "Utensils meant to hold liquids were anointed inside and not outside, but utensils meant to hold dry stuffs were not anointed.
   E. "You may know that they were not consecrated, for it is said, *You shall bring from your dwellings two loaves of bread to be waved, made of two tenths of an ephah* (Leviticus 23:17). Then when do they belong to the Lord? Only after they are baked." [The bread was baked in utensils at home, so the utensils have not been consecrated.]

The exegetes at Pesiqta deRav Kahana have no interest whatsoever in the details at hand. Theirs is not a search for concrete details.

XLIV:II

   3. A. Rabbi says, "Why is it said, . . . *and had anointed and conse-crated it?* And is it not already stated, '. . . and had anointed and consecrated it?'"

     B. "This indicates that with the anointing of these utensils all future utensils were sanctified [so that the sanctification of the tabernacle enjoyed permanence and a future tabernacle or temple did not require a rite of sanctification once again]."

II.1 clarifies the rite of sanctification, aiming at the notion that the act of consecration covered everything at once, leading to the future conclusion, at the end, that that act also covered utensils later on to be used in the cult. II.3 goes over that same ground. II.2 deals with its own issue, pursuing the exegesis of the verse at hand. Its interest in the consecration of the utensils is entirely congruent with II.3, because it wants to know the status of utensils outside of the cult, and, while they serve the purpose of the cult as specified, still, they are not deemed to have been consecrated. That, sum and substance, is the message of the passage: this and that about not very much, apart from the sequence of events that took place on one and the same day, an effort to harmonize and unify diverse tales into a single set of cogent events.

II
Pesiqta deRav Kahana
Pisqa 1

My translation of the critical text of Pesiqta deRav Kahana published by Bernard Mandelbaum, *Pesikta de Rab Kahana. According to an Oxford Manuscript. With Variants from All Known Manuscripts and Genizoth Fragments and Parallel Passages. With Commentary and Introduction* (New York: The Jewish Theological Seminary of America, 1962), I–II. I have further followed Mandelbaum's notes and commentary. I also consulted William G. (Gershon Zev) Braude and Israel J. Kapstein, *Pesikta de-Rab Kahana. R. Kahana's Compilation of Discourses for Sabbaths and Festal Days* (Philadelphia: Jewish Publication Society of America, 1975).[5] The formal traits of the second compilation differ radically.

---

[5]Theirs is not a translation but an eisegetical rendition, more of a literary paraphrase than an academic translation. Moreover, the Hebrew text on which Braude's and Kapstein's translation is based appears to be eclectic, one that they appear to have chosen for the occasion rather than one that is systematic and

Pesiqta deRav Kahana falls into precisely the same structural-formal classification as Genesis *Rabbah* and Leviticus *Rabbah*. It approaches the exegesis of the verse of primary interest, which I call the base verse, by means of a secondary and superficially unrelated verse, which I call the intersecting verse. The latter will be extensively treated, entirely on its own. Then the exegete will move from the intersecting verse to the base verse, showing how the verse chosen from some other passage in fact opens up the deeper meaning of the verse of primary concern. In what follows the intersecting verse, Song of Songs 5:1, is chosen because it refers to *bride*, and the word for *had finished* is formed of the letters KLH, which can be read as *bride*. So in the mind of the exegete, an appropriate intersecting verse will speak of the same matter—KLH = "finish" or "bride"—and the rest follows. But, as we shall see, that intersecting verse imparts its deepest meaning on the base verse, and, in the present instance, the tabernacle on that account is taken as the place in which Israel entered the bridal canopy of God. The clear purpose of the authorship emerges in their treatment of the base verse, Numbers 7:1: teleological–eschatological, beginning, middle, and end. The one important thing about the base verse is the opposite of the main thing that struck the authorship of Sifré to Numbers: its interest in a one-time event on a particular day. To the authorship of Pesiqta deRav Kahana, Scripture presents eternal paradigms and not one-time history.

I:I

    1. A. *I have come back to my garden, my sister, my bride* (Song of Songs 5:1):

       B. R. Azariah in the name of R. Simon said, "[The matter may be compared to the case of] a king who became angry at a noble woman and drove her out and expelled her from his palace.

---

commonly accessible, and therefore it is not readily available to scholars in general. Finally, because they have not analyzed the text from its constitutive components, they have translated (eisegetically) as though one clause derived from the preceding and led to the next, when, in fact, each component was worked out within its own framework and is not necessarily cogent with the others fore and aft. Consequently, their translation harmonizes constantly what seem to me discrete components of discourse. Their penchant for translating not the text but what they conceive (not necessarily without reason) to be its meaning makes the translation attractive and engaging, but in no way a reliable account of what is there in the Hebrew. It has to be checked at every point, though I would not dismiss it as valueless, even as a Hebrew translation. Its lack of accuracy on minor points makes little material difference to its usefulness, but I am in the process of replacing it with something more useful.

After some time he wanted to bring her back. She said, 'Let him renew in my behalf the earlier state of affairs, and then he may bring me back.'

C. "So in former times the Holy One, blessed be He, would receive offerings from on high, as it is said, *And the Lord smelled the sweet odor* (Genesis 8:21). But now he will accept them down below."

2. A. *I have come back to my garden, my sister, my bride* (Song of Songs 5:1):

B. Said R. Hanina, "The Torah teaches you proper conduct,

C. "specifically, that a groom should not go into the marriage canopy until the bride gives him permission to do so: *Let my beloved come into his garden* (Song of Songs 4:16), after which, *I have come back to my garden, my sister, my bride* (Song of Songs 5:1)."

As we shall see, the intersecting verse is fully exposed entirely in its own terms, before we are able to recover the base verse and find out what we learn about that verse from the intersecting one.

3. A. R. Tanhum, son-in-law of R. Eleazar b. Abina, in the name of R. Simeon b. Yosni: "What is written is not, 'I have come into the garden,' but rather, *I have come back to my garden.* That is, 'to my [Mandelbaum] canopy.'

B. "That is to say, to the place in which the principal [presence of God] had been located to begin with.

C. "The principal locale of God's presence had been among the lower creatures, in line with this verse: *And they heard the sound of the Lord God walking about* (Genesis 3:8)."

4. A. [*And they heard the sound of the Lord God walking about* (Genesis 3:8):] Said R. Abba bar Kahana, "What is written is not merely 'going,' but 'walking about,' that is, 'walking away from.'"

B. *And man and his wife hid* (Genesis 3:8):

C. Said R. Aibu, "At that moment the first man's stature was cut down and diminished to one hundred cubits."

5. A. Said R. Isaac, "It is written, *The righteous will inherit the earth* (Psalm 47:29). Where will the wicked be? Will they fly in the air?

B. "Rather, the sense of the clause, *they shall dwell thereon in eternity* is, they shall bring the presence of God to dwell on the earth."

6. A. [Reverting to 3.C,] the principal locale of God's presence had been among the lower creatures, but when the first man sinned, it went up to the first firmament.

B. The generation of Enosh came along and sinned, and it went up from the first to the second.

C. The generation of the flood [came along and sinned], and it went up from the second to the third.

D. The generation of the dispersion . . . and sinned, and it went up from the third to the fourth.

E. The Egyptians in the time of Abraham our father [came along] and sinned, and it went up from the fourth to the fifth.

F. The Sodomites . . . , and sinned, . . . from the fifth to the sixth.

G. The Egyptians in the time of Moses . . . from the sixth to the seventh.

H. And, corresponding to them, seven righteous men came along and brought it back down to earth:

I. Abraham our father came along and acquired merit, and brought it down from the seventh to the sixth.

J. Isaac came along and acquired merit and brought it down from the sixth to the fifth.

K. Jacob came along and acquired merit and brought it down from the fifth to the fourth.

L. Levi came along and acquired merit and brought it down from the fourth to the third.

M. Kahath came along and acquired merit and brought it down from the third to the second.

N. Amram came along and acquired merit and brought it down from the second to the first.

O. Moses came along and acquired merit and brought it down to earth.

P. Therefore it is said, *On the day that Moses completed the setting up of the Tabernacle, he anointed and consecrated it* (Numbers 7:1).

The selection of the intersecting verse, Song of Songs 5:1, rests, as I said, on the appearance of the letters KLH, meaning, "completed," but yielding also the word KLH, meaning, "bride." The exegete wishes to make the point that in building the tabernacle, Moses has brought God down to earth (I.6.P.). This he accomplishes by bringing the theme of "garden, bride" together with the theme of the union of God and Israel. The parable at 1.B then is entirely apt, since it wishes to introduce the notion of God's having become angry with humanity but then reconciled through Israel in the sacrificial cult. I.1.B then refers to the fall from grace, with Israel as the noble spouse who insists that the earlier state of affairs be restored. I.1.C then makes explicit precisely what is in mind, a very effective introduction to the whole. I.2 pursues the exegesis of the intersecting verse, as does I.3, the latter entirely apropos. Because of I.3.C, I.4 is tacked on; it continues the exegesis of the proof-text but has no bearing on the intersecting verse. But I.5 does—at least in its proposition, if not in its selection of proof-texts. I.6 then brings us back to I.3.C, citing the language of the prior component and then making the point of the whole quite explicit. Even with the obvious accretions at I.4 and I.5, the whole hangs together and makes its point—the intersecting verse, Song of Songs 5:1, the base verse Numbers 7:1—in a cogent way.

I:II

1. A. *King Solomon made a pavilion for himself* (Song of Songs 3:9). [The New English Bible: *The palanquin which King Solomon had made for himself was of wood from Lebanon. Its poles he made of silver, its headrest of gold; its seat was of purple stuff, and its lining was of leather*]:

   B. *Pavilion* refers to the tent of meeting.

   C. *King Solomon made a . . . for himself*; he is the king to whom peace [*shalom/shelomoh*] belongs.

2. A. Said R. Judah bar Ilai, "[The matter may be compared to the case of] a king who had a little girl. Before she grew up and reached puberty, he would see her in the marketplace and chat with her, or in alleyways and chat with her. But when she grew up and reached puberty, he said, 'It is not fitting for the dignity of my daughter that I should talk with her in public. Make a pavilion for her, so that I may chat with her in the pavilion.'

   B. "So, to begin with: *When Israel was a child in Egypt, then in my love of him, I used to cry out* (Hosea 11:1). In Egypt they saw me: *And I passed through the land of Israel* (Exodus 12:12). At the sea they saw me: *And Israel saw the great hand*

(Exodus 14:31). At Sinai they saw me: *Face to face the Lord spoke with you* (Deuteronomy 5:4).

C. "But when they received the Torah, they became a fully-grown nation for me. So he said, 'It is not appropriate to the dignity of my children that I should speak with them in public. But make me a tabernacle, and I shall speak from the midst of the tabernacle.'

D. "That is in line with this verse: *And when Moses entered the tent of the presence to speak with God, he heard the voice speaking from above the cover over the ark of the tokens from between the two cherubim: the voice spoke to him* (Numbers 7:89)."

3. A. [*The palanquin which King Solomon had made for himself was of wood from Lebanon. Its poles he made of silver, its headrest of gold; its seat was of purple stuff, and its lining was of leather*] . . . *was of wood from Lebanon. Make for the tabernacle planks of acacia wood as uprights* (Exodus 26:25).

B. *Its poles he made of silver: The hooks and bands on the posts shall be of silver* (Exodus 27:10);

C. *its headrest of gold: Overlay the planks with gold, make rings of gold onto them to hold the bars* (Exodus 26:29);

D. *its seat was of purple stuff: Make a veil of finely woven linen and violet, purple, and scarlet yarn* (Exodus 26:31);

E. *and its lining was of leather:*

F. R. Yudan says, "This refers to the merit accruing on account of the Torah and the righteous."

G. R. Azariah in the name of R. Judah bar Simon says, "This refers to the Presence of God."

4. A. Said R. Aha bar Kahana, "It is written, *And there I shall meet with you* (Exodus 25:22),

B. "to teach that even what is on the outside of the ark-cover is not empty of God's presence."

5. A. A gentile asked Rabban Gamaliel, saying to him, "On what account did the Holy One, blessed be He, reveal Himself to Moses in a bush?"

B. He said to him, "If he had revealed himself to him in a carob tree or a fig tree, what might you have said? It is so as to indicate that there is no place in the earth that is empty of God's presence."

6. A. R. Joshua of Sikhnin in the name of R. Levi: "To what may the tent of meeting be compared?

   B. "To an oceanside cave. The sea tide flows and engulfs the cave, which is filled by the sea, but the sea is not diminished.

   C. "So the tent of meeting is filled with the splendor of the presence of God."

   D. Therefore it is said, *On the day that Moses completed the setting up of the Tabernacle, he anointed and consecrated it* (Numbers 7:1).

Seen by itself, II.1 has no bearing upon the larger context, but it does provide a good exegesis of Song of Songs 3:9 in terms of the theme of the tabernacle. The point of II.2 is that the purpose of the tabernacle was to make possible appropriate communication between a mature Israel and God. Therefore the two items are simply distinct workings of the theme of the tabernacle, one appealing to Song of Songs 3:9, the other to Numbers 7:89.

The introduction at I.II of Song of Songs 3:9, with the explanation that palanquin refers to the tent of meeting, accounts for the exposition of II.3, which reads each phrase of that intersecting verse in line with the proof-texts concerning the tent of meeting. Had I.II.1 been continued by II.3, we should have a smoother statement of the main point. II.4 seems to me to flow from II.3's interest in the tent of meeting; the point of contact is with the viewpoint that God's presence was in the tent. Then II.5 is tacked on for obvious reasons, a story that makes the same point as the exegesis. II.6 goes over the matter yet again. The force of II.6.D is derived only from its redactional function, which is to direct our attention back to our base verse. But while the theme—the tent of meeting or tabernacle—has been worked out, the base verse in its own terms has not been discussed. Tacking it on is only for the purpose of marking the finish of the discourse at hand.

I:III

1. A. [Continuing the exegesis of the successive verses of Song of Songs 3:9ff.] *Come out, daughters of Jerusalem, you daughters of Zion, come out and welcome King Solomon, wearing the crown with which his mother has crowned him, on his wedding day, on his day of joy* (Song of Songs 3:11). [Braude and Kapstein: *Go forth, O younglings whose name Zion indicates that you bear a sign*]:

B. Sons who are marked [a play on the letters that stand for the word, *come out*] for me by the mark of circumcision, by not cutting the corners of the head [in line with Leviticus 19:27], and by wearing show-fringes.

2. A. [... *And welcome*] *King Solomon:*
   B. The king to whom peace belongs.

3. A. Another interpretation: *and welcome King Solomon:*
   B. The King [meaning God] who brings peace through his deeds among his creatures.
   C. He made the fire make peace with Abraham, the sword with Isaac, the angel with Jacob.
   D. It is the King who brings peace among his creatures.
   E. Said R. Yohanan, "*Merciful dominion and fear are with him* (Job 25:2) [that is, are at peace with him]."
   F. Said R. Jacob of Kefar Hanan, "*Merciful dominion* refers to Michael, and *fear* to Gabriel.
   G. "*With him* means that they make peace with him and do not do injury to one another."
   H. Said R. Yohanan, "The sun has never laid eyes on the blemished part of the moon [the black side], nor does a star take precedence over another one, nor does a planet lay eyes on the one above it."
   I. Said Rabbi, "All of them traverse as if it were a spiral staircase."

4. A. It is written, *Who lays the beams of your upper chambers in the waters, who makes the flaming fires your ministers* (Psalm 104:2-3):
   B. R. Simeon b. Yohai taught, "The firmament is of water, the stars of fire, and yet they dwell with one another and do not do injury to one another.
   C. "The firmament is of water and the angel is of fire, and yet they dwell with one another and do not do injury to one another."
   D. Said R. Abin, "It is not the end of the matter [that there is peace between] one angel and another. But even the angel himself is half fire and half water, and yet they make peace."
   E. The angel has five faces—*The angel's body was like beryl, his face as the appearance of lightning, his eyes as torches of fire, his arms and feet like in color to burnished brass, and the*

sound of his words like the sound of a roaring multitude
(Daniel 10:6)—[yet none does injury to the other].

5. A. *So there was hail and fire flashing continually amid the hail*
   (Exodus 9:24):
   B. R. Judah says, "There was a flask of hail filled with fire."
   C. R. Nehemiah said, "Fire and hail, mixed together."
   D. R. Hanin said, "In support of the position of R. Judah is the
   case of the pomegranate in the pulp of which seeds can be
   discerned."
   E. R. Hanin said, "As to Nehemiah's, it is the case of a crystal
   lamp in which are equivalent volumes of water and oil, which
   together keep the flame of the wick burning above the water
   and the oil."

6. A. [*So there was hail and fire flashing continually amid the hail*
   (Exodus 9:24)]: What is the meaning of *flashing continually?*
   B. Said R. Judah bar Simon, "Each one is dying in their
   [Braude and Kapstein, p. 10:] determination to carry out
   their mission."
   C. Said R. Aha, "[The matter may be compared to the case of] a
   king, who had two tough legions, who competed with one
   another, but when the time to make war on behalf of the king
   came around, they made peace with one another.
   D. "So is the case with the fire and hail, they compete with one
   another, but when the time has come to carry out the war of
   the Holy One, blessed be He, against the Egyptians, then: *So
   there was hail and fire flashing continually amid the hail*
   (Exodus 9:24)—one miracle within the other [more familiar
   one, namely, that the hail and fire worked together]."

7. A. [*Come out, daughters of Jerusalem, you daughters of Zion,
   come out and welcome King Solomon,*] *wearing the crown with
   which his mother has crowned him, on his wedding day,* [*on his
   day of joy*] (Song of Songs 3:11):
   B. Said R. Isaac, "We have reviewed the entire Scripture and
   have not found evidence that Beth Seba made a crown for
   her son, Solomon. This refers, rather, to the tent of meeting,
   which is crowned with blue and purple and scarlet."

8. A. Said R. Hunia, "R. Simeon b. Yohai asked R. Eleazar b.
   R. Yose, 'Is it possible that you have heard from your father
   what was the crown with which his mother crowned him?'

B. "He said to him, 'The matter may be compared to the case of a king who had a daughter, whom he loved even too much. He even went so far, in expressing his affection for her, as to call her, "my sister." He even went so far, in expressing his affection for her, as to call her, "my mother."'"

C. "'So at the outset, the Holy One, blessed be He, expressed his affection for Israel by calling them, "my daughter": *Hear, O daughter, and consider* (Psalm 45:11). Then he went so far, in expressing his affection for them, as to call them, "my sister": *My sister, my bride* (Song of Songs 5:1). Then he went so far, in expressing his affection for them, as to call them, "my mother": *Attend to me, O my people, and give ear to me, O my nation* (Isaiah 51:4). The letters that are read as "my nation" may also be read as "my mother."

D. "R. Simeon b. Yohai stood and kissed him on his head.

E. "He said to him, 'Had I come only to hear this teaching, it would have been enough for me.'"

9. A. R. Joshua of Sikhnin in the name of R. Levi: "When the Holy One, blessed be He, said to Moses, 'Make Me a tabernacle,' Moses might have brought four poles and spread over them [skins to make] the tabernacle. This teaches, therefore, that the Holy One, blessed be He, showed Moses on high red fire, green fire, black fire, and white fire.

B. "He said to him, 'Make me a tabernacle.'

C. "Moses said to the Holy One, blessed be He, 'Lord of the ages, where am I going to get red fire, green fire, black fire, and white fire?'

D. "He said to him, 'After the pattern which is shown to you on the mountain (Exodus 25:40).'"

10. A. R. Berekhiah in the name of R. Levi: "[The matter may be compared to the case of] a king who appeared to his household clothed in a garment [Braude and Kapstein, p. 11] covered entirely with precious stones.

B. "He said to him, 'Make me one like this.'

C. "He said to him, 'My lord, O king, where am I going to get myself a garment made entirely of precious stones?'

D. "He said to him, 'You in accord with your raw materials and I in accord with my glory.'

E. "So said the Holy One, blessed be He, to Moses, 'Moses, if you make what belongs above down below, I shall leave My council up here and go down and reduce My Presence so as to be among you down there.'

F. "Just as up there: *seraphim are standing* (Isaiah 6:2), so down below: *boards of shittim-cedars are standing* (Exodus 26:15).

G. "Just as up there are stars, so down below are the clasps."

H. Said R. Hiyya bar Abba, "This teaches that the golden clasps in the tabernacle looked like the fixed stars of the firmament."

11. A. [*Come out, daughters of Jerusalem, you daughters of Zion, come out and welcome King Solomon, wearing the crown with which his mother has crowned him,*] *on his wedding day,* [*on his day of joy*] (Song of Songs 3:11):

B. [Braude and Kapstein, p. 12:] the day he entered the tent of meeting.

C. . . . *on his day of joy:*

D. this refers to the tent of meeting.

E. Another interpretation of the phrase, *on his wedding day, on his day of joy* (Song of Songs 3:11):

F. . . . *on his wedding day,* refers to the tent of meeting.

G. . . . *on his day of joy* refers to the building of the eternal house.

H. Therefore it is said, *On the day that Moses completed the setting up of the Tabernacle, he anointed and consecrated it* (Numbers 7:1).

The exegesis of Song of Songs 3:11 now receives attention in its own terms, our point of departure having been forgotten. III.1 simply provides a play on one of the words of the verse under study. III.2-6 proceed to work on the problem of the name of the king, Solomon. We have a striking and fresh approach at III.2-3: the reference is now to God as King, and the name, Solomon, then is interpreted as God's functionary, as bringing peace among his holy creatures, the patriarchs and the angels, and also among the elements of natural creation. Both topics are introduced and then, at III.4-6, the latter is worked out. God keeps water and fire working together, and to do his bidding they do not injure one another. The proof-text, Exodus 9:24, then leads us in its own direction, but at III.6 discourse returns to the main point.

III.7 moves us on to a fresh issue, namely, Solomon himself. And now we see the connection between the passage and our broader theme, the tabernacle. The Temple is now compared to a crown. III.8 pursues the interpretation of the same clause. But the point of interest is the clause, not the theme under broader discussion, so what we have is simply a repertoire of exegeses of the cited verse. III.9 carries forward the theme of making the tabernacle. It makes the point that Moses was to replicate the colors he had seen on high. I see no connection to the preceding. It is an essentially fresh initiative. III.10 continues along that same line, now making yet another point, which is that the tabernacle on earth was comparable to the abode of God in heaven. III.11 brings us back to our original verse. We take up a clause by clause interpretation of the matter. III.11.H is an editorial subscript, with no connection to the foregoing except a rather general thematic one. But the original interest in working on the theme of the building of the tabernacle as Israel's wedding day to God is well expressed, beginning to end.

I:IV

1. A. *Who has ever gone up to heaven and come down again? Who has cupped the wind in the hollow of his hands? Who has bound up the waters in the fold of his garment? Who has fixed the boundaries of the earth? What is his name or his son's name, if you know it?* (Proverbs 30:4):

   B. . . . *Who has ever gone up to heaven*: this refers to the Holy One, blessed be He, as it is written, *God has gone up to the sound of the trumpet* (Psalm 37:6).

   C. . . . *and come down again: The Lord came down onto Mount Sinai* (Exodus 19:20).

   D. . . . *Who has cupped the wind in the hollow of his hands: In whose hand is the soul of all the living* (Job 12:10).

   E. . . . *Who has bound up the waters in the fold of his garment: He keeps the waters penned in dense cloud-masses* (Job 26:8).

   F. . . . *Who has fixed the boundaries of the earth: Who kills and brings to life* (1 Samuel 2:6).

   G. . . . *What is his name*: His name is the Rock, his name is The Almighty, his name is The Lord of Hosts.

   H. *Or his son's name, if you know it: My son, my first born is Israel* (Exodus 4:22).

2. A. Another interpretation of the verse, *Who has ever gone up to heaven*: Who is the one whose prayer goes up to heaven and brings down rain?

   B. This is one who sets aside the tithes that he owes with his hands, who brings dew and rain into the world.

C. *Who has cupped the wind in the hollow of his hands? Who has bound up the waters in the fold of his garment? Who has fixed the boundaries of the earth?* Who is the one whose prayer does not go up to heaven and bring down rain?

D. This is one who does not set aside the tithes that he owes with his hands, who does not bring dew and rain into the world.

3. A. Another interpretation of the verse, *Who has ever gone up to heaven:*

B. This refers to Elijah, concerning whom it is written, *And Elijah went up in a whirlwind to heaven* (2 Kings 2:11);

C. *... and come down again:*

D. *Go down with him, do not be afraid* (2 Kings 1:16).

E. *Who has cupped the wind in the hollow of his hands:*

F. *Lord, God of Israel, before whom I stand* (1 Kings 17:1).

G. *Who has bound up the waters in the fold of his garment:*

H. *And Elijah took his mantle and wrapped it together and smote the waters and they were divided* (1 Kings 2:8).

I. *Who has fixed the boundaries of the earth:*

J. *And Elijah said, See your son lives* (1 Kings 17:23).

4. A. Another interpretation of the verse, *Who has ever gone up to heaven and come down again:*

B. This refers to Moses, concerning whom it is written, *And Moses went up to God* (Exodus 19:3);

C. *... and come down again:*

D. *And Moses came down from the mountain* (Exodus 19:14).

E. *Who has cupped the wind in the hollow of his hands:*

F. *As soon as I have gone out of the city, I shall spread my hands out to the Lord* (Exodus 9:29).

G. *Who has bound up the waters in the fold of his garment:*

H. *The floods stood upright as a heap* (Exodus 15:8).

I. *Who has fixed the boundaries of the earth:*

J. This refers to the tent of meeting, as it is said, *On the day on which Moses completed setting up the tabernacle* (Numbers 7:1)—for the entire world was set up with it.

5. A. R. Joshua b. Levi in the name of R. Simeon b. Yohai: "What is stated is not 'setting up the tabernacle [without the accusative particle, *et*],' but 'setting up + *the accusative particle* + the tabernacle,' [and since the inclusion of the accusative particle is taken to mean that the object is duplicated, we understand

the sense to be that he set up a second tabernacle along with the first].

B. "What was set up with it? It was the world that was set up with [the tabernacle, that is, the tabernacle represented the cosmos].

C. "For until the tabernacle was set up, the world trembled, but after the tabernacle was set up, the world rested on firm foundations."

D. Therefore it is said, *On the day that Moses completed the setting up of the Tabernacle, he anointed and consecrated it* (Numbers 7:1).

The fresh intersecting verse, Proverbs 30:4, is systematically applied to God, to tithing, then Elijah, finally Moses, at which point the exposition comes to a fine editorial conclusion. I cannot imagine a more representative example of the intersecting verse–base verse exposition. IV.5 is tacked on because it provides a valuable complement to the point of IV.4.

I:V

1. A. Another interpretation of the verse: *On the day that Moses completed the setting up of the Tabernacle, he anointed and consecrated it* (Numbers 7:1):

   B. The letters translated as *completed* are so written that they can be read *bridal*, that is, on the day on which [Israel, the bride] entered the bridal canopy.

2. A. R. Eleazar and R. Samuel bar Nahmani:

   B. R. Eleazar says, "*On the day that Moses completed* means on the day on which he left off setting up the tabernacle day by day."

   C. It has been taught on Tannaite authority: Every day Moses would set up the tabernacle, and every morning he would make his offerings on it and then take it down. On the eighth day [to which reference is made in the verse, *On the day that Moses completed the setting up of the Tabernacle, he anointed and consecrated it*] he set it up but did not take it down again.

   D. Said R. Zeira, "On the basis of this verse we learn the fact that an altar set up on the preceding night is invalid for the offering of sacrifices on the next day."

   E. R. Samuel bar Nahmani says, "Even on the eighth day he set it up and took it apart again."

F. And how do we know about these dismantlings?

G. It is in line with what R. Zeira said, *"On the day that Moses completed* means on the day on which he left off setting up the tabernacle day by day."

3. A. R. Eleazar and R. Yohanan:

B. R. Eleazar said, *"On the day that Moses completed* means on the day on which demons ended their spell in the world.

C. "What is the scriptural basis for that view?

D. *"No evil thing will befall you, nor will any demon come near you* [Braude & Kapstein, p. 15] *by reason of your tent* (Psalm 91:10)—on the day on which demons ended their spell in the world."

E. Said R. Yohanan, "What need do I have to derive the lesson from another passage? Let us learn it from the very passage in which the matter occurs: *May the Lord bless you and keep you* (Numbers 6:24)—keep you from demons."

4. A. R. Yohanan and R. Simeon b. Laqish:

B. R. Yohanan said, *"On the day that Moses completed* means the day on which hatred came to an end in the world. For before the tabernacle was set up, there was hatred and envy, competition, contention, and strife in the world. But once the tabernacle was set up, love, affection, comradeship, righteousness, and peace came into the world.

C. "What is the verse of scripture that so indicates?

D. *"Let me hear the words of the Lord, are they not words of peace, peace to his people and his loyal servants and to all who turn and trust in him? Deliverance is near to those who worship him, so that glory may dwell in our land. Love and fidelity have come together, justice and peace join hands* (Psalm 85:8-10)."

E. Said R. Simeon b. Laqish, "What need do I have to derive the lesson from another passage? Let us learn it from the very passage in which the matter occurs: *and give you peace."*

5. A. [*On the day that Moses completed*] *the setting up of the Tabernacle,* [*he anointed and consecrated it*]:

B. R. Joshua b. Levi in the name of R. Simeon b. Yohai: "What is stated is not 'setting up the tabernacle [without the accusative particle, *et*],' but 'setting up + *the accusative particle* + the tabernacle,' [and since the inclusion of the accusative particle is taken to mean that the object is duplicated, we understand

   the sense to be that he set up a second tabernacle along with
   the first].
C. "What was set up with it? It was the world that was set up
   with [the tabernacle, that is, the tabernacle represented the
   cosmos].
D. "For until the tabernacle was set up, the world trembled, but
   after the tabernacle was set up, the world rested on firm
   foundations."

We work our way through the clause, *on the day that Moses completed.* V.1 goes over familiar ground. It is a valuable review of the point
of stress, the meaning of the word *completed.* V.2 refers to the claim that
from day to day Moses would set up and take down the tent, until on the
day at hand, he left it standing; so the "completed" bears the sense of
ceasing to go through a former procedure. The word under study bears
the further sense of "coming to an end," and therefore at V.3 and 4, we
ask what came to an end when the tabernacle was set up. The matched
units point to demons, on the one side, and hatred, on the other. V.5
moves us along from the word KLT to the following set, *accusative +
tabernacle.*

I:VI

1. A. *On the day that Moses completed* [*the setting up of the Taberna-
      cle*], *he anointed and consecrated it*:
   B. Since it is written, *he anointed and consecrated it,* why does it
      also say, *he anointed them and consecrated them* (Numbers 7:1)?
   C. R. Aibu said, "R Tahalipa of Caesarea, and R. Simeon:
   D. "One of them said, 'After he had anointed each one, he then
      anointed all of them simultaneously.'
   E. "The other of them said, '*And he anointed them* refers to an
      anointing in this world and another anointing in the world to
      come.'"

2. A. Along these same lines: *You shall couple the tent together*
      (Exodus 26:11), *You shall couple the curtains* (Exodus 26:6):
   B. R. Judah and R. Levi, R. Tahalipa of Caesarea and R. Simeon
      b. Laqish:
   C. One of them said, "Once he had coupled them all together, he
      went back and coupled them one by one."
   D. The other said, "*You shall couple the curtains and it shall be
      one,* meaning, one for measuring, one for anointing."

The exposition of the verse continues to occupy our attention, with the problem clear as stated.

I:VII

1. A. *The chief men of Israel, heads of families—that is, the chiefs of the tribes, [who had assisted in preparing the detailed lists—] came forward and brought their offering before the Lord* (Numbers 7:2):

   B. [(Following Braude and Kapstein, p. 16:) The word for *tribes* can mean *rods*, so we understand the meaning to be, they had exercised authority through rods] in Egypt.

   C. *... who had assisted in preparing the detailed lists*—the standards.

The clause by clause interpretation of the base verse does not vastly differ in intent from the interpretation generated by leading the intersecting verse into the base verse. That is to say, in both cases we have a highly allusive and wide-ranging reading of the matter, in which we construct meanings deriving from eternal categories, not one-time events but paradigms, as I said earlier. That trait of the exegetical–eisegetical mind of the later document emerges most strikingly in what follows.

2. A. *... came forward and brought their offering before the Lord, six covered wagons [and twelve oxen, one wagon from every two chiefs and from each one an ox]* (Numbers 7:2):

   B. The six corresponded to the six days of creation.

   C. The six corresponded to the six divisions of the Mishnah.

   D. The six corresponded to the six matriarchs: Sarah, Rebecca, Rachel, Leah, Bilhah, and Zilpah.

   E. Said R. Yohanan, "The six corresponded to the six religious duties that pertain to a king: *He shall not have too many wives* (Deuteronomy 17:17), *He shall not have too many horses* (Deuteronomy 17:16), *He shall not have too much silver and gold* (Deuteronomy 17:17), *He shall not pervert justice, show favor, or take bribes* (Deuteronomy 16:9)."

3. A. The six corresponded to the six steps of the throne. How so?

   B. When he goes up to take his seat on the first step, the herald goes forth and proclaims, *He shall not have too many wives* (Deuteronomy 17:17).

   C. When he goes up to take his seat on the second step, the

herald goes forth and proclaims, *He shall not have too many horses* (Deuteronomy 17:16).

D. When he goes up to take his seat on the third step, the herald goes forth and proclaims, *He shall not have too much silver and gold* (Deuteronomy 17:17).

E. When he goes up to take his seat on the fourth step, the herald goes forth and proclaims, *He shall not pervert justice.*

F. When he goes up to take his seat on the fifth step, the herald goes forth and proclaims, . . . *show favor.*

G. When he goes up to take his seat on the sixth step, the herald goes forth and proclaims, . . . *or take bribes* (Deuteronomy 16:9).

H. When he comes to take his seat on the seventh step, he says, "Know before whom you take your seat."

4. A. *And the top of the throne was round behind* (1 Kings 10:19):

B. Said R. Aha, "It was like the throne of Moses."

C. *And there were arms on either side of the throne by the place of the seat* (1 Kings 10:19):

D. How so? There was a sceptre of gold suspended from behind, with a dove on the top, and a crown of gold in the dove's mouth, and he would sit under it on the Sabbath, and it would touch but not quite touch.

5. A. The six corresponded to the six firmaments.

B. But are they not seven?

C. Said R. Abia, "The one where the King dwells is royal property [not counted with what belongs to the world at large]."

We proceed with the detailed exposition of the verse at hand. The focus of interest, after VII.1, is on the reason for bringing six wagons. The explanations, VII.2 (+3-4), 5, relate to the creation of the world, the Torah, the life of Israel, the religious duties of the King, and the universe above. The underlying motif, the tabernacle as the point at which the supernatural world of Israel meets the supernatural world of creation, is carried forward.

I:VIII

1. A. [. . . *came forward and brought their offering before the Lord, six*] *covered* [*wagons and twelve oxen, one wagon from every two chiefs and from each one an ox*] (Numbers 7:2):

B. The word for covered wagons may be read to yield these meanings:

C. like a lizard skin (Braude and Kapstein, p. 17: "it signifies that the outer surface of the wagons' frames as delicately reticulated as the skin of a lizard"];

D. [and the same word may be read to indicate that the wagons were] decorated, or fully equipped.

E. It has been taught in the name of R. Nehemiah, "They were like a bent bow."

2. A. ... *twelve oxen, one wagon from every two chiefs* ... :

B. This indicates that two chiefs would together bring one wagon, while each tribe gave an ox.

3. A. *These they brought forward before the tabernacle* (Numbers 7:3):

B. This teaches that they turned them into their monetary value and sold them to the congregation at large [so that everyone had a share in the donation].

4. A. *And the Lord spoke to Moses and said,* [*"Accept these from them: they shall be used for the service of the tent of the presence"*]: (Numbers 7:5):

B. What is the meaning of the word, *and said?*

C. R. Hoshaia taught, "The Holy One, blessed be He, said to Moses, 'Go and say to Israel words of praise and consolation.'

D. "Moses was afraid, saying, 'But is it not possible that the holy spirit will abandon me and come to rest on the chiefs?'

E. "The Holy One said to him, 'Moses, had I wanted them to bring their offering, I should have said to you 'say to them,' [so instructing them to do so], but *Take—it is from them* [*at their own volition, not by my inspiration*] (Numbers 7:5) is the language, meaning, they did it on their own volition [and have not received the holy spirit].'"

5. A. And who gave them the good ideas [of making the gift]?

B. It was the tribe of Simeon who gave them the good idea, in line with this verse: *And of the children of Issachar came men who had understanding of the times* (1 Chronicles 12:33).

C. What is the sense of *the times?*

D. R. Tanhuma said, "The ripe hour [*kairos*]."

E. R. Yose bar Qisri said, "Intercalating the calendar."

F. *They had two hundred heads* (1 Chronicles 12:33):

G. This refers to the two hundred heads of sanhedrins that were produced by the tribe of Issachar.

H. *And all of their brethren were subject to their orders* (1 Chronicles 12:33):

I. This teaches that the law would accord with their rulings.

J. They said to the community, "Is this tent of meeting which you are making going to fly in the air? Make wagons for it, which will bear it."

6. A. Moses was concerned, saying, "Is it possible that one of the wagons might break, or one of the oxen die, so that the offering of the chiefs might be invalid?"

B. Said to Moses the Holy One, blessed be He, *They shall be used for the service of the tent of the presence* (Numbers 7:5).

C. "To them has been given a long-term existence."

7. A. How long did they live?

B. R. Yudan in the name of R. Samuel bar Nahman, R. Honia in the name of Bar Qappara, "*In Gilgal they sacrificed the oxen* (Hosea 12:12)."

C. And where did they offer them up?

D. R. Abba bar Kahana said, "In Nob they offered them up."

E. R. Abbahu said, "In Gibeon they offered them up."

F. R. Hama bar Hanina said, "In the eternal house [of Jerusalem] they offered them up."

G. Said R. Levi, "A verse of Scripture supporting the view of R. Hama bar Hanina: *Solomon offered a sacrifice of peace offerings, which he slaughtered for the Lord, twenty-two thousand oxen* (1 Kings 8:63)."

H. It was taught in the name of R. Meir, "They endure even to now, and they never produced a stink, got old, or developed an invalidating blemish."

I. Now that produces an argument a fortiori:

J. If the oxen, who cleaved to the work of the making of the tent of meeting, were given an eternal existence; Israel, who cleave to the Holy One, blessed be He, how much the more so!

K. *And you who cleave to the Lord your God are alive, all of you, this day* (Deuteronomy 4:4).

The exegesis of the verse in its own terms leads us through the several phrases, VIII.1, 2, 3. VIII.4, continuing at VIII.6, with an important complement at VIII.5, goes on to its own interesting question. VIII.7 serves VIII.6 as VIII.6 serves VIII.5.

CONCLUSION

The upshot is very simple. We have two people talking about different things to different people. It seems superfluous at this point to observe that the one group of exegetes have virtually nothing in common with the other, even though, at some few points, the exegetes of Pesiqta deRav Kahana go over ground covered by those in Sifré to Numbers. What one set of sages wishes to know about the verse of Scripture at hand scarcely coincides with the program of the other. The comparison of *midrashim* in this case yields a picture of differences so profound as to call into question the premise with which we started; that the authorships of the two documents did derive from the same movement, share the same viewpoint, and therefore exhibit sufficient traits in common to justify our comparing the exegetical results of the one with the other. Once we undertake the comparison we find nothing in common. Nothing.

When we compare what one authorship thinks important about a verse of Scripture with what another authorship, of the same religious world and of approximately the same period, chooses to emphasize in that same verse, we must conclude that we have the results of different people talking about different things to different people.[6] *Comparative midrash*[7]—that is, comparing exegeses of the same theme or verse of Scripture among the same circles of exegetes—rests on solid foundations in logic.[8] The basis of comparison and contrast is established by points in common. Once we know that two things are like one another, then—and only then—do the points of difference become consequential. Two docu-

---

[6]Compare my article "The Jewish Christian Argument in the First Century. Different People Talking about Different Things to Different People," *Crosscurrents*, 1985, 35:148–158.

[7]See my *Comparative Midrash: The Plan and Program of Genesis Rabbah and Leviticus Rabbah* (Atlanta: Scholars Press for Brown Judaic Studies, 1986).

[8]Compare Jonathan Z. Smith, "What a Difference a Difference Makes," in *Take Judaism for Example* (Chicago: University of Chicago Press, 1983), ed. Jacob Neusner, and his equivalent paper in *"To See Ourselves as Others See Us": Jews, Christians, "Others" in Late Antiquity* (Atlanta: Scholars Press for Brown Judaic Studies, 1985. Studies in the Humanities), ed. Jacob Neusner and Ernest S. Frerichs.

ments in the same canon surely bear broad affinities, having been selected by the consensus of the sages or the faithful as authoritative. They rely upon the opinion or judgment of sages of the same circle. They have been preserved and handed down by the same institutions of the faith. They presumably present basically cogent convictions on the meaning of Scripture. Accordingly, a variety of indicators justifies the judgment that the documents form a solid fit, bearing much in common. Then, it must follow, the work of comparison yields to the exercise of contrast. Being alike, the documents, in their treatment of precisely the same verse of Scripture, produce differences, and these differences make a difference.

The Midrash-compilations of exegeses of the written Torah emerge rich in differences, with sharp definitions from their distinctive viewpoints and particular polemics on the one side, and formal and aesthetic qualities on the other. We deal with a canon, yes, but with a canon made up of highly individual documents. But that, after all, is what a canon is: a mode of classification that takes a library and turns it into a cogent, if composite, statement. A canon comprises separate books that all together make a single statement. In terms of the Judaism of the dual Torah, the canon is what takes scriptures of various kinds and diverse points of origin and turns them into Torah, and commentaries on those scriptures into Torah as well, making them all into the one whole Torah—the Torah of Moses, our rabbi.

Part I

THE SECOND- AND THIRD-CENTURY COMPILATIONS

The Tannaite Midrashim

1

Exodus and Mekhilta Attributed to R. Ishmael

Mekhilta Attributed to R. Ishmael and other writings that focus on pentateuchal books and bear attributions to the same authorities (called Tannaim) of the period before c. 200 C.E. are called *Tannaitic Midrashim*, meaning Midrash-compilations of sayings attributed to those authorities who also appear in the Mishnah. These are Sifra (for Leviticus), Sifré (for Numbers), and Sifré (for Deuteronomy). Collectively, Mekhilta Attributed to R. Ishmael, Sifra, and the two Sifrés are called "Tannaitic Midrashim" and "halakhic Midrashim," meaning Midrash-exegeses on legal passages of the Pentateuch. This latter description is not precise, since all of the documents also cover topics other than legal ones. We do not know when these Midrash-compilations reached closure, but since all of them cite the Mishnah or the Tosefta verbatim, it is assumed that they came to conclusion after the Mishnah, c. 200 C.E. A good guess as to when the work on them was completed is c. 400 C.E. It is generally assumed that they were formed in the Land of Israel.

Mekhilta Attributed to R. Ishmael forms a sustained address to the Book of Exodus, covering Exodus 12:1-23:19, Exodus 31:12-13, and Exodus 35:1-3. It comprises nine tractates, *Pisha* (Exodus 12:1-13:16), *Beshallah* (Exodus 13-17, 14-31), *Shirata* (Exodus 15:1-21), *Vayassa* (Exodus 22:1-27:7), *Amalek* (Exodus 17:8-18:27), *Bahodesh* (Exodus 19:1-20:26), *Neziqin* (Exodus 21:1-22:23), *Kaspa* (Exodus 22:24-23:19), and *Shabbata* (Exodus 31:12-17 and 35:1-3). There are eighty-two sections, subdivided into paragraphs. The division of the Book of Exodus has no bearing on the lections read in the synagogue as we now know them.

Moshe D. Heer maintains that the work was "probably compiled and redacted in Eretz Yisrael not earlier than the end of the fourth century."[1]

Mekhilta Attributed to R. Ishmael is the first scriptural encyclopedia of Judaism. A scriptural encyclopedia joins together expositions of topics, disquisitions on propositions in general precipitated by the themes of scriptural narrative or the dictates of biblical law, and collects and arranges in accord with Scripture's order and program the exegeses—paraphrases or brief explanations—of clauses of biblical verses. While it is generaly thought that that is what Midrash-compilations are meant to accomplish, in fact out of antiquity, it is Mekhilta Attributed to R. Ishmael that conforms to the characterization of such writings just now set forth. In general a Midrash-compilation addresses an urgent question and sets forth a cogent and compelling response to that question. So, in general, a Midrash-compilation in the context of the canonical writings of the Judaism of the dual Torah normally is *not* a scriptural encyclopedia. But Midrash-compilations later on, through medieval and into modern times, are precisely that. Accordingly, in the context of late antiquity, Mekhilta Attributed to R. Ishmael is abnormal, but the document adumbrates how matters would be carried forward for the centuries beyond.[2] Compared to the other writings in its classification, Midrash-compilations of late antiquity, it is exceptional, and its differentiating traits show us that it forms a species unto itself, within the common genus, Midrash-compilation.

A sustained address to approximately half the Book of Exodus, Mekhilta Attributed to R. Ishmael, seen as a whole and in the aggregate, presents a composite of three kinds of materials. The first is a set of ad hoc and episodic exegeses of some passages of Scripture. The second is a group of propositional and argumentative essays in exegetical form, in which theological principles are set forth and demonstrated. The third is a set of topical articles, some of them sustained, many of them well crafted, about important subjects of the Judaism of the dual Torah. Providing this encyclopedia of information concerning theology and normative behavior, however, for the authorship of Mekhilta Attributed to R. Ishmael has not required a sustained demonstration of a position, whether whole or even in part, distinctive to that authorship and distinct

---

[1]M. D. Heer, "Mekhilta of R. Ishmael," *Encyclopaedia Judaica* (Jerusalem: Keter, 1971) 11:1269.
[2]At the end of Chapter 6, I explain how I think this Midrash-compilation addresses a principal problem of theology in its very facticity and laconic mode of merely informative discourse.

from positions set forth by other authorships. This is indicated in two ways. First of all, our authorship has not composed an argument, prevailing through large tracts of the document, that is cogent in all details and accomplishes a main and overriding purpose. Nor has that authorship set forth a statement of important propositions through most of the information, whether topical or exegetical, that it lays out. This is not to suggest, however, that we have a mere conglomerate of unrelated facts. Quite to the contrary, there is no understanding the facts before us without ample access to a complete system, which is to say, the system of the Judaism of the dual Torah of the canon of which our writing forms a principal part. Accordingly, the document before us participates in a system, but its authorship in no way proposes to shape or contribute to the setting forth of the system, other than by rehearsing a corpus of inert facts. Our sample of Mekhilta Attributed to R. Ishmael covers a variety of types of discussions.

Kaspa 5

LXXX:I

    1. A. "The first of the first fruits of your ground you shall bring into the house of the Lord your God":

       B. Why is this passage set forth?

       C. Since Scripture states, "[It shall come to pass, that when you enter the land that the Lord your God is giving you as a heritage, and you possess it and settle in it,] you shall take some of every first fruit of the soil, [which you harvest from the land that the Lord your God is giving you, put it in a basket, and go to the place where the Lord your God will choose to establish his name. You shall go to the priest in charge at that time and say to him, 'I acknowledge this day before the Lord your God that I have entered the land that the Lord swore to our fathers to assign to us.' And the priest shall take the basket from your hand and set it down in front of the altar of the Lord your God. You shall then recite as follows before the Lord your God: 'My father was a fugitive Aramean. He went down to Egypt with meager numbers and sojourned there; but there he became a great and very populous nation. The Egyptians dealt harshly with us and oppressed us; they imposed heavy labor upon us. We cried to the Lord, the God of our fathers, and the Lord heard our plea and saw our plight, our misery, and our oppression. The Lord freed us from Egypt by a mighty hand, by an outstretched arm and awesome power, and by signs and portents. He brought us to this place and gave us this land, a land flowing with milk and honey. Wherefore I now bring the first fruits of the soil which you, O Lord, have given me.' You shall leave it before the Lord your God and bow low before the Lord your God. And you shall enjoy, together with the Levite and the stranger in your midst, all the bounty that the Lord your God has bestowed upon you and your household" (Deuteronomy 26:1-11)].

C. I know only that produce belongs as firstfruits. What about liquids?

D. Scripture states, "you shall bring into the house of the Lord your God":

E. under all circumstances.

F. Then what is the difference between the one and the other?

G. In the case of produce, the farmer brings and makes the required declaration, while in the case of the latter, one brings the liquids but does not make the required declaration.

2. A. "which you harvest from the land":

B. this serves to exclude from the rite share croppers, those who rent the land, holders of land that has been confiscated and resold, and one who has stolen the land.

3. A. "that the Lord your God is giving you":

B. this serves to exclude proselytes and bondservants.

4. A. "you":

B. this excludes women, those with undefined sexual traits, and those bearing the characteristics of both sexes.

5. A. Is the implication then that they are not to bring and also not to make the required declaration?

B. Scripture says, "you shall bring":

C. under all circumstances.

D. Then what is the difference between the one and the other?

E. In the case of the one the farmer brings and makes the required declaration, while in the case of the latter, one brings the firstfruits but does not make the required declaration.

At first glance, we have a single topic, which is the bringing of the firstfruits. But while that topic prevails, there is no focus on the exposition of the topic and its requirements. Rather, we have an exegetical exercise, one that focuses upon the verses spelled out and expounded in sequence. So the presentation proves topically haphazard but exegetically coherent. That is why, in this context, I classify this item as a miscellany. The full power of a topical exposition, by contrast to a miscellany on a given subject, is exposed in what follows. Here we see how our sages do much more than comment episodically on this and that ("commentary"), but prove propositions in a very compelling way.

LXXX:II

1. A. "You shall not seethe a kid in its mother's milk":
   B. R. Ishmael says, "On what account is this rule stated in three passages? It corresponds to the three covenants that the Holy One, blessed be He, made with Israel:
   C. "one at Horeb, one in the plains of Moab, one at Mount Gerizim [Exodus 24:7-8, Deuteronomy 29:11, Deuteronomy 28:29, respectively]."

2. A. ["You shall not seethe a kid in its mother's milk (Exodus 24:7-8, Deuteronomy 29:11, Deuteronomy 28:29)":]
   B. R. Josiah says, "The first constitutes the initial statement of the matter, and no exegetical work is carried on in connection with the initial statement.
   C. "The second serves to deal with the following argument:
   D. "A clean beast in the classification of carrion imparts uncleanness when it is carried, and an unclean beast in the same classification imparts uncleanness when it is carried.
   E. "If you have derived the rule concerning the one that is clean that it is forbidden to boil its meat in the mother's milk, is it possible to maintain that likewise in the case of the unclean beast it should be forbidden to boil its meat in its mother's milk?
   F. "Scripture states, 'in its mother's milk,'
   G. "not in the milk of an unclean beast.
   H. "And as to the third usage, it makes the point that it is not forbidden to do so in the milk of a human being."

3. A. ["You shall not seethe a kid in its mother's milk (Exodus 24:7-8, Deuteronomy 29:11, Deuteronomy 28:29)":]
   B. R. Jonathan says, "On what account is this matter repeated three times?
   C. "One applies to a domesticated beast, the second to a wild beast, the third to fowl."

4. A. ["You shall not seethe a kid in its mother's milk (Exodus 24:7–8, Deuteronomy 29:11, Deuteronomy 28:29):"]

   B. Abba Hanin in the name of R. Eliezer says, "On what account is this matter repeated three times?

   C. "One applies to a large beast, one to goats, one to sheep."

5. A. ["You shall not seethe a kid in its mother's milk (Exodus 24:7–8, Deuteronomy 29:11, Deuteronomy 18:29):"]

   B. R. Simeon b. Eleazar says, "On what account is this matter repeated three times?

   C. "One applies to a large beast, one to a small beast, one to a wild beast."

6. A. ["You shall not seethe a kid in its mother's milk (Exodus 24:7–8, Deuteronomy 29:11, Deuteronomy 28:29):"]

   B. Simeon b. Yohai says, "On what account is this matter repeated three times?

   C. "One serves to prohibit eating it, one to derive benefit from it, and the third to cooking with it under any circumstances."

7. A. Another treatment of the passage, ["You shall not seethe a kid in its mother's milk (Exodus 24:7–8, Deuteronomy 29:11, Deuteronomy 28:29):"]

   B. One applies to cooking both in the Land and abroad, one to the period when there is a house [temple], and one afterward. [This is now spelled out.]

   C. Since Scripture says, "The first of the first fruits of your ground you shall bring into the house of the Lord your God," and we have therefore derived the rule that the law governing firstfruits applies, in the place in which the firstfruits are brought, but we have not derived the rule that the prohibition of ["seething a kid in its mother's milk"] applies when firstfruits do not apply, and to areas in which the firstfruits are not brought.

   D. Scripture states, "You shall not eat anything that dies of itself" (Deuteronomy 14:21), and further, "You shall not seethe a kid in its mother's milk."

   E. This indicates that just as the prohibition of carrion applies both in the Land and abroad, both when the house is standing and when the house is not standing, so the prohibition of "You shall not seethe a kid in its mother's milk" applies both in the Land and abroad, both when the house is standing and when the house is not standing.

8. A. ["You shall not seethe a kid in its mother's milk (Exodus 24:7-8, Deuteronomy 29:11, Deuteronomy 28:29)":]

 B. R. Akiva says, "On what account is this matter repeated three times?

 C. "One is to encompass, in particular, a domesticated beast, the second a wild beast, the third fowl."

9. A. [Another comment concerning the statement, "You shall not seethe a kid in its mother's milk":]

 B. R. Yosé the Galilean says, "Scripture states, 'You shall not eat anything that dies of itself' (Deuteronomy 14:21), and further, 'You shall not seethe a kid in its mother's milk.'

 C. "The meat of what can be forbidden under the count of carrion falls into the classification of what is forbidden under the count of 'You shall not seethe a kid in its mother's milk.'

 D. "Then does fowl, the meat of which is forbidden under the count of carrion fall into the classification of what is forbidden under the count of 'You shall not seethe a kid in its mother's milk'?

 E. "Scripture says, 'in its mother's milk,' so excluding fowl, the mother of which has no milk.

 F. "An unclean beast, further, is forbidden whether it is properly slaughtered or carrion."

10. A. "You shall not seethe a kid in its mother's milk":

 B. I know only that the prohibition applies to seething. How do I know that it applies also to eating the meat that has been seethed?

 C. It is an argument a fortiori:

 D. If the Passover offering, which is not subject to an explicit prohibition as to not seething it, is subject to a prohibition against eating it [should it be seethed], meat that has been cooked in milk, which is subject to a specific prohibition against seething, surely should be subject to a prohibition against eating.

 E. No, if you have invoked that rule in the case of the Passover, which may not be cooked with anything, and which therefore also is subject to a prohibition as to being eaten,

F. will you say the same of meat in milk? For it is not subject to a prohibition against being cooked in any manner at all, and therefore it should be subject to a prohibition against being eaten.

G. R. Akiva says, "This argument is not the way to go. Rather:

H. "If the sinew of the thigh-vein, which is not subject to a prohibition as to being cooked, is subject to a prohibition as to being eaten, the matter of meat in milk, which is subject to a prohibition as to being cooked, surely should be subject to a prohibition as to being eaten.

I. "No, if you have invoked that rule in connection with the sinew of the thigh-vein, the prohibition of which comes prior to the giving of the Torah, and therefore it is subject to a prohibition as to being eaten, will you say the same of milk in meat, the prohibition of which does not come prior to the giving of the Torah, and therefore it should not be subject to a prohibition as to being eaten?

J. "Lo, carrion forms an anomaly that proves the contrary, for its prohibition was not announced prior to the giving of the Torah, yet the prohibition extends to eating it. It will then provide an example for meat in milk, so that, even though the prohibition concerning it was not announced prior to the giving of the Torah, nonetheless it should be subject to a prohibition against being eaten.

K. "No, if you have invoked the case of carrion, which imparts uncleanness when it is carried, and therefore it also is forbidden as to eating, will you say the same of meat in milk, which does not impart uncleanness when it is carried, and therefore should not be forbidden as to eating?

L. "Lo, the rule concerning forbidden fat and blood will provide an analogy, for these do not impart uncleanness when they are carried, yet they are forbidden as to being eaten. They then will prove concerning meat in milk, that, even though it does not impart uncleanness when it is carried, it should nonetheless be forbidden as to being eaten.

M. "No, if you have invoked the case of forbidden fat and blood, on account of eating which one incurs the liability of extirpation, will you say the same of meat in milk, on account of which one does not incur the liability of extirpation, and therefore no prohibition as to eating [but merely as to seething] should apply!

N. "Accordingly, Scripture states, 'you shall not eat it' (Deuteronomy 12:24), which encompasses meat in milk, indicating that it will be forbidden as to eating."

11. A. [On the same matter of prohibiting not only seething but also eating,] Issi says, "'You shall not eat the life with the flesh' (Deuteronomy 12:23):

B. "This serves to encompass meat in milk, indicating that it is subject to a prohibition against being eaten."

12. A. [On the same matter of prohibiting not only seething but also eating,] Issi b. Gur Arye says, "Here we find reference to holiness [at Deuteronomy 14:21] and there also we find a reference to holiness [at Exodus 22:30].

B. "Just as at the one passage the prohibition pertains against eating, so at the other it pertains also to eating."

13. A. I know only that the prohibition extends to [seething and to] eating. How about deriving benefit [from meat cooked in milk]?

B. You may offer the following argument a fortiori:

C. if produce of fruit trees during the first three years after planting, in which case no transgression has been committed [for example, by the planting of the orchard], is forbidden both as to eating and as to all other benefit,

D. meat cooked in milk, in which case a transgression already has been committed, surely should be forbidden both as to eating and as to all other benefit!

E. No, if you take that view in the case of produce of fruit trees during the first three years after planting, in which case the produce has never not been subject to a prohibition, and therefore such produce is forbidden both as to eating and as to all other benefit, will you say the same of meat cooked in milk, in which case the meat assuredly has been free of all prohibition [prior to its being cooked in the milk], and therefore it should not be forbidden both as to eating and as to all other benefit?

F. Lo, leaven on Passover forms an anomaly to the rule, for it was once free of all prohibition [prior to Passover], yet it is forbidden both as to eating and as to all other benefit. It therefore provides an appropriate analogy for the case of meat in milk, for even though it was once free of all prohibition, yet it too should be forbidden both as to eating and as to all other benefit.

G. No, if you have invoked the case of leaven on Passover, on account of which one incurs the liability of extirpation, and therefore it is forbidden both as to eating and as to all other benefit, will you say the same of meat in milk, on account of which one does not incur the liability of extirpation, and therefore it should not be forbidden both as to eating and as to all other benefit?

H. Now lo, an anomaly derives from the case of mixed seeds in a vineyard [for example, wheat sown in a vineyard], for on its account liability to extirpation is not incurred, and yet the crop grown there is prohibited [not only as to eating but also as to] all benefit.

I. That anomaly will then prove concerning the case of meat in milk, that even though one does not on account of eating such meat incur liability to extirpation, nonetheless, a prohibition as to deriving benefit does apply.

J. Rabbi says, "'or you may sell it to a foreigner . . . you shall not seethe a kid' (Deuteronomy 14:21):

K. "The Torah has said, when you sell it, you may not seethe it and then sell it.

L. "Lo, you have derived the rule that what meat in milk may not be used for any benefit whatsoever."

14. A. "You shall not seethe a kid in its mother's milk":

B. I know only the prohibition against seething it in the milk of its mother. How about the milk of its sister?

C. You may present the following argument a fortiori:

D. if in the case of its mother, with whom the beast may enter the corral for tithing, it is forbidden to seethe the beast with her milk; in the case of its sister, with whom the beast may not enter the corral for tithing, surely it should be forbidden to seethe its meat in her milk.

E. How about the beast's own milk with its meat?

F. You may present the following argument a fortiori:

G. if in a case in which the law has permitted use of "produce with produce," for example, as to slaughter [for one may slaughter them on the same day], the law nonetheless prohibits the offspring with the mother, here, in which the law forbids offspring with offspring [Lauterbach, III, p. 194, n. 11: "The kid and its mother's milk are both the produce of the mother. The animal, so to speak, is the parent of its own milk"], we surely should forbid produce with parent.

H. How about the milk of goats for use with the meat of lambs?

I. You may present the following argument a fortiori:

J. if in a case in which the law has permitted offspring with offspring, as in the matter of mating, the law has forbidden offspring with mother, here, in which case the law has prohibited offspring with offspring, as to mating, surely the law should forbid offspring with mother.

K. The same reasoning applies, moreover, to the use of goat's milk for cooking beef.

L. Then why does Scripture speak of a kid?

M. Because its mother produces a lot of milk.

15. A. ["You shall not seethe a kid in its mother's milk":]

B. Rabbi says, "Here we find a reference to 'its mother,' and elsewhere we find 'its mother' (Leviticus 22:27).

C. "Just as reference to 'its mother' in the latter passage speaks of the mother of ox, sheep, or goat, so here, 'its mother' encompasses an ox, sheep or goat."

16. A. "You shall not seethe a kid in its mother's milk":

B. It is meat in milk that you are forbidden to seethe, but not all other things are prohibited.

C. For one might have constructed the following encompassing classification:

D. if meat in milk, in which case this by itself is permitted, and that by itself is permitted, lo, together they are subject to prohibition as to seething,

E. all other things in the Torah that are prohibited, in which case this is prohibited on its own and that is prohibited on its own, surely together should be subject to prohibition as to seething.

F. Scripture is explicit: "You shall not seethe a kid in its mother's milk":

G. It is meat in milk that you are forbidden to seethe, but not all other things are prohibited.

17. A. "You shall not seethe a kid in its mother's milk":

B. I know only that the rule applies to ordinary beasts. How do

> I know that it applies also to beasts that have been conse-
> crated?
>
> C. You may argue as follows:
> D. If the prohibition applies to unconsecrated beasts, should it
> not apply also to consecrated beasts?
> E. No, if you have invoked the rule for unconsecrated beasts,
> which cannot be slaughtered through pinching the neck, will
> you say the same of consecrated beasts, in which case there is
> no prohibition against slaughter through pinching the neck?
> F. Scripture says, "In the house of the Lord your God you shall
> not seethe a kid in its mother's milk."

This is a classic exposition of a topic or a theme, ringing the changes on all the anticipated problems, systematically working through, in particular, the methodical-analytical program of inclusion and exclusion. The contrast to the treatment of firstfruits in the foregoing now may be drawn. Not only so, but, within this massive and forceful topical exposition, we also discern propositional exercises. A quick review of the whole shows us that propositions enter in when a given question is answered. But the whole in my judgment is so obviously a unitary composition, with a beginning, middle, and an end, that we must treat the topical exposition as primary, the propositional disquisitions as secondary. A closer look shows why.

We begin, II.1, with the problem of the several passages in which the same rule occurs, and that work, starting with a theological point, works through a variety of inclusionary propositions, II.2-8. The next problem, II.9, asks about the comparison between this prohibition and the one of carrion. That forms an interlude. The next sequence, beautifully articulated, moves from not seething to not eating, from not eating to not deriving benefit, II.10-13. The next inclusionary problem concerns the origin of the milk: not only the mother, but all other beasts, II.14-15. II.16 then provides the first exclusion, not a very formidable one, and II.17, the second and final exclusion. In all, the program is logical, orderly, and so far as I can imagine, complete. It is one of the finest thematic-legal expositions, built upon a well-composed logical structure, and in our document, a model for the assessment of all others.

The following passage presents the proposition that Israel is saved through attaining merit, a proposition only implicitly represented by the disputes concerning details of what merit, in particular, effected Israel's redemption from Egypt.

Pisha 5

V:I

1. A. "and you shall keep it [until the fourteenth day of this month, when the whole assembly of the congregation of Israel shall kill their lambs in the evening]":

    B. On what account did Scripture advance the purchase of the beast for the Passover offering by four days prior to its slaughter?

    C. R. Mattia b. Heresh would say, "Lo, Scripture says, 'Now when I passed by you and look on you, and behold, your time was the time of love' (Ezekiel 16:8)—

    D. "the time to carry out the oath that the Holy One, blessed be He, had taken to our father Abraham that he would redeem his sons had come, and yet they did not have in hand religious duties to carry out so that they might be redeemed.

    E. "For it is said, 'Your breasts were fashioned and your hair was grown, yet you were naked and bare' (Ezekiel 16:8), that is to say, naked of all religious obligations.

    F. "Accordingly, the Holy One, blessed be He, assigned to them two religious duties, the religious duty concerning the Passover offering, and the one concerning circumcision,

    G. "so that they would carry out these duties and so be redeemed.

    H. "For it is said, 'And when I passed by you, and saw you wallowing in your blood, I said to you, "In your blood live"' (Ezekiel 16:6); 'As for you also, because of the blood of your covenant I sent forth your prisoners out of the pit that had no water' (Zechariah 9:11).

    I. "That explains why Scripture advanced the purchase of the beast for the Passover offering by four days prior to its slaughter,

    J. "for one receives the reward for doing a deed only when the deed is actually done."

    K. R. Eleazar Haqqappar says, "[That explanation cannot serve.] Now is it not the case that the Israelites had in hand four religious duties of which the entire age is not worthy?; they were not suspect as to fornication or as to gossip, had not changed their name, and had not changed their language.

L. "How do we know that they were not suspect as to fornication? 'And the son of an Israelite woman whose father was
an Egyptian went out' (Leviticus 24:10). This testifies to the
praise that is coming to Israel, for among them was only
this particular one alone, and Scripture singles it out in their
regard. [That was the sole act of fornication in Israel in
Egypt.]"

M. So it is spelled out in tradition: "A garden shut up is my
sister, my bride; a spring shut up, a fountain sealed" (Song
of Songs 4:12).

N. "A garden shut up": this refers to the men.

O. "A spring shut up": this refers to the women.

P. R. Nathan says, "'A garden shut up': this refers to the
married women.

Q. "'A spring shut up': this refers to the betrothed women."

R. Another teaching concerning the verse, "A garden shut up
is my sister, my bride; a spring shut up, a fountain sealed"
(Song of Songs 4:12):

S. This refers to the two possibilities for sexual relations [vagi-
nal, anal, neither of which served].

T. [Reverting to Eleazar's statement:] "How do we know that
they were not suspect as to gossip but expressed love for one
another?

U. "'But every woman shall ask of her neighbor . . .' (Exodus
3:22)

V. "Now they had this instruction in hand for twelve months,
and you do not find that a single one of them informed
against his fellow.

W. "How do we know that they had not changed their name?

X. "For just as their genealogies when they went down to
Egypt [consisted in the names] Reuben, Simeon, Levi and
Judah, so their genealogies when they came up out of Egypt
involved the names Reuben, Simeon, Levi and Judah.

Y. "So Scripture says, 'And they declared their pedigrees after
their families by their fathers' houses' (Numbers 1:18); 'The
angel who has redeemed me from all evil bless the lads and
let my name be named in them' (Genesis 48:16).

Z. "How do we know that they had not changed their language?

AA. "It is said, 'Who made you a ruler and judge over us' (Exodus 2:14), which shows that they were speaking Hebrew.

BB. "Further: 'That is my mouth that speaks to you' (Genesis 45:12); 'And they said, "The God of the Hebrews has met with us'" (Exodus 5:3); 'And there came one that had escaped and told Abram the Hebrew' (Genesis 14:13).

CC. "So on what account did Scripture advance the purchase of the beast for the Passover offering by four days prior to its slaughter?

DD. "The reason is that the Israelites in Egypt were [Lauterbach:] steeped in idol-worship.

EE. "Idol-worship outweighs all the rest of the religious duties that are in the Torah: 'Then it shall be, if it be done in error by the congregation, it being hid from their eyes' (Numbers 15:24).

FF. "[In the cited passage, which refers to idolatry committed without intention,] Scripture singles out this religious duty and treats it as a matter entirely unto itself. And what is it? It is idol-worship. [Hence avoidance of idolatry outweighs all other religious duties.]"

GG. You maintain that at the cited passage reference is made to idolatry, but perhaps it refers to any one of the other religious duties to which the Torah makes reference.

HH. When Scripture says, "And when you err and do not do all these commandments" (Numbers 15:22), the reference to "all these commandments" serves to call attention to a single religious duty, [thus bearing the following proposition:]

II. just as one who violates all the religious duties thereby breaks off [heaven's] yoke and annuls the covenant and [Lauterbach:] misrepresents the Torah,

JJ. so one who violates a single religious duty likewise thereby breaks off [heaven's] yoke and annuls the covenant and [Lauterbach:] misrepresents the Torah.

KK. And what religious duty is that? It is idol-worship,

LL. for through it one removes the yoke [of heaven], annuls the covenant, and [Lauterbach:] misrepresents the Torah.

MM. For it is said, "in transgressing his covenant [and has gone and served other gods and worshipped them]" (Deuteronomy 17:2-3).

NN. And how on the basis of Scripture do we know that one who violates all the religious duties thereby breaks off [heaven's] yoke and annuls the covenant and [Lauterbach:] misrepresents the Torah?

OO. Scripture says, "That you should enter the covenant of the Lord your God" (Deuteronomy 29:11).

PP. "Covenant" refers only to the Torah: "These are the words of the covenant which the Lord commanded Moses" (Deuteronomy 28:69).

QQ. [Continuing the statement broken off at FF:] He therefore said to them, "Leave off idol-worship and attach yourself to the religious duties [and assigning them the religious duty at hand was the first step in that process, hence purchasing the beast was done before the rite itself by four days]."

2. A. R. Judah b. Baterah says, "Lo, Scripture says, 'but they did not listen to Moses because of their broken spirit and the cruel bondage in which they were held' (Exodus 6:9).

B. "Now can you imagine a person who gets good news and does not celebrate?

C. "'A male child has been born to you'—will he not celebrate?

D. "'Your master is emancipating you'—will he not celebrate?

E. "If so, why does Scripture say, 'but they did not listen to Moses because of their broken spirit and the cruel bondage in which they were held' (Exodus 6:9)?

F. "The reason is that giving up idol-worship really bothered them.

G. "And so Scripture states: 'And I said to them, "Cast you away every one the detestable things of his eyes and do not defile yourselves with the idols of Egypt" (Ezekiel 20:7); 'But they rebelled against me and would not obey . . . but I did it for my name's sake' (Ezekiel 20:8–9).

H. "This is in line with the verse of Scripture: 'The Lord spoke to Moses and Aaron and commanded them concerning the Israelites' (Exodus 6:13),

I. "commanding them, in particular, about giving up idol-worship."

This enormous sustained discussion sets forth two distinct explanations of the same fact. The first was that it was through religious duties that Israel was to be redeemed, and this preparation of the rite well in advance was the religious duty to which redemption from Egypt would serve as reward. Eleazar Haqqappar does not concede that this was the sole religious duty to Israel's credit. Rather, he sees the preparation for Passover as the antidote to the idolatry in which Israel was steeped. The premise of both positions of course is clear; the dispute concerns a detail. Both parties concur that it is through the merit attained through carrying out religious duties that Israel is redeemed from Egypt. The rather sizable interpolations pose no problems. I.2 then is tacked on because of its emphasis on the power of idolatry over the Israelites in Egypt.

As to an example of a broad proposition demonstrated through a variety of cases—propositions deriving from methodical-analytical work—we may consider the following, which exemplifies the taxon as I have defined it. I give two instances to show a uniform and well-composed program of methodical-analytical inquiry, quite different from the assembly of miscellaneous paraphrases or amplifications of discrete materials, such as we saw previously.

Neziqin 16

LXXIII:I

1. A. "If a man delivers to his neighbor [an ass or an ox or a sheep or any beast to keep, and it dies or is hurt or is driven away, without any one's seeing it, an oath by the Lord shall be between them both to see whether he has not put his hand to his neighbor's property; and the owner shall accept the oath, and he shall not make restitution]":
   B. R. Ishmael says, "Liability is incurred only if he will make a deposit with him and explicitly state to him, 'Here! Keep this for me.'
   C. "But if he merely said to him, 'Keep your eye on it,' lo, the other is exempt [from all responsibility for the loss of the object]."

2. A. "an ass or an ox or a sheep or any beast to keep":
   B. I know only the rule covering an ass, ox, or sheep.
   C. How about all other sorts of beasts?
   D. Scripture says, "or any beast to keep."
   E. Then why should I not read only, "or any beast to keep?" Why specify, "an ass or an ox or a sheep or any beast to keep?"
   F. Should I have read only "and all beasts," I might have inferred that liability is incurred only if one will deposit with the householder every beast.
   G. Scripture specifies, "an ass or an ox or a sheep."
   H. This serves to impose liability for each species unto itself.

    I. And why does Scripture say, "or any beast to keep?"

    J. Scripture comes to tell you that in the case of any generalization which serves to add details to particularizations, everything is encompassed by the generalization.

3. A. "'and it dies':

    B. "the death must be of natural causes.

    C. "'or is hurt':

    D. "It must be a wild beast that injures it.

    E. "'or is driven away':

    F. "It must be driven away by thieves.

    G. "Still, might I maintain that for injury or capture, whether or not the householder could have saved the beast, he should be liable?

    H. "Scripture states, 'and it dies':

    I. "Just as the indicative trait of death is that it is not possible for the farmer to save the beast and so he is exempt from having to make restitution, so in any case in which it is not possible for him to save it, he is exempt from having to make restitution,"

    J. Said to him R. Akiva, "My lord, you draw an analogy for a case in which there is a possibility [of saving the beast] from a case in which there is no possibility of saving the beast, that is, from the case of death, which can only be by the hand of heaven, for a case of injury or capture, which may or may not be because of the hands of heaven or the action of man."

    K. He then reverted and imposed the generative analogy of theft.

4. A. R. Ishmael says, "'If it is torn by beasts, let him bring it as evidence; he shall not make restitution for what has been torn'—

    B. "there is a case of an animal torn by beasts in which one pays, and there is a case of an animal torn by beasts in which one does not pay."

5. A. "without anyone's seeing it":

    B. Witnesses refers to suitable witnesses.

6. A. "without anyone's seeing it, an oath by the Lord shall be between them both":

    B. lo, if there is a suitable witness, the household is exempt on all counts.

7. A. "without anyone's seeing it, an oath by the Lord shall be between them both":

   B. It is an oath with the four-lettered name of God.

   C. From this case you derive the generative analogy for the conduct of all oaths that are listed in the Torah, for all other occasions for taking an oath that are listed in the Torah are given without further specification, while Scripture has spelled out for you the rule applying in one of them,

   D. namely, it is an oath with the four-lettered name of God.

   E. I therefore apply the same detail to all other oaths in the Torah, that they are to be oaths with the four-lettered name of God.

8. A. "between them both":

   B. excluding heirs [who in such a case do not have to take an oath as to the conduct of their father, about which they cannot be fully informed].

9. A. "between them both":

   B. This excludes a case in which the opposing party is suspect concerning oaths.

10. A. "between them both":

    B. This indicates that the presiding judge may not impose an oath against one's will.

11. A. R. Nathan says, "'an oath by the Lord shall be between them both':

    B. "this indicates that the oath applies to both of them."

12. A. "to see whether he has not put his hand to his neighbor's property":

    B. What is involved is misappropriation for one's own use.

    C. You maintain that what is involved is misappropriation for one's own use. But perhaps culpability is incurred whether or not there is misappropriation for one's own use.

    D. Lo, I construct the following argument:

    E. Here we find reference to "whether he has not put his hand to his neighbor's property," and elsewhere we find the same language.

    F. Just as here, what is required is an oath, so elsewhere, what is required is an oath.

G. Just as here, the four-lettered name of God is used, so elsewhere, the four-lettered name of God is used.

H. Just as elsewhere the oath must be taken in court, so here it must be in court.

I. Just as elsewhere, "putting the hand" means misappropriation for one's own use, so here, "putting the hand" means misappropriation for one's own use.

J. Just as elsewhere, it is "for every breach of trust," so here, the oath covers "for every breach of trust."

13. A. "and the owner shall accept the oath, and he shall not make restitution":

B. In this connection sages have said:

C. All those who take an oath do so and are not required to make restitution.

14. A. "and the owner shall accept the oath, and he shall not make restitution":

B. In this connection sages have said:

C. The owner of the carcass takes care of the carcass that is his [and disposes of it].

The familiar reading begins at I.2, which sorts out the particularization and the generalization. Then we have a sequence of exclusionary exegeses, I.3, 4, 5, 6. I.7 generalizes beyond the limits of our passage, which is no longer a case subject to generalization into a law, but rather a type subject to extension to other cases of the same type, a quite different thing. This shows how the word "exegesis" for the passage at hand covers a considerable variety of transformations indeed. The exclusions resume at I.8, 9, 10, 11. I.12 is a familiar exercise, also of exclusion, lifted from the prior discussion. I.13, 14 link our passage to legal writings.

LXXIII:II

1. A. "But if it is stolen from him, [he shall make restitution to its owner. If it is torn by beasts, let him bring it as evidence; he shall not make restitution for what has been torn]":

B. This passage refers to a paid bailee, and the prior one to an unpaid bailee.

C. You maintain that this passage refers to a paid bailee, and the prior one to an unpaid bailee. But perhaps this passage refers to an unpaid bailee, and the prior one to a paid bailee?

D. You may construct the following argument:

E. Since one who hires a beast is liable for what happens, and [in the case at hand] the bailee likewise is liable, just as the one who rents the beast is one who derives benefit from it, so the bailee who has to pay must be one who derives benefit from it.

F. That excludes an unpaid bailee, who does not require benefit from the beast.

G. Lo, you have the choice of adopting not the second but only the first formulation of matters.

H. This passage refers to a paid bailee, and the prior one to an unpaid bailee.

2. A. "But if it is stolen from him":

B. I have the rule only governing theft. How do I know the rule covering the beast's being lost?

C. Lo, you construct the following argument:

D. Since the theft is on account of insufficient guardianship, and the loss is on account of insufficient guardianship, if you have derived the rule governing the beast that is stolen, that one is liable to pay restitution, so in the case of the beast that is lost, one should be liable for making restitution.

3. A. "But if it is stolen from him":

B. R. Yosé the Galilean says, "This encompasses one that is lost."

4. A. ". . . from him":

B. this excludes the shepherd's boy.

5. A. ". . . from him":

B. this includes the shepherd.

6. A. "If it is torn by beasts, let him bring it as evidence; [he shall not make restitution for what has been torn]":

B. "That is, the hide," the words of R. Josiah.

C. "Even though there is no direct proof, there is at least an indication: 'Thus says the Lord, as the shepherd rescues out of the mouth of the lion two legs or a piece of an ear' (Amos 3:12).

D. R. Ahai b. R. Josiah says, "'If it is torn by beasts, let him bring it as evidence': let him bring witnesses that it was torn and then he will be exempt from having to pay restitution."

E. R. Jonathan says, "'If it is torn by beasts, let him bring it as evidence': let him bring the owner to the torn beast and then he will be exempt from having to make restitution."

7. A. "he shall not make restitution for what has been torn":
   B. Or might he have to make restitution for what has been torn?
   C. The following argument suggests so:
   D. Since the loss of the beast is on account of insufficient guardianship, and the animal's being torn is on account of insufficient guardianship, if you have derived the rule governing the beast that is lost, that one is liable to pay restitution, so in the case of the beast that is torn by a beast, one should be liable for making restitution.
   E. Accordingly, "he shall not make restitution for what has been torn," and he might have to make restitution for what has been torn.

8. A. What is a case of a beast that is torn in which one has to make restitution?
   B. For example, a beast that is torn by a cat or a fox.
   C. And how can one prove it on the authority of the Torah?
   D. Scripture says, "for what has been torn":
   E. just as a case of tearing of a beast bears the indicative trait that it is possible to save the beast and one is liable to make restitution, so in any case in which it is possible to save the beast, one is liable to make restitution.
   F. What is a case of a beast that is torn in which one does not have to make restitution?
   G. For example, a beast torn by a wolf, lion, bear, tiger, leopard, or snake.
   H. And how can one prove it on the authority of the Torah?
   I. Scripture says, "and it dies":
   J. just as a case of tearing of a beast bears the indicative trait that it is impossible to save the beast and one is not liable to make restitution, so in any case in which it is impossible to save the beast, "he shall not make restitution for what has been torn."

9. A. "If a man borrows anything of his neighbor, [and it is hurt or dies, the owner not being with it, he shall make full restitution. If the owner was with it, he shall not make restitution; if it was hired, it came for its hire]":
   B. Scripture has removed the borrower from the classification of the guardian and treated that case by itself.

10. A. "of his neighbor":

    B. This indicates that the borrower is liable only at the point that he has removed the beast out of the domain of the owner.

11. A. "and it is hurt or dies":

    B. I know only the case of the beast's being hurt or its dying.

    C. How do I know the rule governing the case in which it is kidnapped?

    D. Lo, you construct the following argument:

    E. Here we find reference to death, and elsewhere we find a reference to death "If a man delivers to his neighbor [an ass or an ox or a sheep or any beast to keep, and it dies or is hurt or is driven away"].

    F. Just as death treated there forms a category encompassing also the beast's being hurt or being kidnapped,

    G. so death here forms a category encompassing also the beast's being hurt or being kidnapped.

    H. As to theft or loss?

    I. You may compose the following argument a fortiori:

    J. if in a case in which one is not liable in the case of death, one is liable in the case of loss or theft, here, in a case in which one is liable for the death of the beast, it is surely reasonable to suppose that we should impose liability also for the loss or theft of the beast.

12. A. "the owner not being with it, he shall make full restitution. If the owner was with it, he shall not make restitution":

    B. Scripture indicates that once the beast left the domain of the person from whom it was borrowed to the domain of the person who has borrowed it, even for a single moment,

    C. then, in the presence of the owner, the borrower is exempt; not in the presence of the owner, the borrower is liable.

13. A. "if it was hired, it came for its hire":

    B. Might I understand that the one who rented the beast takes an oath and is exempt from all further compensation?

    C. Lo, you construct the following argument from analogy:

    D. Since the paid bailee derives benefit, and the one who rents the beast gives a benefit [to the owner], if you have derived the rule governing the one who is a paid bailee that he takes an oath in the case of unavoidable accidents and pays in the case of theft or loss, so the one who rents out the beast should take an oath in the case of unavoidable accidents and pay in the case of theft or loss.

E. Lo, the unpaid bailee forms an analogy, for he gives benefit to the owner of the beast, yet he is exempt from having to pay compensation. He then should give evidence in the case of the one who hires out the beast, that even though he gives benefit to the owner, he should be exempt from having to pay.

F. You may state the following distinction:

G. The one who collects a fee for guarding the beast derives benefit for himself and also gives a benefit to the owner, while the one who hires out the beast also derives benefit for himself and also benefits the owner. But let the unpaid bailee present an anomaly, for while he gives benefit to the owner, he does not derive benefit for himself.

H. Only the one who collects a fee for guarding the beast derives a benefit for himself and also benefits the owner, and likewise the one who hires out the beast derives benefit for himself and also gives a benefit to the owner.

I. If, then, you have derived the rule governing the one who collects a fee for guarding the animal that he takes an oath in the case of unavoidable accidents and pays restitution in the case of theft or loss, so the one who rents out the beast likewise should take an oath in the case of unavoidable accidents and pay restitution in the case of theft or loss.

J. That is why Scripture says, "if it was hired, it came for its hire." [Lauterbach: "If it be a hireling, he loses his hire."]

We proceed to a new topic, beginning with a distinction, well demonstrated indeed, between the types of bailees under discussion. This involves a very acute reading, but, as we see, the reading of the (well established) distinction is solidly founded on the text. Inclusionary and exclusionary work starts at II.2 and moves on through II.3–6. Here again the case of Scripture is transformed into a general rule. II.7 establishes the important principle expressed at II.7.B now by adopting as valid a classification proposed herein. II.8 presents a neat pair. II.11 reverts to the inclusionary approach, beginning with the distinction between the rule set forth in the current chapter and the one provided in the prior chapter, then showing that the same principles apply in both. Here again the independent construction of a classification is accepted. The next interesting argument is at II.13, which asks about the comparison of the paid bailee and the unpaid one, that is, the same problem as just addressed. There can be no doubt that the exposition at hand begins with a well-conceived program and task and accomplishes goals that the exegete-compilers had in mind when they constructed the work.

2

Leviticus and Sifra

A remarkably cogent and well-crafted compilation, Sifra—an address to the Book of Leviticus—uses three forms to make three points. The first, the dialectical, is the demonstration that if we wish to classify things, we must follow the taxa dictated by Scripture rather than relying solely upon the traits of the things we wish to classify. The second, the citation-form, invokes the citation of passages of the Mishnah or the Tosefta in the setting of Scripture. The third is what I call commentary-form, in which a phrase of Scripture is followed by an amplifying clause of some sort. The forms of the document admirably express the polemical purpose of the authorship at hand. What they wished to prove was that a taxonomy resting on the traits of things without reference to Scripture's classifications cannot serve. They further wished to restate the oral Torah in the setting of the written Torah. And, finally, they wished to accomplish the whole by rewriting the written Torah. The dialectical form accomplishes the first purpose, the citation-form the second, and the commentary-form the third.

The simple commentary-form is familiar in Mekhilta Attributed to R. Ishmael, in which a verse, or an element of a verse, is cited, and then a very few words explain the meaning of that verse. Second is the complex form, in which a simple exegesis is augmented in some important way, commonly by questions and answers, so that we have more than simply a verse and a brief exposition of its elements or of its meaning as a whole. The authorship of the Sifra time and again wished to show that prior documents, Mishnah or Tosefta, cited verbatim, require the support of exegesis of Scripture for important propositions, presented in the Mishnah and the Tosefta not on the foundation of exegetical proof at all. In the main, moreover, the authorship of Sifra tends not to attribute its materials to specific authorities, and most of the pericopae containing attributions are shared with Mishnah and Tosefta.

Every example of a complex form, that is, a passage in which we have more than a cited verse and a brief exposition of its meaning, may be called *dialectical*, that is, moving or developing an idea through questions and answers, sometimes implicit, but commonly explicit. What *moves* is the argument, the flow of thought, from problem to problem. The movement is generated by the raising of contradictory questions and theses. There are several subdivisions of the dialectical exegesis, so distinctive as to be treated by themselves. But all exhibit a flow of logical argument, unfolding in questions and answers characteristic, in the later literature, of the Talmud. One important subdivision of the stated form consists of those items, somewhat few in number but all rather large in size and articulation, intended to prove that logic alone is insufficient, and that only through revealed law will a reliable view of what is required be attained. The polemic in these items is pointed and obvious; logic (DYN) never wins the argument, though at a few points in the text flaws seem to suggest disjunctures in the flow of logic. There are a few instances of this form in Mekhilta Attributed to R. Ishmael.

The rhetorical plan of Sifra leads us to recognize that the exegetes, while working verse by verse, in fact have brought a considerable program to their reading of the book of Leviticus. It concerns the interplay of the Oral Torah, represented by the Mishnah, with the written Torah, represented by the Book of Leviticus. That question demanded, in their view, an answer comprising not mere generalities. They wished to show their results through details, masses of details, and, like the rigorous philosophers that they were, they argued essentially through an inductive procedure, amassing evidence that in its accumulation made its point. The syllogism I have identified concerning the priority of the revelation of the Written Torah in the search for truth is nowhere expressed in so many words, because the philosopher–exegetes of the rabbinic world preferred to address an implicit syllogism and to pursue or to test that syllogism solely in a sequence of experiments of a small scale. Therefore Sifra's authorship finds in the Mishnah and Tosefta a sizable laboratory for the testing of propositions. We have then to ask, at what points do Sifra and Mishnah and Tosefta share a common agenda of interests, and at what points does one compilation introduce problems, themes, or questions unknown to the other? The answer to these questions is that Sifra and Mishnah and Tosefta form two large concentric circles, sharing a considerable area in common. Sifra, however, exhibits interests peculiar to itself. On the criterion of common themes and interests, Mishnah and Tosefta and Sifra exhibit a remarkable unity. If I had to compare the rhetorical program of Sifra's authorship with that of their counterparts in our document, I should say that the latter group has taken over and vastly expanded the program selected by the former. To clarify these general remarks, let us now address a particular chapter of Sifra and out of its details form a theory of the repertoire of forms on which our authorship has drawn.

PARASHAT VAYYIQRA DIBURA DENEDABAH

Parashah 7

XIV:I

1. A. ["If his offering to the Lord is a burnt offering of birds, he shall choose [bring near] his offering from turtledoves or pigeons. The priest shall bring it to the altar, pinch off its head, and turn it into smoke on the altar; and its blood shall be drained out against the side of the altar. He shall remove its crop with its contents and cast it into the place of the ashes, at the east side of the altar. The priest shall tear it open by its wings, without severing it, and turn it into smoke on the altar, upon the wood that is on the fire. It is a burnt offering, an offering by fire, of pleasing odor to the Lord" (Leviticus 1:14–17)]:
   B. "[The priest] shall bring it [to the altar]":
   C. What is the sense of this statement?
   D. Since it is said, "he shall choose [bring near] his offering from turtledoves or pigeons," one might have supposed that there can be no fewer than two sets of birds.
   E. Accordingly, Scripture states, "[The priest] shall bring it [to the altar]" to indicate, [by reference to the "it,"] that even a single pair suffices.

Reduced to its simplest syntactic traits, the form consists of the citation of a clause of a verse, followed by secondary amplification of that clause. We may call this commentary-form, in that the rhetorical requirement is citation plus amplification. Clearly, the form sustains a variety of expressions, for example, the one at hand: "what is the sense of this statement . . . since it is said . . . accordingly Scripture states. . . ." But for

our purposes there is no need to differentiate within the commentary-
form.

2. A. "The priest shall bring it to the altar, pinch off its head":
   B. Why does Scripture say, "The priest . . . pinch off . . .?"
   C. This teaches that the act of pinching off the head should be
      done only by a priest.
   D. But is the contrary to that proposition not a matter of logic:
   E. if in the case of a beast of the flock, to which the act of
      slaughter at the north side of the altar is assigned, the partici-
      pation of a priest in particular is not assigned, to the act of
      pinching the neck, to which the act of slaughter at the north
      side of the altar is not assigned, surely should not involve the
      participation of the priest in particular?
   F. That is why it is necessary for Scripture to say, "The priest . . .
      pinch off . . . ,"
   G. so as to teach that the act of pinching off the head should be
      done only by a priest.

3. A. Might one compose an argument to prove that one should
      pinch the neck by using a knife?
   B. For lo, it is a matter of logic.
   C. If to the act of slaughter [of a beast as a sacrifice], for which
      the participation of a priest is not required, the use of a correct
      utensil is required, for the act of pinching the neck, for which
      the participation of a priest indeed is required, surely should
      involve the requirement of using a correct implement!
   D. That is why it is necessary for Scripture to say, "The priest . . .
      pinch off . . . "

4. A. Said R. Akiva, "Now, would it really enter anyone's mind that
      a non-priest should present an offering on the altar?
   B. "Then why is it said, 'The priest . . . pinch off . . . ?'
   C. "This teaches that the act of pinching the neck must be done
      by the priest using his own finger [and not a utensil]."

5. A. Might one suppose that the act of pinching may be done either
      at the head [up by the altar] or at the foot [on the pavement
      down below the altar]?
   B. It is a matter of logic:
   C. If in the case of an offering of a beast, which, when presented

as a sin-offering is slaughtered above [at the altar itself] but
when slaughtered as a burnt offering is killed below [at the
pavement, below the altar], in the case of an offering of fowl,
since when presented as a sin-offering it is slaughtered down
below, surely in the case of a burnt offering it should be done
down below as well!

D. That is why it was necessary for Scripture to make explicit
[that it is killed up by the altar itself:] "The priest shall bring
it to the altar, pinch off its head, and turn it into smoke on the
altar."

E. The altar is explicitly noted with respect to turning the offering into smoke and also to pinching off the head.

F. Just as the offering is turned into smoke up above, at the altar
itself, so the pinching off of the head is to be done up above, at
the altar itself.

The form at hand is to be characterized as a dialectical-exegetical
argument, in which we move from point to point in a protracted, yet very
tight, exposition of a proposition. The proposition is both implicit and
explicit. The implicit proposition is that "logic" does not suffice, a matter
vastly spelled out in uniting the Dual Torah. The explicit proposition
concerns the subject matter at hand. We may identify the traits of this
form very simply: citation of a verse or clause plus a proposition that
interprets that phrase, then "it is a matter of logic" followed by the
demonstration that logic is insufficient for the determination of taxa.

XIV:II

1. A. ". . . pinch off its head":
   B. The pinching off of the head is done at the shoulder.
   C. Might one suppose that it may be done at any other location?
   D. It is a matter of logic. Lo, I shall argue as follows:
   E. Here an act of pinching off at the neck is stated, and elsewhere we find the same [Leviticus 5:8: "He shall bring them
   to the priest, who shall offer first the one for the sin offering,
   pinching its head at the nape without severing it"].
   F. Just as pinching off at the neck in that passage is to be done
   at the nape of the neck, so pinching off at the neck in the
   present context is to be done at the nape of the neck.
   G. Perhaps the analogy is to be drawn differently, specifically,
   just as the pinching stated in that other passage involves

pinching the neck without dividing the bird [Leviticus 5:8: "without severing it"], so the importance of the analogy is to yield the same rule here.

H. In that case, the priest would pinch the neck without severing it.

I. Accordingly, [the ambiguous analogy is such as to require] Scripture to state, "... pinch off its head."

We have an example of the dialectical exegesis of the limitations of logic for definition of taxa.

2. A. "[turn it into smoke on the altar;] and its blood shall be drained out":

B. Can one describe matters in such a way?

C. Specifically, after the carcass is turned into smoke, can one drain out the blood?

D. But one pinches the neck in accord with the way in which one turns it into smoke:

E. Just as we find that the turning of the carcass into smoke is done up to the head by itself and then the body by itself, so in the act of pinching the neck, the head is by itself and the body is by itself.

3. A. And how do we know that in the case of turning a carcass into smoke, the head is done by itself?

B. When Scripture says, "The priest [shall tear it open by its wings, without severing it,] and turn it into smoke on the altar" (Leviticus 1:17),

C. lo, the turning of the body into smoke is covered by that statement.

D. Lo, when Scripture states here, "pinch off its head, and turn it into smoke on the altar," it can only mean that the head is to be turned into smoke by itself.

E. Now, just as we find that the turning of the carcass into smoke is done up to the head by itself and then the body by itself, so in the act of pinching the neck, the head is by itself and the body is by itself.

II.2 and 3 present in a rather developed statement the simple exegetical form. The formal requirement is not obscured, however, since all we have is the citation of a clause followed by secondary amplification. This version of commentary-form obviously cannot be seen as identical to the other; but so far as the dictates of rhetoric are concerned, there is no material difference, since the variations affect only the secondary amplification of the basic proposition, and in both cases, the basic proposition is set forth by the citation of the verse or clause followed by a sentence or two of amplification.

XIV:III

1. A. "... and its blood shall be drained out [against the side of the altar]":
   B. all of its blood: he takes hold of the head and the body and drains the blood out of both pieces.

This is commentary-form.

2. A. "... against the side of the altar":
   B. not on the wall of the ramp up to the altar, and not on the wall of the foundation, nor on the wall of the courtyard.

3. A. It is to be on the upper half of the wall.
   B. Might one suppose it may be on the lower half of the wall?
   C. It is a matter of logic: in the case of the sacrifice of a beast, which, if done as a sin-offering, has its blood tossed on the upper part of the wall, and if done as a burnt offering, has its blood tossed on the lower part of the wall,
   D. in the case of the sacrifice of a bird, since, if it is offered as a sin offering, the blood is tossed at the lower half of the wall, should logic not dictate that if it is offered as a burnt offering, its blood should be tossed on the lower part of the wall as well?
   E. That is why it is necessary for Scripture to frame matters in this way:
   F. "The priest shall bring it to the altar, pinch off its head, and turn it into smoke on the altar; and its blood shall be drained out against the side of the altar,"
   G. the altar is noted with respect to turning the carcass into smoke and also with reference to the draining of the blood.
   H. Just as the act of turning the carcass into smoke is done at the topside of the altar, so the draining of the blood is done at the topside of the altar.

This is the dialectical–exegetical form. Now we come to a third usage.

4. A. How does the priest do it?
   B. The priest went up on the ramp and went around the circuit. He came to the southeastern corner. He would wring off its head from its neck and divide the head from the body. And he drained off its blood onto the wall of the altar [Mishnah Zebahim 6:5B–E].
   C. If one did it from the place at which he was standing and downward by a cubit, it is valid. R. Simeon and R. Yohanan ben Beroqah say, "The entire deed was done only at the top of the altar" (Tosefta Zebahim 7:9C–D].

What we have now is the verbatim citation of a passage of the Mishnah or of the Tosefta, joined to its setting in the exegetical framework of Sifra by some sort of joining formula. We shall call this formal convention Mishnah-citation form. Its formal requirement is simply appropriate joining language.

XIV:IV
1. A. "He shall remove its crop [with its contents and cast it into the place of the ashes, at the east side of the altar]":
   B. this refers to the bird's crop.
   C. Might one suppose that one should extract the crop surgically with a knife?
   D. Scripture says, ". . . with its contents."
   E. He should remove it with its contents [including the innards, or, alternatively, the feathers].
   F. Abba Yosé b. Hanan says, "He should remove the intestines with it."

A variation on commentary-form, we have secondary development at IV.1.C. I am not inclined to think a sizable catalogue of variations on commentary-form will materially advance our inquiry.

Now that we see clearly how the framers of Sifra make their statements, let us turn to the question of what they wish to say. For its topical program the authorship of Sifra takes the Book of Leviticus. For propositions Sifra's authorship presents episodic and ad hoc sentences. If we ask how these sentences form propositions other than amplifications of points made in Leviticus itself, and how we may restate those propositions in a coherent way, so far as I can see, nothing sustained and coherent emerges. Without leading the reader through all 257 chapters of Sifra, I state simply that Sifra does not constitute a propositional document transcending its precipitating text. But that in no way bears the implication that the document's authorship merely collected and arranged this and that about the Book of Leviticus. This matter requires amplification, first negatively, then positively.

We must conclude for three reasons that Sifra does not set forth propositions in the way in which the Rabbah-compilations and Sifré to Deuteronomy do. Firstly, in general I fail to see a topical program distinct from that of Scripture, nor do I find it possible to set forth important propositions that transcend the cases at hand. Sifra remains wholly within Scripture's orbit and range of discourse, proposing only to expand and clarify what it finds within Scripture. Where the authorship moves beyond Scripture, it is not toward fresh theological or philosophical thought, but rather to a quite different set of issues altogether, concerning Mishnah and Tosefta. When we describe the topical program of the document, the blatant and definitive trait of Sifra is simple: the topical program and order derive from Scripture. Just as the Mishnah defines the topical program and order for Tosefta, the Yerushalmi, and the Bavli, so Scripture does so for Sifra. It follows that Sifra takes as its structure the plan and program of the written Torah, in contrast to decisions of the framers or compilers of Tosefta and the two Talmuds.

Secondly, for sizable passages, the sole point of coherence for the discrete sentences or paragraphs of Sifra's authorship derives from the base verse of Scripture that is subject to commentary. That fact corresponds to the results of form-analysis and the description of the logics of cogent discourse. While, as we have noted, the Mishnah holds thought together through propositions of various kinds, with special interest in demonstrating propositions through a well-crafted program of logic of a certain kind, Sifra's authorship appeals to a different logic altogether. It is one which I have set forth as fixed associative discourse. This is not a propositional logic—by definition.

The third fundamental observation draws attention to the paramount position, within this restatement of the written Torah or the oral Torah. We may say very simply that, in a purely formal and superficial sense, a sizable proportion of Sifra consists simply of the association of completed statements of the oral Torah with the exposition of the written Torah, the whole re-presenting as one whole Torah, the dual Torah received by Moses at Sinai (speaking within the Torah-myth). Even at the very surface we observe a simple fact. Without the Mishnah or the Tosefta, our authorship would have had virtually nothing to say about passage after passage of the written Torah. A deeper knowledge of Sifra, set forth in my complete translation, has shown, furthermore, that far more often than citing the Mishnah or the Tosefta verbatim, our authorship cites principles of law or theology fundamental to the Mishnah's treatment of a given topic, even when that particular passage of the Mishnah or the Tosefta is not cited verbatim.

It follows that the three basic and definitive traits of Sifra, are: first, its total adherence to the topical program of the written Torah for order and plan; second, its very common reliance upon the phrases or verses of the written Torah for the joining into coherent discourse of discrete thoughts, for example, comments on, or amplifications of, words or phrases; and third, its equally profound dependence upon the oral Torah for its program of thought, the problematic that defines the issues the authorship wishes to explore and resolve.

This brings us to the positive side of the picture. Sifra in detail presents no paramount propositions. Sifra as a whole demonstrates a highly distinctive and vigorously demonstrated proposition. While in detail we cannot reconstruct a topical program other than that of Scripture, viewed in its indicative and definitive traits of rhetoric, logic, and implicit proposition, Sifra does take up a well-composed position on a fundamental issue, namely, the relationship between the written Torah, represented by the Book of Leviticus, and the oral Torah, represented by the passages of the Mishnah deemed by the authorship of Sifra to be pertinent to the Book of Leviticus. In a simple and fundamental sense, Sifra joins the two Torahs into a single statement, accomplishing a re-presentation of the written Torah in topic and in program and in the logic of cogent discourse, and within that rewriting of the written Torah, a re-presentation of the oral Torah in its paramount problematic and substantive propositions.

Stated simply, the written Torah provides the form, the oral Torah, the content. What emerges is not merely a united, dual Torah, but *The* Torah, stated whole and complete, in the context defined by the Book of Leviticus. Here the authorship of Sifra presents, through its re-presentation, The Torah as a proper noun, all together, all at once, and, above all, complete and utterly coherent. In order to do so, our authorship has constructed through its document, first, the sustained critique of the Mishnah's *Listenwissenschaft*, and second, the defense of the Mishnah's propositions on the foundation of scriptural principles of taxonomy, hierarchical classification in particular.

First, we shall observe a sequence of cases in which Sifra's author-ship demonstrates that *Listenwissenschaft*—collecting data and selecting the ones with shared traits that permit us to form a list and identify the rule that is common to the list; that is, standard method in natural history—is a self-evidently valid mode of demonstrating the truth of propositions. Second, we shall note, in the same cases, that *the* source of the correct classification of things is Scripture and only Scripture. With-out Scripture's intervention into the taxonomy of the world, we should have no knowledge at all of which things fall into which classifications and therefore are governed by which rules. Let us begin with a sustained example of the right way of doing things. Appropriately, the opening composition of Sifra shows us the contrast between relying on Scrip-ture's classification, and the traits imputed by Scripture to the taxa it identifies, and appealing to categories not defined and endowed with indicative traits by Scripture.

PARASHAT YAYYIQRA DIBURA DENEDABAH

Parashah 1

I:I

1. A. "The Lord called [to Moses] and spoke [to him from the tent of meeting, saying, 'Speak to the Israelite people and say to them']" (Leviticus 1:1):

   B. He gave priority to the calling over the speaking.

   C. That is in line with the usage of Scripture.

   D. Here there is an act of speaking, and in connection with the encounter at the bush [Exodus 3:4: "God called to him out of the bush, 'Moses, Moses'"], there is an act of speaking.

   E. Just as in the latter occasion, the act of calling is given priority over the act of speaking [even though the actual word, "speaking" does not occur, it is implicit in the framing of the verse], so here, with respect to the act of speaking, the act of calling is given priority over the act of speaking.

2. A. No [you cannot generalize on the basis of that case,] for if you invoke the case of the act of speaking at the bush, which is the first in the sequence of acts of speech [on which account there had to be a call prior to entry into discourse],

B. will you say the same of the act of speech in the tent of meeting, which assuredly is not the first in a sequence of acts of speech [so there was no need for a preliminary entry into discourse through a call]?

C. The act of speech at Mount Sinai [Exodus 19:3] will prove to the contrary, for it is assuredly not the first in a sequence of acts of speech, yet, in that case, there was an act of calling prior to the act of speech.

3. A. No, [the exception proves nothing,] for if you invoke in evidence the act of speech at Mount Sinai, which pertained to all the Israelites, will you represent it as parallel to the act of speech in the tent of meeting, which is not pertinent to all Israel?

B. Lo, you may sort matters out by appeal to comparison and contrast, specifically:

C. The act of speech at the bush, which is the first of the acts of speech, is not of the same classification as the act of speech at Sinai, which is not the first act of speech.

D. And the act of speech at Sinai, which is addressed to all Israel, is not in the same classification as the act of speech at the bush, which is not addressed to all Israel.

4. A. What they have in common, however, is that both of them are acts of speech, deriving from the mouth of the Holy One, addressed to Moses, in which case, the act of calling comes prior to the act of speech,

B. so that, by way of generalization, we may maintain that every act of speech which comes from the mouth of the Holy One to Moses will be preceded by an act of calling.

5. A. Now, if what the several occasions have in common is that they all involve an act of speech, accompanied by fire, from the mouth of the Holy One, addressed to Moses, so that the act of calling was given priority over the act of speaking, then every case in which there is an act of speech, involving fire, from the mouth of the Holy One, addressed to Moses, should involve an act of calling prior to the act of speech.

B. But then an exception is presented by the act of speech at the tent of meeting, in which there was no fire.

C. [That is why it was necessary for Scripture on this occasion to state explicitly,] "The Lord called [to Moses and spoke to him

from the tent of meeting, saying, 'Speak to the Israelite people
and say to them']" (Leviticus 1:1).

D. That explicit statement shows that, on the occasion at hand,
priority was given to the act of calling over the act of speaking.

I:II

1. A. ["The Lord called to Moses and spoke to him from the tent of
meeting, saying, 'Speak to the Israelite people and say to
them'" (Leviticus 1:1)]: Might one suppose that the act of
calling applied only to this one act of speaking?

    B. And how on the basis of Scripture do we know that on the
occasion of all acts of speaking that are mentioned in the
Torah, [there was a prior act of calling]?

    C. Scripture specifies, "from the tent of meeting,"

    D. which bears the sense that on every occasion on which it was
an act of speaking from the tent of meeting, there was an act
of calling prior to the act of speaking.

2. A. Might one suppose that there was an act of calling only prior
to the acts of speech alone?

    B. How on the basis of Scripture do I know that the same
practice accompanied acts of saying and also acts of commanding?

    C. Said R. Simeon, "Scripture says not only, '. . . spoke, . . .' but
'. . . and he spoke,' [with the inclusion of the *and*] meant to
encompass also acts of telling and also acts of commanding."

The exercise of generalization addresses the character of God's meeting with Moses. The point of special interest is the comparison of the
meeting at the bush and the meeting at the tent of meeting. In question
is whether all acts of God's calling and talking with, or speaking to, the
prophet are the same, or whether some of these acts are of a different
classification from others. In point of fact, we are able to come to a
generalization, worked out at I:I.5.A. And that permits us to explain why
there is a different usage at Leviticus 1:1 from what characterizes
parallel cases. I:II.1–2 proceeds to generalize from the case at hand to
other usages entirely, a very satisfying conclusion to the whole. I separate I:II from I:I because had I:I ended at I.5, it could have stood
complete and on its own, and therefore I see I:II as a brief appendix. The
interest for my argument should not be missed. We seek generalizations,
governing rules, that are supposed to emerge by the comparison and

contrast of categories or of classifications. The way to do this is to follow the usage of Scripture, that alone. And the right way of doing things is then illustrated. Now we seek rules that emerge from Scripture's classification.

I.IV

1. A. How on the basis of Scripture do we know that every act of speech involved the call to Moses, Moses [two times]?

   B. Scripture says, "God called to him out of the bush, 'Moses, Moses'" (Exodus 3:4).

   C. Now when Scripture says, "And he said," it teaches that every act of calling involved the call to Moses, Moses [two times].

2. A. And how on the basis of Scripture do we know, furthermore, that at each act of calling, he responded, "Here I am"?

   B. Scripture says, "God called to him out of the bush, 'Moses, Moses,' and he said, 'Here I am'" (Exodus 3:4).

   C. Now when Scripture says, "And he said," it teaches that in response to each act of calling, he said, "Here I am."

3. A. "Moses, Moses" (Exodus 3:4), "Abraham, Abraham" (Genesis 22:11), "Jacob, Jacob" (Genesis 46:2), "Samuel, Samuel" (1 Samuel 3:10).

   B. This language expresses affection and also means to move to prompt response.

4. A. Another interpretation of "Moses, Moses":

   B. This was the very same Moses both before he had been spoken with [by God] and also afterward.

The final unit completes the work of generalization which began with the opening passage. The point throughout is that there are acts of calling and speech, and a general rule pertains to them all. IV.3 and IV.4 conclude with observations outside of the sought for generalization. The first of the two interprets the repetition of a name, the second, a conclusion particular to Moses personally. These seem tacked on. The first lesson in the rehabilitation of taxonomic logic is then clear. Let me state the proposition, which is demonstrated over and over again in rhetoric and logic: *Scripture provides reliable taxa and dictates the indicative characteristics of those taxa.*

The next step in the argument is to maintain that Scripture *alone* can set forth the proper names of things: classifications and their hierarchical order. How do we appeal to Scripture to designate the operative classifications? Here is a simple example of the alternative mode of classification, one that does not appeal to the traits of things but to the utilization of names by Scripture. What we see is how by naming things in one way, rather than in another, Scripture orders all things, classifying and, in the nature of things, also hierarchizing them.

PARASHAT VAYYIQRA DIBURA DENEDABAH

Parashah 4

VII:V

1. A. "... and Aaron's sons the priests shall present the blood and throw the blood [round about against the altar that is at the door of the tent of meeting]":

   B. Why does Scripture make use of the word "blood" twice [instead of using a pronoun]?

   C. [It is for the following purpose:] How on the basis of Scripture do you know that if blood deriving from one burnt offering was confused with blood deriving from another burnt offering, or if blood deriving from one burnt offering with blood deriving from a beast that had been substituted therefore, or if blood deriving from a burnt offering with blood deriving from an unconsecrated beast, should the mixture nonetheless be presented?

   D. It is because Scripture makes use of the word "blood" twice [instead of using a pronoun].

2. A. Is it possible to suppose that while if blood deriving from beasts in the specified classifications, it is to be presented, for the simple reason that if the several beasts while alive had been confused with one another, they might be offered up,

   B. but how do we know that even if the blood of a burnt offering were confused with that of a beast killed as a guilt offering, [it is to be offered up]?

   C. I shall concede the case of the mixture of the blood of a burnt offering confused with that of a beast killed as a guilt offering, it is to be presented, for both this one and that one fall into the classification of Most Holy Things.

D. But how do I know that if the blood of a burnt offering were confused with the blood of a beast slaughtered in the classification of peace offerings or of a thanksgiving offering, [it is to be presented]?

E. I shall concede the case of the mixture of the blood of a burnt offering confused with that of a beast slaughtered in the classification of peace offerings or of a thanksgiving offering, [it is to be presented], because the beasts in both classifications produce blood that has to be sprinkled four times.

F. But how do I know that if the blood of a burnt offering were confused with the blood of a beast slaughtered in the classification of a firstling, or a beast that was counted as tenth, or of a beast designated as a passover, [it is to be presented]?

G. I shall concede the case of the mixture of the blood of a burnt offering confused with that of a beast slaughtered in the classification of firstling, or a beast that was counted as tenth, or of a beast designated as a passover, [it is to be presented], because Scripture uses the word "blood" twice.

H. Then while I may make that concession, might I also suppose that if the blood of a burnt offering was confused with the blood of beasts that had suffered an invalidation, it also may be offered up?

I. Scripture says, ". . . its blood," [thus excluding such a case].

J. Then I shall concede the case of a mixture of the blood of a valid burnt offering with the blood of beasts that had suffered an invalidation, which blood is not valid to be presented at all.

K. But how do I know that if such blood were mixed with the blood deriving from beasts set aside as sin offerings to be offered on the inner altar, [it is not to be offered up]?

L. I can concede that the blood of a burnt offering that has been mixed with the blood deriving from beasts set aside as sin offerings to be offered on the inner altar is not to be offered up, for the one is offered on the inner altar, and the other on the outer altar [the burnt offering brought as a free will offering, under discussion here, is slaughtered at the altar ". . . that is at the door of the tent of meeting," not at the inner altar].

M. But how do I know that even if the blood of a burnt offering was confused with the blood of sin offerings that are to be slaughtered at the outer altar, it is not to be offered up?

N. Scripture says, ". . . its blood," [thus excluding such a case].

In place of the rejecting of arguments resting on classifying species into a common genus, we now demonstrate how classification really is to be carried on. It is through the imposition upon data of the categories dictated by Scripture: Scripture's use of language. That is the force of this powerful exercise. V.1 sets the stage, simply pointing out that the use of the word "blood" twice encompasses a case in which blood in two distinct classifications is somehow confused in the process of the conduct of the cult. In such a case it is quite proper to pour out the mixture of blood deriving from distinct sources, for example, beasts that have served different, but comparable purposes. We then systematically work out the limits of that rule, showing how comparability works, then pointing to cases in which comparability is set aside. Throughout the exposition, we invoke the formulation of Scripture, subordinating logic, or in our instance, the process of classification of like species to the dictation of Scripture. I cannot imagine a more successful demonstration of what the framers wish to say.

In what follows, we shall see an enormous, coherent, and beautifully articulated exercise in the comparison and contrast of many things of a single genus. The whole holds together, because Scripture makes possible the statement of all things within a single rule. That is, as we have noted, precisely what the framers of the Mishnah proposed to accomplish. Our authorship maintains that only by appeal to the Torah is this feat of learning possible. If, then, we wish to understand all things together and at once under a single encompassing rule, we had best revert to the Torah, with its account of the rightful names, positions, and order, imputed to all things.

PARASHAT VAYYIQRA DIBURA DENEDABAH

Parashah 11

XXII:I

1. A. [With reference to Mishnah Menahot 5:5:] There are those [offerings which require bringing near but do not require waving, waving but not bringing near, waving and bringing near, neither waving nor bringing near. These are offerings which require bringing near but do not require waving: the meal offering of fine flour, and the meal offering prepared in the baking pan, and the meal offering prepared in the frying pan, and the meal offering of cakes, and the meal offering of

wafers, and the meal offering of priests, and the meal offering of an anointed priest, and the meal offering of Gentiles, and the meal offering of women, and the meal offering of a sinner. R. Simeon says, "The meal offering of priests and of the anointed priest—bringing near does not apply to them, because the taking of a handful does not apply to them. And whatever is not subject to the taking of a handful is not subject to bringing near,"] [Scripture] says, "When you present to the Lord a meal offering that is made in any of these ways, it shall be brought [to the priest who shall take it up to the altar]":

B. What requires bringing near is only the handful alone. How do I know that I should encompass under the rule of bringing near, the meal offering?

C. Scripture says explicitly, "meal offering."

D. How do I know that I should encompass all meal offerings?

E. Scripture says, using the accusative particle, "the meal offering."

2. A. I might propose that what requires bringing near is solely the meal offering brought as a free will offering.

B. How do I know that the rule encompasses an obligatory meal offering?

C. It is a matter of logic.

D. Bringing a meal offering as a free will offering and bringing a meal offering as a matter of obligation, form a single classification. Just as a meal offering presented as a free will offering requires bringing near, so the same rule applies to a meal offering of a sinner [brought as a matter of obligation], which should likewise require bringing near.

E. No, if you have stated that rule governing bringing near in the case of a free will offering, on which oil and frankincense have to be added, will you say the same of the meal offering of a sinner [Leviticus 5:11], which does not require oil and frankincense?

F. The meal offering brought by a wife accused of adultery will prove to the contrary, for it does not require oil and frankincense, but it does require bringing near [as is stated explicitly at Numbers 5:15].

G. No, if you have applied the requirement of bringing near to the meal offering brought by a wife accused of adultery, which also requires waving, will you say the same of the meal offering of a sinner, which does not have to be waved?

H. Lo, you must therefore reason by appeal to a polythetic analogy [in which not all traits pertain to all components of the category, but some traits apply to them all in common]:

I. the meal offering brought as a free will offering, which requires oil and frankincense, does not in all respects conform to the traits of the meal offering of a wife accused of adultery, which does not require oil and frankincense, and the meal offering of the wife accused of adultery, which requires waving, does not in all respects conform to the traits of a meal offering brought as a free will offering, which does not require waving.

J. But what they have in common is that they are alike in requiring the taking up of a handful and they are also alike in that they require bringing near.

K. I shall then introduce into the same classification the meal offering of a sinner, which is equivalent to them as to the matter of the taking up of a handful, and also should be equivalent to them as to the requirement of being drawn near.

L. But might one not argue that the trait that all have in common is that all of them may be brought equally by a rich or a poor person and require drawing near, which then excludes from the common classification the meal offering of a sinner, which does not conform to the rule that it may be brought equally by a rich or a poor person, [but may be brought only by a poor person,] and such an offering also should not require being brought near!

M. [The fact that the polythetic classification yields indeterminate results means failure once more, and, accordingly,] Scripture states, "meal offering,"

N. with this meaning: the same are the meal offering brought as a free will offering and the meal offering of a sinner, both this and that require being brought near.

The elegant exercise draws together the various types of meal offerings and shows that they cannot form a classification of either a monothetic or a polythetic character. Consequently, Scripture must be invoked to supply the proof for the classification of the discrete items. The important language is at I.2.H–J: these differ from those, and those from these, but what they have in common is. . . . Then we demonstrate, with our appeal to Scripture, the sole valid source of polythetic classification, I.2.M. And this is constant throughout Sifra.

The strength of argument of our authorship is manifest in its capacity to demonstrate how diverse things relate through common points, so long as the commonalities derive from a valid source. And that leads us to the central and fundamental premise of all: Scripture, its picture of the classifications of nature and supernature, its account of the rightful names and order of all things, is the sole source for that encompassing and generalizing principle that permits scientific inquiry into the governing laws to take place. This tripartite subject of (1) the transformation of case to rule in Leviticus through the exercise of exclusion and inclusion; (2) the movement from rule to system and structure, hence the interest in taxonomy based on Scripture's classification system; and (3) the reunification of the two Torahs into a single statement, effected in part through commentary, in part through extensive citation of passages of the Mishnah and of the Tosefta—this is what I take to be the topic addressed by Sifra, together with its simple problematic: the relationship of the two Torahs not only in form but at the deepest structures of thought.

Sifra and the other documents of its class do not merely assemble this and that, forming a hodgepodge of things people happen to have said. In the case of each document we can answer the question of topic as much as of rhetoric and logic: Why this, not that? That is to say, why discuss this topic in this pattern of language and resort to this logic of cogent discourse, rather than treating some other topic in a different set of language patterns and relying on other modes of making connections and drawing conclusions? These are questions that we have now answered for Sifra. The writings before us, seen individually and as a group, stand neither wholly autonomously nor forming a continuity of discourse, whether in rhetoric, or in logic, or in topic and problematic. They are connected. They intersect at a few places but not over the greater part of their territory. For—as I argued in the Prologue—they are not compilations but freestanding compositions. They are not essentially the same, but articulately differentiated. They are not lacking all viewpoint, serving a single undifferentiated task of collecting and arranging whatever was at hand. Quite to the contrary, these documents emerge as sharply differentiated from one another and clearly defined, each through its distinctive viewpoint and particular polemic on one side, and formal and aesthetic qualities on the other.

3

Numbers and Sifré to Numbers

Were we to face the task of writing an encyclopedia article on Sifré to Numbers, we would want to answer these questions: (1) Where, when, and by whom was the book written? (2) What is the book about? (3) Does the author propose to argue a particular case, and, if so, what polemic does he propose to advance? Yet another range of questions—is it a book or an anthology, a cogent statement or a composite?—might also attract our attention. Defining the document demands classifying it, and describing the document requires stating its main points of emphasis. In other words, just what is Sifré to Numbers, what sort of a book is it, and what particular example of that sort of book is it? These questions define the work of introducing a book—any book. The answers to these and other questions constitute the definition of this book. They tell us what it is: its context, composition, and contents.

The character and contents of Sifré to Numbers allows no answer to any of these questions. To deal with all of them, we have to move beyond the limits of the book itself, through an exercise of comparison and contrast. But even reaching the point of comparison and contrast will require considerable preliminary analysis. Let us speak first of context. The book reaches us under particular auspices, so we turn first to the institutional medium by which Sifré to Numbers has come down from antiquity to our own day: the medium of Judaism. Sifré to Numbers is a holy book. Let us start there, and there, too, we shall conclude.

Books such as Sifré to Numbers, that form part of the canon of Judaism, that is, of "the one whole Torah of Moses our rabbi revealed by God at Sinai," do not contain answers to questions of definition that ordinarily receive answers within the pages of a given book. In antiquity, books or other important writings, for example, letters and treatises, bore the name of the author or at least an attribution, Aristotle's or Paul's name, or the attribution to Enoch or Baruch or Luke. No document in the canon of Judaism produced in late antiquity has a named author, let alone a clear-cut date of composition, a defined place or circumstance in which it was written, a sustained and ongoing argument to which we can readily gain access, or any of the other usual indicators by which we define the authorship, and therefore its context and circumstance. Internal evidence alone testifies; there is nothing on the surface to tell us who is telling us these things and why: what is at issue? So the canon of which our document forms a part presents single books as episodes in a timeless, ahistorical setting: Torah revealed to Moses by God at Mount Sinai, but written down long afterward. This theological conviction about the canon overall denies us information to introduce the book at hand, that is to say, what it is. Without the usual indicators, then, how are we to read our document on its own terms, to answer the question: what is this book? When, where, why was it written? What does it mean?

Lacking clear answers to these questions, we turn to the evidence the document does provide: its salient traits of plan and program. By plan I mean simply the literary traits before us. The intellectual program, so far as we can define it, derives from those same literary traits: from *how* the book's authorship presents its messages, we hope to learn *what* important points that authorship proposed to impart. So these two go together: form and meaning, structure and sustained polemic. Proposing to define the document at hand, we begin from the outside, with formal traits, and work our way inward, toward the deciphering of the messages contained within those recurrent points of interest and stress. Only by seeing the document whole and all at once can we gain the rudiments of a definition. Describing, and so defining bits and pieces would yield no encompassing description of the whole. If we ask, then, what is this book, we begin with the entire document.

If we focus, as we must, on intrinsic traits exhibited within the words of the document itself, we do not know much more than that the book forms part of a canon of books. We know this because Sifré to Numbers persistently refers to another book, specifically, sections of the Book of Numbers. (But the selection of the sections chosen for treatment, specified in the table of contents, conforms to no clear pattern and so cannot find explanation by reference to some larger task or plan.) Still, the fact that the authorship declares its dependence upon another authorship—a fact deriving from entirely intrinsic traits, inductively discovered—testifies to the canonical context in which our document comes into being. In point of fact, all we know about Sifré to Numbers is that it forms a document organized around another document, or, in conventional language, it is a commentary to a text.

What does this mean? Simply this: were we to approach our document without knowing that the authors use as their point of departure—the organization and formal program of their book—an already available book written by someone else, we would understand very little in the book at hand. Sifré to Numbers, read out of alignment with the Book of Numbers, presents unintelligible gibberish. To state matters affirmatively, we define the present book only when we can describe its relationship to the book that forms the trellis for its vine. Even after we know that we have a commentary to a text, we still possess little more knowledge of the program and purpose of Sifré to Numbers than we did previously. For (to revert to the list of things we do not know) we still do not know who wrote the book, for what purpose, with the intent of advancing what ideas or program. We do not even know what made the author select as the organizing structure for his book the Book of Numbers in particular, or whether some other book would have served his purpose just as well.

Nonetheless, when we have worked out the points our authorship wishes to make in the reading of the Book of Numbers, we shall have come a long way toward defining the purpose and polemic of Sifré to Numbers. All propositions must emerge, in a commentary to a text, out of the relationship between the commentary and the text. And since that relationship, by definition, proves fixed and consistent, we indeed can say what, over all, in form and in the implications of form, the authorship proposed to demonstrate: its main points. These, as we shall see, concern specific propositions, exemplified in the reading of the Book of Numbers. But these same points could have been made, and in fact were made, through the systematic reading of at least one other pentateuchal book, the Book of Leviticus, as we saw in the previous chapter. So it is not the Book of Numbers that has dictated the program of Sifré to Numbers. It is a sustained program, defined and set forth by the authorship at hand, that has told that authorship what, in the Book of Numbers, demands comment, and what comment must be made.

The upshot? The extrinsic traits of the document at hand tell us practically nothing about the book and do not permit us to define it. So we cannot say what Sifré to Numbers is and is not, who wrote it, to make what point, when, why, where, and on and on. And if we cannot answer these questions, we also cannot make sense of the document before us. We know what it says, but we do not know what it means. Lacking all context, Sifré to Numbers provides merely a set of formal observations.

We simply do not know what the book is, even though we can say what is in the book (and even define the meanings of words and phrases in the interstices of discourse). But where shall we look to find a context for description? The answer is the internal traits. The sole fact in hand is the document itself. For even the context—the canonical setting—is imputed by others, by circumstance and sentiment beyond the pages of the book.

Inductive evidence derives from the way in which the authorship at hand has organized and expressed its ideas. The document rests upon clear-cut choices of formal and rhetorical preference, so it is, from the viewpoint of form and mode of expression, cogent. Formal choices prove uniform and paramount. How to discover the forms of discourse? To begin with I analyze one *pisqa*, to show its recurrent structures. These as a matter of hypothesis I describe and categorize. Then, I proceed to survey two more *pisqaot* to see whether or not a single cogent taxonomic structure provides a suitable system of classification for diverse units of discourse. On that basis we can describe the incremental message, the cumulative effect, of the formal traits of speech and thought revealed in the uniform rhetoric and syntax of the document. The framers or redactors followed a set of rules which we are able to discern. These rules lead us deep into the interior of our authorship: people say things the way they mean to say them, and how they express their ideas imparts meaning to what they say.

We proceed to the definition of the forms of Sifré to Numbers. These forms I call literary structures. A literary structure is a set of rules that dictates those recurrent conventions of expression, organization, or proportion, that are *extrinsic* to the message of the author. The conventions at hand bear none of the particular burden of the author's message, so they are not idiosyncratic but systemic and public. A literary structure imposes upon the individual writer a limited set of choices about how he will convey his message. Or the formal convention will limit an editor or redactor to an equally circumscribed set of alternatives about how to arrange received materials. These conventions then form a substrate of the literary culture that preserves and expresses the world view and way of life of the system at hand. When we can define the literary structures, we also can ask about the program of thought—recurrent modes of analysis and exercises of conflict and resolution—that dictate the content of the commentary. How I think and what the syntax of my language and thought permits me to say, dictates what I shall think and why I shall think it: this, not that.

How are we to recognize the presence of such structures? On the basis of forms that merely appear to be patterned or extrinsic to particular meaning and so entirely formal, we cannot allege that we have in hand a fixed, literary structure. Such a judgment would prove subjective. Nor shall we benefit from bringing to the text at hand recurrent syntactic or grammatical patterns shown in *other* texts, even of the same canon of literature, to define conventions for communicating ideas. Quite to the contrary, we find guidance in a simple principle: *A text has to define its own structures for us.*

This its authors do by repeatedly resorting to a severely circumscribed set of linguistic patterns and literary conventions and to no others. These patterns, we shall soon see, dictate not only formal syntax and principles of composition but also logical analysis and the propositions of argument. On the basis of inductive evidence alone, a document will testify that its authors adhere to a fixed canon of literary forms and that these forms guide the authors to the propositions for, or against, which they choose to argue: the program of the book, not only its plan. If demonstrably present, these forms present an author or editor with a few choices on how ideas are to be organized and expressed in intelligible— again, therefore, public—compositions. So internal evidence alone testifies to the literary structures of a given text.

The adjective "recurrent" constitues a redundancy when joined to the noun "structure." To state matters negatively—we cannot know that we have a structure if the text under analysis does not repeatedly resort to the presentation of its message through that disciplined structure external to its message on any given point. And, it follows self-evidently, we do know that we have a structure when the text in hand repeatedly follows recurrent conventions of expression, organization, or proportion *extrinsic* to the message of the author. The literary structures or patterns find definition in entirely formal and objective facts: the placement of the key-verse subject to discussion in the composition at hand, the origin of that verse. No subjective or impressionistic judgment intervenes.

How shall we proceed to identify the structures of the document before us? It seems to me we had best move first to the analysis of a single *pisqa*. We seek, within that *pisqa*, to identify what holds the whole together. For this purpose I shall try to describe what I conceive to be the underlying and repeated structures of formulation or pattern. These I do one by one, simply experimenting with the possibility that a way of forming ideas will recur and so constitute a pattern. The description of course is inductive: I say what I see. The reader can check every step and form his or her own judgments. The second step then is to see whether what I have identified exemplifies formations beyond itself or forms a phenomenon that occurs in fact only once or at random. For the first exercise, we take up Pisqa 6, and for the second, Pisqaot 59 and 107, the former brief, the latter long.

VI:I

1. A. ". . . every man's holy thing shall be his; whatever any man gives to the priest shall be his" (Numbers 5:10).
   B. All manner of consecrated produce originally was covered by the general principle stated here: ". . . every man's holy thing shall be his; whatever any man gives to the priest shall be his."
   C. Scripture thus drew all Holy Things and assigned them to the priest, among them omitting reference only to the thanksgiving offering, peace offering, Passover offering, tithe of cattle, produce in the status of Second Tithe, and fruits of an orchard in the fourth year after its planting, all of which are to belong to the farmer [not to the priest].

The form consists of the citation of an opening verse, followed by an issue stated in terms extrinsic to the cited verse. That is to say, no word or phrase of the base verse (that is, the cited verse at the beginning) attracts comment. Rather a general rule of exegesis is invoked. I.1.C then introduces a broad range of items not at all subject to attention in the verse at hand. The formal traits: [1] citation of a base verse from Numbers, [2] a generalization ignoring clauses or words in the base verse, [3] a further observation without clear interest in the verse at hand. But the whole is linked to the theme of the base verse—and to that alone. So an extrinsic exegetical program comes to bear. We shall provisionally call this the extrinsic exegetical form. In due course the extrinsic patterns will undergo their own differentiation, as will the corresponding internal ones.

VI:II

1. A. ". . . every man's holy thing shall be his; whatever any man gives to the priest shall be his" (Numbers 5:10).
   B. On the basis of this statement you draw the following rule:
   C. If a priest on his own account makes a sacrificial offering, even though it falls into the week [during which] another priestly watch than his own [is in charge of the actual cult, making the offerings and receiving the dues], lo, that priest owns the priestly portions of the offering, and the right of

offering it up belongs to him [and not to the priest ordinarily on duty at that time, who otherwise would retain the rights to certain portions of the animal] [Tosefta Menahot 13:17].

What we have is simply a citation of the verse plus a law in prior writing (Mishnah, Tosefta) which the verse is supposed to sustain. The formal traits require [1] citation of a verse, with or without comment, followed by [2] verbatim citation of a passage of the Mishnah or the Tosefta. What we have is a formal construction in which we simply juxtapose a verse, with or without intervening words of explanation, with a passage of the Mishnah or the Tosefta.

VI:III

1. A. ". . . every man's holy thing shall be his; whatever any man gives to the priest shall be his" (Numbers 5:10).
   B. "Why does Scripture make this statement?
   C. "Because, with reference to the fruit of an orchard in the fourth year after its planting, it is said, 'And in the fourth year all their fruit shall be holy, an offering of praise to the Lord' (Leviticus 19:24), [I do not know whether the sense is that] it is holy for the farmer or holy for the priesthood. Accordingly, Scripture says, '. . . every man's holy thing shall be his; whatever any man gives to the priest shall be his,' Scripture thereby speaks of produce of an orchard in the fourth year after its planting, indicating that it should belong to the farmer." the words of R. Meir.
   D. R. Ishmael says, "It is holy to the farmer."
   E. "You maintain that it is holy for the farmer. Or is it holy for the priesthood? Lo, this is how you may logically [rather than by reference to the exegesis, III. B–C, based on Scripture] deal with the problem:
   F. "Produce in the status of second tithe is called holy, and the fruit of an orchard in the fourth year after its planting is called holy. If I draw the analogy to produce in the status of second tithe, which belongs only to the farmer, then likewise produce of an orchard in the fourth year after its planting should belong only to the farmer."
   G. No, produce separated as heave-offering [for priestly use] proves to the contrary, for it too is called Holy, but it belongs only to the priest. And that furthermore demonstrates for produce of an orchard in the fourth year after its planting

that even though it is called holy, it should belong only to the priesthood.

H. "You may then offer [the following argument to the contrary, showing the correct analogy is to be drawn not to heave-offering but to produce in the status of second tithe, as follows:] the correct separation of produce in the status of second tithe involves bringing the produce to the holy place [of Jerusalem, where it is to be eaten], and, along these same lines, produce of an orchard in the fourth year after its planting likewise involves bringing that produce to the holy place. If, therefore, I draw the rule for produce in the status of second tithe, maintaining that it belongs to the owner, so produce of an orchard in the fourth year after its planting likewise should belong only to the owner."

I. [No, that argument can be disproved from another variety of produce entirely:] lo, produce designated as first fruits will prove to the contrary, for such produce likewise has to be brought to the holy place, but it belongs only to the priest. So produce in that classification will prove for produce of an orchard in the fourth year after its planting, showing that even though it has to be brought to the holy place, it also should belong only to the priests. [So the labor of classification continues.]

J. "You may compose [the following argument to reply to the foregoing:] The [result of the] separation of produce in the status of second tithe falls into the classification of holy and has to be brought to the holy place, but further is subject to redemption [in that one can redeem the actual fruit and replace it with ready cash, and one may then bring that cash to Jerusalem and buy for it produce to be eaten in Jerusalem under the rules governing second tithe]. Produce of an orchard in the fourth year after its planting likewise is called holy, has to be brought to the holy place, and is subject to the rules of redemption. But let the matter of heave-offering not come into the picture, for even though it is called holy, it does not have to be brought to the holy place [but is eaten wherever it is located], and let the matter of first fruit likewise not enter the picture, for even though it is produce that has to be brought to the holy place, it is not called holy."

K. Lo, there is the case of the firstling, which *is* called holy, and which has to be brought to the holy place, but which belongs only to the priesthood. [So we can now provide an appropriate analogy.] And that case will prove [the rule for other sorts of produce subject to the same traits, specifically] produce of an orchard in the fourth year after its planting, for, even though it is called holy, and even though it has to be brought to the holy place, it should belong only to the priesthood.

L. "You may invoke the consideration of separating [the produce into one of its several classifications]. Let me call to account three distinct considerations in a single exercise:

M. "[1] Food in the status of second tithe is called holy, requires delivery to the holy place, and is subject to the rules of redemption,

N. "[2] Produce of an orchard in the fourth year after its planting is called holy, requires delivery to the holy place, and is subject to the rules of redemption.

O. "[1] But let not food that has been designated as heave-offering enter into consideration. For even though it is called holy, it does not require delivery to the holy place,

P. "And [2] let not first fruits enter into consideration. For even though it requires delivery to the holy place, it is not called holy.

Q. "Nor should [3] the firstling enter into consideration. For even though it is called holy and requires delivery to the holy place, it is not subject to the rules of redemption.

R. "Let me then draw the appropriate analogy from the correct source, and let me then compose a logical argument on the basis of the correct traits of definition.

S. "I shall draw an analogy on the basis of three shared traits from one matter to another, but I shall not drawn an analogy from something which exhibits three traits to something which does not share these same traits, but only one or two of them.

T. "If then I draw an analogy to produce in the status of second tithe, which belongs only to the owner, so too in the case of produce of an orchard in the fourth year after its planting, it should belong only to the owner."

2. A. R. Joshua says, "What is called holy belongs to the owner.

B. "You maintain that what is called holy belongs to the owner. But perhaps it belongs only to the priesthood?

C. "Scripture states, 'But in the fifth year you may eat of their fruit that they may yield more richly for you' (Leviticus 19:25). To whom does the increase go? To him to whom the produce already has been assigned [that is to say, the farmer, not the priesthood]."

We have a debate on whether reason unaided by Scripture can prevail. III.1.A–C prove essential to what is to follow, since Ishmael's purpose is not merely to make his point, III.1.D, but to demonstrate that logic, without Scripture, can sustain that same point, III.1.E–T. The form of argument is fairly standard throughout our document, with a series of arguments by analogy. We prove that the item at hand is like another item and therefore follows its rule, or is unlike that item and therefore follows the opposite of its rule. The argument is formalized to an extreme, and there are very few variations among exempla of this form, though one—the matter of length—should not be missed. The exegesis of the verse at hand plays no substantial role, beyond its initial introduction. What is critical is the issue of the reliability of logic. The base verse before us contributes virtually nothing and in no way serves as the foundation for the composition at hand, which is sustained and handsomely executed. The fundamental issue, of course, transcends the subject matter: can we, on the basis of unaided reason, reach the correct conclusions (which, as a matter of fact, we already know)? Ishmael shows we can, while Meir, then Joshua offer a narrowly exegetical proof for the same proposition.

VI:IV

1. A. ". . . every man's holy thing shall be his; whatever any man gives to the priest shall be his" (Numbers 5:10).

   B. Why is this verse articulated? Because it is said, "All the holy offerings which the people of Israel present to the Lord I give to you [priests]" (Numbers 18:19). Might I infer that the priests may seize these gifts by force?

   C. Scripture says, ". . . every man's holy thing shall be his; whatever any man *gives* to the priest shall be his" (Numbers 5:10).

   D. This indicates that the gratitude for the benefit of holy things belongs to the farmer [and the priest cannot seize the things by force but must accept them as gifts and give gratitude to the farmer for assigning those gifts to him in particular].

The verse itself is clarified in contrast with another verse that makes the same point. Now the focus is on the base verse and not a broader issue. We may call this an intrinsic exegetical form, in that the focus of exegesis is on the verse, which is cited and carefully spelled out.

VI:V

1. A. ". . . every man's holy thing shall be his; whatever any man gives to the priest shall be his" (Numbers 5:10).

B. Lo, if one has taken the measure of the produce on the ground, and further produce is added to the pile, is it possible that I may invoke in connection with the pile as a whole the verse, ". . . every man's holy thing shall be his" (Numbers 5:10) [so that the farmer now owns all of the produce]?

C. Scripture states, ". . . whatever any man gives to the priest shall be his." [The priest retains the right to the produce originally designated but cannot stake a claim on the priestly share of the additional produce.]

D. Or is it possible that even if one has measured out the designated produce in a basket, and further produce is added to what has been designated, I may invoke in that regard, ". . . every man's holy thing shall be his"?

E. Scripture states, ". . . whatever any man gives to the priest shall be his." [The priest retains the right to the produce originally designated.]

2. A. R. Yose says, "Lo, if one has paid the priest the redemption money for his first born son within the thirty days after birth, but the infant has died, might I invoke in that case, '. . . whatever any man gives to the priest shall be his' [the priest's]? [Then the priest would not have to return the money.] [No, for] Scripture further states, '. . . every man's holy thing shall be his.' [The priest does have to return the money.]

B. "If the child dies after thirty days, the money may not be recovered from the priest's possession, and I recite in that connection, '. . . whatever any man gives to the priest shall be his [the priest's].'"

Once again the apparent contradiction between the two clauses of the verse is smoothed out, by assigning each statement to a different circumstance. The exegesis of the verse then forms the center of interest. Thus the classification is the intrinsic exegetical form. We may now define the formal conventions of Pisqa 6. The first I call *extrinsic exeget-*

ical form. The form consists of the citation of an opening verse, followed
by an issue stated in terms extrinsic to the cited verse. That is to say, no
word or phrase of the base verse (the cited verse at the beginning)
attracts comment. Rather, a general rule of exegesis is invoked. C then
introduces a broad range of items not at all subject to attention in the
verse at hand. The formal traits are: (1) citation of a base verse from
Numbers, (2) a generalization ignoring clauses or words in the base
verse, (3) a further observation without clear interest in the verse at
hand. But the whole is linked to the theme of the base verse—and to that
alone. So an extrinsic exegetical program comes to bear.

The second is the *intrinsic exegetical form.* Here the verse itself is
clarified. In the first instance, the exegesis derives from the contrast
with another verse that is making the same point. But the formal trait
should not be missed. It is that the focus is on the base verse and not on a
broader issue. We may call this an intrinsic exegetical form, in that the
focus of exegesis is on the verse, which is cited and carefully spelled out.
We shall know that we have it when the base verse is cited, clause by
clause or in other ways, and then given an ample dose of attention.

The distinction between extrinsic and intrinsic exegesis emerges
from a simple formal trait: do verses other than the base verse, that is, the
verse of the Book of Numbers under discussion, play a considerable part?
Are there many such verses besides the base one, or only a few? Do those
many verses deal with the topic of the base verse or other topics? If the
former, then they may serve to illuminate the verse under discussion, if
the latter, then all the verses together, including the one chosen from the
Book of Numbers, may serve to demonstrate a given proposition external
to all of the proof-texts. These questions find answers not in impressions
but in simple facts: number of verses other than the base verse, origins of
those other verses. No one can answer those questions merely on the
basis of subjective impressions. But we have now to move quickly to the
promised differentiation within the two gross categories, extrinsic and
intrinsic. The other forms of this document are familiar to us from Sifra,
so let us turn immediately to the literary structures of Sifré to Numbers
59 and 105. Since we already know the repertoire, I simply signify the
form I think is before us.

XLIX:I

1. A. "Now the Lord said to Moses, 'Say to Aaron and tell him,
When you set up the lamps, [the seven lamps shall give light
in front of the menorah.' And Aaron did so. He set up its
lamps to give light in front of the menorah, as the Lord

commanded Moses. And this was the workmanship of the menorah, hammered work of gold; from its base to its flowers, it was hammered work; according to the pattern which the Lord had shown Moses, so he made the menorah]" (Numbers 8:1–4):

B. Why is this passage spelled out?

C. Because Scripture says, "Make seven lamps for this and mount them to shed light over the space in front of it" (Exodus 25:37).

D. On this basis should I infer that all of the lights should illuminate the entire face of the menorah?

E. Scripture says, ". . . shall give light in front of the menorah."

F. It is so that the lamps will converge on the menorah and the menorah on the lamps. How so? Three will go toward the east, three to the west, one in the middle, so that all of them converge on the middle one.

G. On this basis R. Nathan says, "The one in the middle is the most honored of them all."   Intrinsic-exegetical

XLIX:I

2. A. ". . . Say to Aaron":

B. Because the entire matter depends on the action of Aaron, Aaron is included in the statement to begin with.

Intrinsic-exegetical

3. A. ". . . and tell him":

B. Lo, in this way Aaron is admonished.

Intrinsic-exegetical

4. A. ". . . When you set up the lamps":

B. [Since the word for "set up" and the word for "steps" make use of the same root, the sense is:] make steps [for the menorah].

Intrinsic-exegetical

5. A. ". . . in front of the lampstand":

B. Make for the menorah a front and an inner part.

Intrinsic-exegetical

6. A. ". . . the seven lamps shall give light [in front of the lampstand]":

B. May I infer that they should give light at all times?

C. Scripture says, ". . . from dusk to dawn before the Lord" (Leviticus 24:3).

D. May I infer that then the priest should put out the lamp?

E. Scripture says, ". . . from dusk to dawn before the Lord continually" (Leviticus 24:3).

F. How so? The seven lamps will give light from evening to morning, "before the Lord continually."

G. The sense is that the westernmost lamp should be kept burning continually, and from that the lamp is to be kindled at dusk. Intrinsic-exegetical

7. A. ". . . the seven lamps shall give light [in front of the menorah]":

B. May I infer that they should give light at all times?

C. Scripture says, ". . . from dusk to dawn before the Lord" (Leviticus 24:3).

D. May I infer that then the priest should put out the lamp? Intrinsic-exegetical

CVII:I

1. A. "The Lord said to Moses, 'Say to the people of Israel, When you come into the land you are to inhabit']" (Numbers 15:1-16):

B. R. Ishmael says, "Scripture's purpose is to indicate that the Israelites were obligated to bring drink offerings [to accompany animal offerings] only after they had entered the land." Intrinsic-exegetical

2. A. [Continuing the thesis of Ishmael:] Scripture addresses the period after the division and inheritance [settlement] of the Land.

B. You say that Scripture addresses the period after the division and settlement of the Land. But perhaps it speaks of the time immediately upon their entry into the Land [and before the division and settlement]?

C. Scripture says, "When you come into the land which the Lord your God is giving to you and have inherited it and settled in it" (Deuteronomy 17:14).

D. Since the word "coming" is mentioned without further specification, and, further, Scripture has given you details of the meaning of the word in one of the cases in which it occurs, namely, that "coming" speaks only after actual inheritance and settlement, so here too, in all places in which the word "coming" occurs in the Torah, it speaks only of the case after the inheritance and settlement. Intrinsic-exegetical

3. A. And the further fact is that every such passage refers to your dwelling *in* the land [and not outside of it].
   B. Said to him R. Akiva, "Since Scripture says, 'It is a Sabbath to the Lord in all your dwellings' (Leviticus 23:3), may I draw the inference that that is both in the land and outside of the land?"
   C. Said to him R. Ishmael, "It is not a necessary inference at all. Just as the most minor of religious duties pertain both outside of the land and in the land, the Sabbath, a principal religious duty, all the more so should apply in the land as well as outside of the land."   Extrinsic-exegetical

4. A. Said one of the disciples of R. Ishmael, "The verse of Scripture comes to tell you that an individual was obligated to bring drink offerings only after the entry into the land."
   B. R. Simeon b. Yohai says, "Scripture comes to tell you in regard to drink offerings that they are to be offered on a high place [before the building of the Temple]."
   C. Abba Hanin says in the name of R. Eliezer, "Why is this statement made? It is because one might have reasoned thus: since we find that the number of garments used for the cult in the eternal house [the Temple in Jerusalem] is greater than the number of garments to be worn in the tent of meeting, so we should require more drink offerings in the eternal house than the number of drink offerings required in the tent of meeting.
   D. "Scripture therefore states, '. . . and you offer to the Lord from the herd or from the flock an offering by fire or a burnt offering or a sacrifice,' to indicate that even though the number of garments used for the cult in the eternal house [the Temple in Jerusalem] is greater than the number of garments to be worn in the tent of meeting, we should not require more drink offerings in the eternal house than drink offerings in the tent of meeting."   Extrinsic-exegetical

CVII:II
1. A. ". . . and you offer to the Lord from the herd or from the flock an offering by fire [or a *burnt offering* or a *sacrifice*, to fulfill a vow or as a freewill offering, or at your appointed feasts]":
   B. May I infer that whatever is offered as an offering by fire requires a drink offering?

C. Scripture refers specifically to a burnt offering.

D. I know only that that is the case of a *burnt offering.*

E. How do I know that the same rule applies to peace offerings?

F. Scripture alludes to a *sacrifice.*

G. How about a thank offering?

H. Scripture refers to a sacrifice.

I. Is the implication that one bring drink offerings with these and likewise with a sin offering or a guilt offering?

J. Scripture states, ". . . to fulfill a vow or as a freewill offering": I have therefore encompassed within the rule [that drink offerings are required] only Holy Things that are brought on account of a vow or a freewill offering.

K. Then the inference is that I exclude these [a sin offering or a guilt offering, which do not require drink offerings], but then I should further exclude a burnt offering brought in fulfillment of an obligation on the pilgrim festivals [since that would be excluded by the rule that what is brought on one's own option requires the drink offerings].

L. When Scripture makes explicit reference to "at your appointed feasts," Scripture encompasses the obligatory burnt offering brought on festivals. [That sort of offering requires drink offerings as well.]

M. Then the inference is that one encompasses in the requirement of bringing drink offerings a burnt offering brought as a matter of obligation on pilgrim festivals and likewise a sin offering that also is brought as a matter of obligation on festivals.

N. Scripture says, ". . . you offer to the Lord from the herd or from the flock." An animal "from the herd" was encompassed by the general rule but singled out from the general rule to teach you a trait of the encompassing rule itself.

O. That is, specifically, just as an animal of the herd is brought on account of a vow or as a freewill offering and requires drink offerings, so whatever is brought on account of a vow or as a freewill offering requires drink offerings.

P. Then a sin offering and a guilt offering are excluded, for these do not come on account of keeping a vow or as a thank offering [but only when the obligation is imposed on account of an inadvertent violation of the law], and so these do not require drink offerings.

This is a masterpiece of dialectical exegesis, already familiar from sifra, in which a single line of thought is spun out through a variety of possibilities. The exegesis is moving, as it progresses from point to point, but remains cogent. I cannot imagine how a more uniform composition could have been written. At every point each issue is addressed to the base verse, and every conceivable problem of analogical logic has been worked out. And the base verse is always in focus.

CVII:III

1. A. "'. . . from the herd or from the flock an offering by fire or a burnt offering or a sacrifice, to fulfill a vow or as a freewill offering, or at your appointed feasts, to make a pleasing odor to the Lord':

   B. "Why is this stated?

   C. "Since it is said, '. . . and you offer to the Lord from the herd or from the flock an offering by fire or a burnt offering or a sacrifice,' I might infer that the same rule applies to a burnt offering brought of fowl, namely, that drink offerings should be required.

   D. "Scripture specifies, '. . . from the herd or from the flock,' to indicate that burnt offerings of fowl do not require drink offerings," the words of R. Josiah.

   E. R. Jonathan says, "Such an argument is not required. For in any case it is said, '. . . or a sacrifice.' Just as a sacrifice always derives from a beast, so a burnt offering under discussion here involves a beast [and not fowl, so drink offerings are not required for fowl].

   F. "Why then does Scripture say, '. . . from the herd or from the flock an offering by fire or a burnt offering or a sacrifice, to fulfill a vow or as a freewill offering, or at your appointed feasts, to make a pleasing odor to the Lord'?

   G. "Because Scripture says, 'and you offer to the Lord from the herd or from the flock an offering by fire.'

   H. "The point is, if someone has said, 'Lo, incumbent on me is a burnt offering and peace offerings,' should I infer that he should bring the two of them simultaneously [of the same species]?

   I. "Scripture says, '. . . from the herd or from the flock,' to indicate that one brings a beast of this species by itself and one of that species by itself."   Intrinsic-exegetical

2. A. On the basis of the present passage, furthermore, you may

derive the rule governing the animal to be designated as a Passover offering.

B. Since Scripture says, "Your lamb shall be without blemish, a male a year old; you shall take it from the sheep or from the goats" (Exodus 12:5), the meaning is, from this species by itself or from that species by itself.

C. You say that one should take a beast from this species by itself or from that species by itself.

D. Or perhaps one may bring from both species simultaneously?

E. Scripture says, "If his gift for a burnt offering is from the flock, from the sheep or goats, he shall offer a male without blemish" (Leviticus 1:10).

F. Now that statement produces an argument a fortiori: if a burnt offering, which is a weighty matter, is suitable if it derives from a single species, a Passover, which is a lighter-weight offering, all the more so that it should be valid if it comes from one species. Then why does Scripture say, ". . . you shall take it from the sheep or from the goats"? To indicate, from this species by itself or from that species by itself. Extrinsic-exegetical

CVII:IV

1. A. ". . . then [the one who brings the offering] shall offer": (Numbers 15:1–16):

B. I know only that a man is subject to the rule. How do I know that the woman also is required [to bring drink offerings]?

C. Scripture says, "*The one who brings* the offering"—encompassing all cases. Intrinsic-exegetical

2. A. ". . . then [the one who brings the offering] shall offer": (Numbers 15:1–16):

B. R. Nathan says, "This passage forms the generative analogy for all cases in which one voluntarily brings a meal offering, that he should bring no less than a tenth ephah of fine flour and a log of oil." Intrinsic-exegetical

3. A. ". . . then he who brings his offering shall offer to the Lord a cereal offering of a tenth of an ephah of fine flour, mixed with a fourth of a hin of oil, and wine for the drink offering, a fourth of a hin":

B. The oil is for stirring and the wine for a drink offering. Intrinsic-exegetical

CVII:V

1. A. ". . . [then he who brings his offering shall offer to the Lord a
cereal offering of a tenth of an ephah of fine flour, mixed with
a fourth of a hin of oil, and wine for the drink offering, a
fourth of a hin,] you shall prepare with the burnt offering, or
for the sacrifice, for each lamb": (Numbers 15:1-16):

   B. Why is the statement made, [that is, ". . . you shall prepare
with the burnt offering, or for the sacrifice, for each lamb"]?

   C. Since Scripture says, ". . . you offer to the Lord from the herd
or from the flock an offering by fire or a burnt offering or a
sacrifice," if then someone has said, "Lo, incumbent on me is a
burnt offering, lo, incumbent on me are peace offerings,"
might I infer that one may bring a single drink offering to
cover both pledges?

   D. Scripture states, ". . . you shall prepare with the burnt offering, or for the sacrifice, for each lamb" so as to indicate that
one brings drink offerings for this beast by itself and for that
beast by itself. [The partitive language of Scripture is explicit
that a burnt offering or a sacrifice requires individual drink
offerings.]   Intrinsic-exegetical

   E. Abba Hanin says in the name of R. Eliezer, "The contrary
rule might have appeared logical: if in a case in which the
rites required for an offering are the same, namely, the rites
for an ox as a burnt offering and the rites for a lamb as a burnt
offering [since both are subject to the same rule governing the
burnt offering], the two offerings are not equivalent as to the
requirement of drink offerings, in a case in which the rites
required for the one are *not* the same as the rites required for
the other, namely, the rites for a lamb as a burnt offering as
compared with the rites required for a lamb as a peace offering
[the burnt offering is wholly consumed by the altar fire, the
peace offering yields meat for the priest and the *sacrificer* and
his family], is it not reasonable to suppose that the rule
regarding drink offerings should not be the same? [In fact, the
rule *is* the same, so logic would have misled us.]

   F. "On that account Scripture says, '. . . you shall prepare with
the burnt offering, or for the sacrifice,' to indicate that even
though the rites required for the lamb as a burnt offering are
not the same as the rites required for a lamb as a peace

offering, nonetheless they are equivalent to the requirement of drink offerings."

Dialectical Exegesis—the Fallacy of Logic

2. A. R. Nathan says, "'. . . you shall prepare with the burnt offering,' refers to the burnt offering brought by the leper. '. . . for the sacrifice,' refers to the sin offering brought by him. '. . . *or* for the sacrifice' then encompasses his guilt offering."

   B. R. Jonathan says, "'. . . for each lamb,' encompasses the burnt offering brought by a woman after childbirth, who has to bring drink offerings, a rule which we have not derived anywhere else in the entire Torah.

   C. "Or perhaps it speaks only of the ram?

   D. "When Scripture says, '. . . for a ram you shall prepare for a cereal offering two-tenths of an ephah of fine flour mixed with a third of a hin of oil; *and for the drink offering* you shall offer a third of a hin of wine,' lo, reference is made to the ram. So how shall I interpret the statement, '. . . for each lamb'? It is to encompass the burnt offering brought by a woman after childbirth, who has to bring drink offerings, a rule which we have not derived anywhere else in the entire Torah."

   E. Another matter: ". . . for each lamb" encompasses the eleventh lamb produced in the tithing of the flock.

Intrinsic-exegetical

CVII:VI

1. A. ". . . for a ram you shall prepare for a cereal offering":

   B. The purpose of Scripture is to distinguish the drink offerings of a lamb from the drink offerings of a ram. [There is a different rule for each classification of animal.]

   C. For one might have reasoned to the contrary: an animal taken from the herd requires drink offerings, and an animal taken from the flock requires drink offerings. If therefore I draw an analogy to the animal taken from the herd, in which case the Torah has not distinguished the drink offerings brought for a calf from those brought for a full-grown ox, so the law should not distinguish the drink offerings brought for a lamb from the drink offerings brought for a ram. [They should be the same in all cases.]

D. So Scripture states, ". . . for a ram you shall prepare for a cereal offering":

E. The purpose of Scripture is to distinguish the drink offerings of a lamb from the drink offerings of a ram. [Even though such a distinction does not cover the calf and the ox, it does cover the lamb and the ram.]

Dialectical Exegesis—the Fallacy of Logic

2. A. Abba Hanin says in the name of R. Eliezer, "Why is this statement made? It is because reason would have led me to a different conclusion.

B. "Specifically: if in a case in which Scripture required many drink offerings, Scripture did not distinguish among the drink offerings required for a calf from those required for an ox, in a case in which Scripture did not demand many drink offerings, is it not reasonable that we should not require more for a ram than a lamb?

C. "Scripture says, '. . . for a ram you shall prepare for a cereal offering.' Scripture thus makes the point that even though Scripture has diminished the number of drink offerings that are required, it has made an increase whether for a lamb or for a ram."

D. Another matter: ". . . for a ram you shall prepare for a cereal offering": Scripture thereby encompasses a ram brought as a burnt offering, and so on.

Dialectical Exegesis—the Fallacy of Logic

CVII:VII

1. A. ". . . [for a ram] you shall prepare for a cereal offering two-tenths of an ephah of fine flour [mixed with a third of a hin of oil; and for the drink offering you shall offer a third of a hin of wine, a pleasing odor to the Lord]:

B. Why is this statement made?

C. Since logic would have led to the contrary conclusion: since the lamb brought with the sheaf of first grain requires two-tenths of fine flour, and the ram that is brought as a burnt offering requires two-tenths of fine flour, if I draw an analogy to the lamb that is brought with the sheaf of first grain, in which case even though the number of tenths is doubled, the number of drink offerings is not doubled, so in the case of the ram brought as a burnt offering, even though the law has required double the number of tenths, we should not double the number of drink offerings.

D. Scripture thus says, ". . . for a ram you shall prepare for a cereal offering two-tenths of an ephah of fine flour mixed with a third of a hin of oil; and for the drink offering you shall offer a third of a hin of wine," so informing us that just as the Torah has doubled the number of tenths to be brought with it, so it has doubled the volume of drink offerings.

Dialectical Exegesis—the Fallacy of Logic

2. A. ". . . and for the drink offering you shall offer a third of a hin of wine":

B. Oil for mixing with the flour, wine for mixing a drink offering.

Intrinsic-exegetical

3. A. ". . . a pleasing odor to the Lord":

B. "It is a source of pleasure for me, for I have spoken and my will has been done."

Intrinsic-exegetical

4. A. "And when you prepare a bull for a burnt offering [or for a sacrifice, to fulfill a vow or for peace offerings to the Lord, then one shall offer with the bull a cereal offering of three-tenths of an ephah of fine flour, mixed with half a hin of oil, and you shall offer for the drink offering half a hin of wine, as an offering by fire, a pleasing odor to the Lord]":

B. The bull as a burnt offering was covered by the foregoing general statements. Why then has it been singled out? It is to teach a rule governing the encompassing law, specifically:

C. just as a bull may be brought in fulfillment of a vow or as a freewill offering and requires drink offerings, so whatever is brought in fulfillment of a vow or as a freewill offering requires drink offerings.

D. Excluded are the sin offering and the guilt offering, which are not brought merely in fulfillment of a vow or as a freewill offering and which do not require drink offerings.

Intrinsic-exegetical

CVII:VIII

1. A. "[And when you prepare a bull] for a burnt offering or for a sacrifice [to fulfill a vow or for peace offerings to the Lord, then one shall offer with the bull a cereal offering of three-tenths of an ephah of fine flour, mixed with half a hin of oil,

and you shall offer for the drink offering half a hin of wine, as an offering by fire, a pleasing odor to the Lord]":

B. Why is this statement made?

C. Because it is said, "as an offering by fire," if one has said, "Lo, incumbent on me is a burnt offering, lo, incumbent on me are burnt offerings as peace offerings," I might infer that he may bring a single drink offering for both of them.

D. Scripture says, ". . . for a burnt offering or for a sacrifice," so indicating that one brings drink offerings for this one by itself and for that one by itself.

E. Might one then maintain that even if one has said, "Lo, incumbent on me are five oxen for a burnt offering, five oxen for peace offerings," that he may bring a single drink offering for all of them?

F. Scripture says, "for a burnt offering or for a sacrifice," so indicating that one brings drink offerings for each one by itself. Intrinsic-exegetical

2. A. Abba Hanin in the name of R. Eliezer says, "Why is this statement made?

B. "For reason might have produced an error, namely:

C. "if in a case in which the rites of a lamb brought as a burnt offering are the same as the rites of an ox brought as a peace offering, is it not reasonable that the drink offerings should not be the same?

D. "Scripture therefore says, '. . . for a burnt offering or for a sacrifice,' indicating that even though the rites of an ox brought as a burnt offering are not the same as the rites of an ox brought as a peace offering, they are the same as to drink offerings."

Dialectical Exegesis—the Fallacy of Logic

CVII:IX

1. A. "[And when you prepare a bull for a burnt offering or for a sacrifice, to fulfill a vow or for peace offerings to the Lord,] then one shall offer with the bull a cereal offering of three tenths of an ephah of fine flour, mixed with half a hin of oil, and you shall offer for the drink offering half a hin of wine, as an offering by fire, a pleasing odor to the Lord":

B. The oil is for mixing with the flour, and the wine for mixing a drink offering. Intrinsic-exegetical

2. A. ". . . as an offering by fire, a pleasing odor to the Lord:"
    B. It is offered on grills.
    C. You say that the offering by fire is placed on grills. But perhaps it is placed directly on the flames?
    D. If you make that rule, you will turn out to extinguish the bonfire, while the Torah has said, "A *perpetual* fire will be lit on the altar, it shall not go out" (Leviticus 6:6).
    E. Lo, how shall I interpret the statement of the Torah, ". . . as an offering by fire, a pleasing odor to the Lord"?
    F. It is to be placed on grills.
                                    Dialectical exegesis, Intrinsic

3. A. ". . . as an offering by fire, a pleasing odor to the Lord":
    B. "It is a pleasure to me that I spoke and my will was carried out."
                                    Intrinsic-exegetical

CVII:X

1. A. "Thus it shall be done for *each* bull or ram or for *each* of the male lambs or the kids, according to the number that you prepare, so shall you do with every one according to their number":
    B. Scripture thus stresses that there is no difference between the drink offerings brought for a calf and the drink offerings brought for an ox.
    C. For one might have reasoned wrongly, as follows: the animal drawn from the flock requires drink offerings, and so does one drawn from the herd. If I draw an analogy, in that the Torah has made a distinction between the drink offerings required for a lamb and those required for a ram, so I should draw a distinction between the drink offerings required for a calf and those required for an ox.
    D. So the Torah specifies to the contrary: "Thus it shall be done for each bull [or ram or for each of the male lambs or the kids]," indicating that the Torah has made no distinction between the drink offerings brought for a calf and those brought for an ox.
                                    Intrinsic-exegetical

2. A. Abba Hanin in the name of R. Eliezer says, "Why is this statement made? Because logic would have made us err, specifically, in a case in which the law has diminished the number of drink offerings, it has demanded more for a ram than a lamb, in a case in which the law has demanded many drink

offerings, is it not reasonable that the law should require more for an ox than a calf?

B. "So the Torah specifies to the contrary: 'Thus it shall be done for each bull [or ram or for each of the male lambs or the kids],' indicating that the Torah has made not demanded more drink offerings for an ox than those to be brought for a calf."

Dialectical Exegesis—the Fallacy of Logic

CVII:XI

1. A. "[Thus it shall be done for] each bull or ram [or for each of the male lambs or the kids, according to the number that you prepare, so shall you do with every one according to their number. All who are native shall do these things in this way, in an offering by fire, a pleasing odor to the Lord]":

B. Why is this point stressed?

C. It is because logic would have suggested otherwise: since we find that the Torah has made a distinction between the drink offerings required of a one-year-old beast and those to be brought for a two-year-old beast, so the Torah should distinguish the drink offerings brought for a two-year-old beast from those brought for a three-year-old.

D. Scripture says, ". . . or for each ram," indicating that even though the Torah has distinguished the drink offerings brought for a one-year-old beast from those for a two-year-old, the Torah does not distinguish those brought for a two-year-old from those brought for a three-year-old.

Dialectical Exegesis—the Fallacy of Logic

2. A. ". . . or for each of the male lambs or the kids":

B. Why is this stated?

C. It is because logic would have suggested otherwise: since we find that the Torah has made a distinction between the drink offerings required for a lamb from those required for a ram, so the Torah should distinguish between the drink offerings brought for a female lamb from those brought for a sheep.

D. So Scripture states, ". . . or for each of the male lambs or the kids."

Dialectical Exegesis—the Fallacy of Logic

CVII:XII

1. A. ". . . according to the number that you prepare, so shall you do with every one according to their number":

B. I know only that the law covers those listed. How do I know that the law covers beasts that are declared to be substitutes for the beasts at hand?

C. Scripture says, ". . . according to the number that you prepare."

Intrinsic-exegetical

2. A. "'. . . according to the number that you prepare':

B. "This means that one may not give less.

C. "But is it the law that if one wants to give more, he may do so?

D. "Scripture says, '. . . so shall you do with every one according to their number,'" the words of R. Josiah.

E. R. Jonathan says, "Such a proof is not required. For lo, in any event it is said, 'All who are native shall do these things in this way.'"

Intrinsic-exegetical

3. A. "All who are native shall do these things":

B. This means that one may not give less.

C. But is it the law that if one wants to give more, he may do so?

D. Scripture says, "according to their number."

E. Or if one wants to give double, may he give double?

F. Scripture says, "so shall you do with every one"—in accord with the number applying to each of them.

Scriptural basis for a passage of the Mishnah

G. On this basis sages have ruled:

H. The priests may mix together [and offer as one] the drink offerings brought with oxen with those brought with other oxen, the ones brought with rams with those brought with other rams, those brought with lambs with those brought with other lambs, those brought with an animal brought by an individual and those brought with an animal offered by the community, those brought on a given day with those brought on the preceding day. But they may not mix the drink offerings brought with lambs and those brought with oxen or those brought with rams [Mishnah Menahot 9:4].

I. They have further ruled:

J. He who says, "Lo, incumbent on me is a gift of wine," a log of wine he may not bring, two he may not bring, three he may bring. If he said four, five he may not bring, six he may bring. From that point, he may bring [any volume]. Just as the community brings wine as a matter of obligation, so an indi-

vidual is permitted to make a voluntary gift of wine. [Mishnah
Menahot 12:4J: They do not volunteer as a freewill offering a
single log of wine, two or five. But they volunteer as a freewill
offering three, four, or six, and any number more than six.]

L.   ". . . so shall you do with every one": this serves to encompass
the eleventh [beast designated as tithe of the flock].

A-F = Intrinsic Exegesis;
G-L = Scriptural basis for a passage of the Mishnah

CVII:XIII

1. A. "All who are native shall do these things in this way":
   B. Why is this said?
   C. Since it is said, "If its testicles have been crushed or bruised,
   torn or cut, you shall not present it to the Lord . . . You shall
   not procure any such creature from a foreigner and present it
   as food for your God. [Their deformity is inherent in them, a
   permanent defect, and they will not be acceptable on your
   behalf]" (Leviticus 22:25),
   D. [one might have argued:] *these* you shall not acquire from
   them, but you may acquire from them unblemished beasts.
   E. Now that I have learned that a Gentile may offer a burnt
   offering, I have grounds to propose a logical argument as at
   the outset:
   F. An Israelite brings a burnt offering, and a Gentile brings a
   burnt offering. Then just as an Israelite brings drink offerings, so does a Gentile bring drink offerings?
   G. Scripture says, "All who are native shall do these things in this
   way," meaning, "These things does an Israelite do, bringing
   drink offerings, but a Gentile does not bring drink offerings."
   H. Might one maintain then that his burnt offering should not
   require drink offerings at all?
   I. Scripture says, "In this way," meaning, as sages have ruled: If
   a Gentile sent a burnt offering from overseas and did not send
   the cost of drink offerings with it, the drink offerings are to
   derive from community funds.

Dialectical exegesis, Intrinsic

We have found that five forms encompass all of the literary structures of the three pisqaot we have reviewed. Now let us ask the obvious
question: so what? By recognizing these forms, I think, we may describe

the incremental message, the cumulative effect, of the formal traits of speech and thought revealed in the uniform rhetoric and syntax of the document. So I ask this question: What do the formal structures of our document emphasize, and what (as in the case of stories about sages) do they ignore? Let us rapidly review them, highlighting their main traits.

Extrinsic-exegetical form The form consists of the citation of an opening verse, followed by an issue stated in terms extrinsic to the cited verse. The formal traits: (1) citation of a base verse from Numbers, (2) a generalization ignoring clauses or words in the base verse, (3) a further observation without clear interest in the verse at hand. The form yields a syllogism proved by a list of facts beyond all doubt.

Intrinsic-exegetical form The verse itself is clarified. The focus is on the base verse and not on a broader issue. There are diverse versions of this exercise, some consisting only of a verse or a clause and a statement articulating the sense of the matter, others rather elaborate. But the upshot is always the same.

Dialectical exegesis A sequence of arguments about the meaning of a passage, in which the focus is on the meaning of the base verse. This is the internal-exegetical counterpart to the ongoing argument on whether logic works. Now logic pursues the sense of a verse, but the results of logic are tested, forthwith and one by one, against the language at hand, for example, why is this stated? Or, you say it means X but why not Y? Or, if X, then what about Y? if Y, then what about Z? All of these nicely articulated exegetical programs impose a scriptural test on the proposals of logic.

Dialectical exegesis: The fallacy of logic uncorrected by exegesis of Scripture The formal indicator is the presence of the question: Is it not a matter of logic? in one of several versions. The exegesis of the verse at hand plays no substantial role.

Scriptural basis for a passage of the Mishnah What we have is simply a citation of the verse plus a law in a prior writing (Mishnah, Tosefta) which the verse is supposed to sustain. The Mishnah's or the Tosefta's rule then cannot stand as originally set forth, that is, lacking any exegetical foundation. On the contrary, the rule, verbatim, rests on a verse of Scripture, given with slight secondary articulation: verse, then Mishnah-sentence. That suffices, the point is made.

Let us now characterize the formal traits of Sifré to Numbers as a commentary. These we have reduced to two classifications, based on the point of origin of the verses that are catalogued or subjected to exegesis: exegesis of a verse in the Book of Numbers in terms of the theme or problems of that verse, hence, intrinsic exegesis; exegesis of a verse in Numbers in terms of a theme or polemic not particular to that verse, hence, extrinsic exegesis. The implicit message of the external category proves simple to define, since the several extrinsic classifications turn out to form a cogent polemic. Let me state the recurrent polemic of external exegesis. Scripture supplies hard facts, which, properly classified, generate syllogisms. By collecting and classifying facts of Scripture, therefore, we may produce firm laws of history, society, and Israel's everyday life. The diverse compositions in which verses from various books of the Scriptures are compiled in a list of evidence for a given proposition—whatever the character or purpose of that proposition— make that one point. And given their power and cogency, they make the point stick.

Scripture alone supplies reliable basis for speculation. Laws cannot be generated by reason or logic unguided by Scripture. Efforts at classification and contrastive-analogical exegesis, in which Scripture does not supply the solution to all problems, prove few and far between (and always in Ishmael's name, for whatever that is worth). This polemic forms the obverse of the point above. So when extrinsic issues intervene in the exegetical process, they coalesce to make a single point. Let me state that point with appropriate emphasis on the recurrent and implicit message of the forms of external exegesis:

Scripture stands paramount; logic, reason, analytical processes of classification and differentiation, secondary. Reason not built on scriptural foundations yields uncertain results. The Mishnah itself demands scriptural bases.

What about the polemic present in the intrinsic exegetical exercises? This clearly does not allow for ready characterization. As we saw, at least three intrinsic exegetical exercises focus on the use of logic, specifically, the logic of classification, comparison and contrast of species of a genus, in the explanation of the meaning of verses of the Book of Numbers. The internal dialectical mode, moving from point to point as logic dictates, underlines the main point already stated: logic produces possibilities, Scripture chooses among them. Again, the question, Why is this passage stated? commonly produces an answer generated by further verses of Scripture, for example, this matter is stated here to clarify what otherwise would be confusion left in the wake of other verses. So Scripture produces problems of confusion and duplication, and Scripture—not logic, not differentiation, not classification—solves those problems.

To state matters simply: Scripture is complete, harmonious, perfect. Logic not only does not generate truth beyond the limits of Scripture but also plays no important role in the harmonization of difficulties yielded by what appear to be duplications or disharmonies. These forms of internal exegesis then make the same point that the extrinsic ones do. In so stating, of course, we cover all but the single most profuse category of exegesis, which we have treated as simple and undifferentiated: (1) verse of Scripture or a clause, followed by (2) a brief statement of the meaning at hand. Here I see no unifying polemic in favor of, or against, a given proposition. The most common form also proves the least pointed: X bears this meaning, Y bears that meaning, or, as we have seen, citation of verse X, followed by, [what this means is]. Whether simple or elaborate, the upshot is the same.

What can be at issue when no polemic expressed in the formal traits of syntax and logic finds its way to the surface? What do I do when I merely clarify a phrase? Or, to frame the question more logically: what premises must validate my *intervention*, that is, my willingness to explain the meaning of a verse of Scripture? These seem to me propositions that must serve to justify the labor of intrinsic exegesis as we have seen its results here:

1. My independent judgment bears weight and produces meaning. I—that is, my mind—may therefore join in the process.
2. God's revelation to Moses at Sinai requires my intervention. I have the role, and the right, to say what that revelation means.
3. What validates my entry into the process of revelation is the correspondence between the logic of my mind and the logic of the document.

   Why do I think so? Only if I think in accord with the logic of the revealed Torah can my thought processes join issue in clarifying what is at hand: the unfolding of God's will in the Torah. To state matters more accessibly: if the Torah does not make statements in accord with a syntax and a grammar that I know, I cannot understand the Torah enough to explain its meaning. But if I can join in the discourse of the Torah, it is because I speak the same language of thought, syntax and grammar at the deepest levels of my intellect.

4. Then to state matters affirmatively and finally: since a shared logic of syntax and grammar joins my mind to the mind of God as

revealed in the Torah, I can say what a sentence of the Torah means. So I too can amplify, clarify, expand, revise, rework: that is to say, create a commentary.

It follows that the intrinsic exegetical forms stand for a single proposition:

While Scripture stands paramount, and logic, reason, analytical processes of classification and differentiation are secondary; nonetheless, man's mind joins God's mind when he receives and sets forth the Torah.

Can we then state in a few words and in simple language what the formal rules of the document tell us about the purpose of Sifré to Numbers? Beyond all concrete propositions, the document as a whole, through its fixed and recurrent formal preferences or literary structures makes two complementary points.

1. *Reason unaided by Scripture produces uncertain propositions.*
2. *Reason operating within the limits of Scripture produces truth.*

With the perspective provided by our analysis of the way in which the authorship expresses its ideas, we see how truly remarkable a document we have in Sifré to Numbers, a work no less compelling in its intellectual power than Sifra. We shall now see that, in a different way, Sifré to Deuteronomy proves equally persuasive.

4

Deuteronomy and Sifré to Deuteronomy

The fundamental rhetorical structure of Sifré to Deuteronomy, from beginning to end, is defined by verses of the Book of Deuteronomy. These will be cited, and then whole verses or clauses will systematically dictate the arrangement of materials. The structure of the document, therefore, finds its definition in verses of the Book of Deuteronomy. But the "commentary-form" as structure plays a misleadingly paramount role, for that structure that dictates a form, a language pattern, in fact sustains and holds together a wide variety of forms. Once the overall arrangement of a given sequence of units of thought is established through the base verse—that is, the verse of the Book of Deuteronomy that stands at the head—we may find a variety of formalized patterns.

To be sure, as in Sifré to Numbers, one is exegetical, in that what we have is a clause followed by a sentence or two expanding on that clause or imputing meaning to it. And that is "commentary-form." The citation of a sentence of one document, followed by an arrangement of words, ordinarily as a simple declarative sentence, independent of that document, in the most primitive level defines the exegetical form. But that form may develop in a number of different ways. What is important at the outset is the distinction between the fundamental structure of the document as a whole, which finds definition in the Book of Deuteronomy, and the forms of patterned language within the whole units of thought of which our composition is made up. These forms sometimes do, and sometimes do not, appeal to phrases or sentences of the Book of Deuteronomy as part of the rhetorical pattern at hand. So, in all, we must

107

distinguish form from structure, for my claim that Sifré to Deuteronomy
adheres to highly formalized patterns of language proves trivial if all I
mean is that the document is structured around the Book of Deuteronomy. This is something we knew when we opened it. In our search for
regularities of language patterning, let us now work our way through
Sifré to Deuteronomy, Pisqa 1, to provide an example of the forms that
characterize the document as a whole.

SIFRÉ TO DEUTERONOMY

Pisqa 1

I:I

1. A. "These are the words that Moses spoke to all Israel in Trans-
   jordan, in the wilderness, that is to say in the Arabah, opposite
   Suph, between Paran on the one side and Tophel, Laban,
   Hazeroth, and Dizahab, on the other" (Deuteronomy 1:1):
   B. ["These are the words that Moses spoke" (Deuteronomy 1:1):]
   Did Moses prophesy only these alone? Did he not write the
   entire Torah?
   C. For it is said, "And Moses wrote this Torah" (Deuteronomy
   31:9).
   D. Why then does Scripture say, "These are the words that
   Moses spoke" (Deuteronomy 1:1)?
   E. It teaches that [when Scripture speaks of the words that one
   spoke, it refers in particular to] the words of admonition.
   F. So it is said [by Moses], "But Jeshurun waxed fat and kicked"
   (Deuteronomy 32:15).

2. A. So too you may point to the following:
   B. "The words of Amos, who was among the herdsmen of Tekoa,
   which he saw concerning Israel in the days of Uzziah, king of
   Judah, and in the days of Jeroboam, son of Joash, king of
   Israel, two years before the earthquake" (Amos 1:1):
   C. Did Amos prophesy only concerning these [kings] alone? Did
   he not prophesy concerning a greater number [of kings] than
   any other?
   D. Why then does Scripture say, "These are the words of Amos,
   [who was among the herdsmen of Tekoa, which he saw concerning Israel in the days of Uzziah, king of Judah, and in the

days of Jeroboam, son of Joash, king of Israel, two years before the earthquake]" (Amos 1:1)?

E. It teaches that [when Scripture speaks of the words that one spoke, it refers in particular to] the words of admonition.

F. And how do we know that they were words of admonition?

G. As it is said, "Hear this word, you cows of Bashan, who are in the mountain of Samaria, who oppress the poor, crush the needy, and say to their husbands, 'Bring, that we may feast'" (Amos 4:1).

H. ["And say to their husbands, 'Bring, that we may feast'"] speaks of their courts.

3. A. So too you may point to the following:

B. "And these are the words that the Lord spoke concerning Israel and Judah" (Jeremiah 30:4).

C. Did Jeremiah prophesy only these alone? Did he not write two [complete] scrolls?

D. For it is said, "Thus far are the words of Jeremiah" (Jeremiah 51:64)

E. Why then does Scripture say, "And these are the words [that the Lord spoke concerning Israel and Judah]" (Jeremiah 30:4)?

F. It teaches that [when the verse says, "And these are the words that the Lord spoke concerning Israel and Judah" (Jeremiah 30:4)], it speaks in particular of the words of admonition.

G. And how do we know that they were words of admonition?

H. In accord with this verse: "For thus says the Lord, 'We have heard a voice of trembling, of fear and not of peace. Ask you now and see whether a man does labor with a child? Why do I see every man with his hands on his loins, as a woman in labor and all faces turn pale? Alas, for the day is great, there is none like it, and it is a time of trouble for Jacob, but out of it he shall be saved'" (Jeremiah 30:5-7).

4. A. So too you may point to the following:

B. "And these are the last words of David" (2 Samuel 23:1).

C. And did David prophesy only these alone? And has it further-more not been said, "The spirit of the Lord spoke through me, and his word was on my tongue" (2 Samuel 23:2)?

D. Why then does it say, "And these are the last words of David" (2 Samuel 23:1)?

E. It teaches that, [when the verse says, "And these are the last words of David" (2 Samuel 23:1)], it refers to words of admonition.

F. And how do we know that they were words of admonition?

G. In accord with this verse: "But the ungodly are as thorns thrust away, all of them, for they cannot be taken with the hand" (2 Samuel 23:6).

5. A. So too you may point to the following:

B. "The words of Kohelet, son of David, king in Jerusalem" (Kohelet 1:1).

C. Now did Solomon prophesy only these words? Did he not write three and a half scrolls of his wisdom in proverbs?

D. Why then does it say, "The words of Kohelet, son of David, king in Jerusalem" (Kohelet 1:1)?

E. It teaches that [when the verse says, "The words of Kohelet, son of David, king in Jerusalem" (Kohelet 1:1)], it refers to words of admonition.

F. And how do we know that they were words of admonition?

G. In accord with this verse: "The sun also rises, and the sun goes down . . . the wind goes toward the south and turns around to the north, it turns round continually in its circuit, and the wind returns again—that is, east and west [to its circuits]. All the rivers run into the sea" (Kohelet 1:5-7).

H. [Solomon] calls the wicked sun, moon, and sea, for [the wicked] have no reward [coming back to them].

We may now identify a very blatant form, one that we have not observed in either Sifra or Sifré to Numbers. It is the propositional form, one in which a variety of verses makes one important point. The passage proposes to demonstrate a philological fact, which is that, under the stated conditions, "words" refers in particular to words of admonition. The form is repeated and readily discerned. A verse is cited, and then a question addressed to that verse, followed by an answer, which bears in its wake secondary expansion. The whole composition in each case in the composite rests upon the intersection of two verses, a base verse, e.g., at I.1, Deuteronomy 1:1, and then a secondary verse which challenges the superficial allegation of the base verse, at I.1, Deuteronomy 31:9. This yields "it teaches that," followed by yet a third verse, this one proving the proposed proposition. That this form is indeed fixed and patterned is shown by the fivefold repetition. Clearly we have nothing like a commentary on a clause of a phrase of a verse. The opening word of Deuteronomy, "words . . ." serves solely as a joining clause, that is, allowing us to tack on the first of the five exercises—and the rest in its wake. We may classify the pattern as a mode of stating and developing a syllogism, aiming at proving a particular proposition concerning word usages. Standing by itself, what we have is simply a very carefully formalized syllogism that makes a philological point, which is that the word "words of . . ." bears the sense of "admonition" or "rebuke." Five proofs are offered. We know that we reach the end of the exposition when, at I.5.H, there is a minor gloss, breaking the perfect form. That is a common mode of signaling the conclusion of discourse on a given point.

I:II

    1. A. " . . . to all Israel":

        B. [Moses spoke to the entire community all at once, for] had he admonished only part of them, those who were out at the market would have said, "Is this what you heard from the son of Amram? And did you not give him such-and-such an answer? If we had been there, we should have answered him four or five times for every word he said!"

Here we have the exegetical form with an implicit proposition. The form before us is that simple commentary-form, to which I alluded earlier. It involves only a clause of a base verse followed by an explanation of some fact or detail carried by that clause. But the simplicity should not deceive us into missing the highly formalized character of discourse and the effective way in which discourse not only holds together but makes a clearly discernible point. What holds the whole together, that is, II.1.A, B, is a question that II.1.A raises and II.1.B presupposes. The further question of how a sequence of exegetical forms constitutes a sustained composition—if it does make up such a composition—will engage our attention later. The exegetical form is subject to infinite expansion. It can be repeated for any number of statements, none of them having anything in common with any other in context, all of them linked to the single clause subject to discussion.

    2. A. Another matter concerning "[. . . to all Israel]":

        B. This teaches that Moses collected all of them together, from the greatest to the least of them, and he said to them, "Lo, I shall admonish you. Whoever has an answer—let him come and say it."

A mark of exegetical form—self-evidently—is that it [1] confronts only a single passage and [2] does not proceed to very complicated formal expansion. We proceed to the next word in the base verse, but now our comment is particular to the verse. The explanation of why Moses spoke to everyone is then clear. On the one hand, it was to make certain that there was no one left out, thus II.1. On the other, it was to make certain that everyone had a say, thus II.2. These two points then complement each other.

I:III

1. A. Another matter concerning " . . . to all Israel":
   B. This teaches that all of them were subject to admonition but quite able to deal with the admonition.

This is a composite of sayings of sages on a single proposition. This will be made up of sayings—X says, or said X—followed by diverse ways of saying the same thing or of developing the same point. What joins the whole are [1] a shared theme focused upon [2] a single proposition, resting on the authority of, not Scripture, but [3] named sages.

2. A. Said R. Tarfon, "By the Temple service! [I do not believe] that there is anyone in this generation who can accept admonition."
   B. Said R. Eleazar ben Azariah, "By the Temple service! [I do not believe] that there is anyone in this generation who can accept admonition."
   C. Said R. Akiva, "By the Temple service! [I do not believe] that there is anyone in this generation who knows how to give an admonition."
   D. Said R. Yohanan b. Nuri, "I call to give testimony against me, heaven, and earth, [if it is not the case that] more than five times was R. Akiva criticized before Rabban Gamaliel in Havney, for I would lay complaints against him, and [Gamaliel therefore] criticized him. Nonetheless, I know that [each such criticism] added to [Akiva's] love for me.
   E. "This carries out the verse, 'Do not criticize a scorner, lest he hate you, but reprove a wise person, and he will love you' (Proverbs 9:8)."

III.1 and 2 are quite separate units of thought, each making its own point. Shall we say that all we have, at I:I-III is a sequence of three quite

disparate propositions? In that case, the authorship before us has presented nothing more than a collection of relevant comments on discrete
clauses. I think otherwise. It seems to me that in I:I-III, as the distinct
and complete units of thought unfold, we have a proposition, fully exposed, composed by setting forth two distinct facts, which serve as
established propositions to yield a syllogism. But the syllogism is not
made explicitly, rather it is placed on display by the (mere) juxtaposition
of facts and then the final proposition, I:III.1, followed by a story making
the same point as the proposition. The exegesis now joins the (established) facts(1) that Moses rebuked Israel and (2) that all Israel was
involved. The point is (3) that Israel was able to deal with the admonition
and did not reject it. I:II then contains a story that makes explicit and
underlines the virtue spun out of the verse. Akiva embodies that virtue,
the capacity—the wisdom—to accept rebuke. The upshot, then, is that
the authorship wished to make a single point in assembling into a single
carefully ordered sequence I:I-III, and it did so by presenting two distinct propositions, at I:I, I:II, and then, at I:III, recast the whole by
making a point drawing upon the two original, autonomous proofs.
Joining I:I and I:II led directly to the proposition at which the authorship was aiming. We have much more than an assembly of information
on diverse traits or points of verses, read word by word. It is, rather, a
purposeful composition, made up of what clearly are already available
materials.

Next comes the exegetical form with an implicit proposition. We
have another example of a rather neatly defined formal construction. In
this case a sequence of brief exegeses is so arranged as to make a point
that is not made explicit, but that is readily uncovered through the
repetition, in specific cases, of a general and overriding principle.

I:IV

1. A. "On the other side of the Jordan" (Deuteronomy 1:1):
   B. This teaches that he admonished them concerning things that
   they had done on the other side of the Jordan.

I:V

1. A. "In the wilderness" (Deuteronomy 1:1):
   B. This teaches that he admonished them concerning things that
   they had done in the wilderness.

2. A. Another matter concerning "In the wilderness" (Deuteronomy 1:1):

B. This teaches that they would take their little sons and daughters and toss them into Moses' bosom and say to him, "Son of Amram, what ration have you prepared for these? What living have you prepared for these?"

C. R. Judah says, "Lo, Scripture says [to make this same point], 'And the children of Israel said to them, "Would that we had died by the hand of the Lord in the land of Egypt [when we sat by the fleshpots, when we ate bread ... for you have brought us forth to this wilderness to kill the whole assembly with hunger]" (Exodus 16:3).'"

3. A. Another matter concerning "In the wilderness" (Deuteronomy 1:1):

B. This encompasses everything that they had done in the wilderness. The exposition continues, with the insertion of V. 2 as an illustration of what is at issue.

I:VI

1. A. "In the Plain" (Deuteronomy 1:1):

B. This teaches that he admonished them concerning things that they had done in the Plains of Moab.

C. So Scripture says, "And Israel dwelt in Shittim and the people began to commit harlotry with the daughters of Moab" (Numbers 25:1).

I:VII

1. A. "Over against Suph [the sea]" (Deuteronomy 1:1):

B. This teaches that he admonished them concerning things that they had done at the sea.

C. For they rebelled at the sea and turned their back on Moses for three journeys.

2. A. R. Judah says, "They rebelled at the sea, and they rebelled within the sea.

B. "And so Scripture says, 'They rebelled at the sea, even in the sea itself' (Psalm 106:7)."

3. A. Is it possible to suppose that he admonished them only at the outset of a journey? How do we know that he did so between one journey and the next?

B. Scripture says, "Between Paran and Tophel" (Deuteronomy 1:1).

4. A. "Between Paran and Tophel" (Deuteronomy 1:1):

 B. [The word Tophel bears the sense of] disparaging words with which they disparaged the manna.

 C. And so does Scripture say, "And our soul loathed this light bread" (Numbers 21:5).

 D. [God] said to them, "Fools! Even royalty choose for themselves only light bread, so that none of them should suffer from vomiting or diarrhea. For your part, against that very act of kindness that I have done for you, you bring complaints before me.

 E. "It is only that you continue to walk in the foolishness of your father, for I said, 'I will make a helpmeet for him' (Genesis 2:18), while he said, 'The woman whom you gave to be with me gave me of the tree and I ate' (Genesis 3:12)."

The words of admonition, now fully exposed, apply to a variety of actions of the people. That is the main point of I:IV–VII. The matter is stated in a simple way at I:IV, V.1 (with an illustration at I:V.2), I:V.3, I:VI, I:VII. After the five illustrations of the proposition that the admonition covered the entire past, we proceed to a secondary expansion, I:VII.2, 3, which itself is amplified at I:VII.4. The main structure is clear, and the proposition is continuous with the one with which we began: Moses admonished Israel, all Israel, which could take the criticism, and covered the entire list of areas where they had sinned, which then accounts for the specification of the various locations specified by Deuteronomy 1:1. When we realize what is to come, we understand the full power of the proposition, which is syllogistic though in exegetical form. It is to indicate the character and encompassing program of the Book of Deuteronomy—nothing less.

I:VIII

1. A. "And Hazeroth" (Deuteronomy 1:1):

 B. [God] said to them, "Ought you not to have learned from what I did to Miriam in Hazeroth?

 C. "If to that righteous woman, Miriam, I did not show favor in judgment, all the more so to other people!"

2. A. Another matter: Now if Miriam, who gossiped only against her brother, who was younger than herself, was punished in this way, one who gossips against someone greater than himself, all the more so!

3. A. Another matter: Now if Miriam, whom when she spoke, no person heard, but only the Omnipresent alone, in line with this verse, "And the Lord heard ... " (Numbers 12:2), was punished, one who speaks ill of his fellow in public all the more so!

We have a theme, but the theme also bears within itself a distinct proposition. The basic point is made at the outset, and the case is then amplified. The sin with which Moses now admonished the people was that of gossiping, and the connection to Miriam is explicit. The argument that each place name concerns a particular sin thus is carried forward. The entire discourse exhibits remarkable cogency. The phrase-by-phrase exegesis in this instance masks the propositional intention.

The following I call the particular proposition and the generalizing parable. The requirement of this rhetorical composite is unexpected. We begin with the exegetical form, meaning, we cite a clause and say a few words about it. But the upshot is to yield a proposition, phrased in very particular language. This proposition then is restated out of all relationship to its particularity of case or circumstance, in terms of great generality and applicability to a timeless world of everyday life.

I:IX

1. A. "And DiZahab (Deuteronomy 1:1);
   B. [Since the place name means, "of gold," what he was] saying to them [was this:] "Lo, [following Finkelstein] everything you did is forgiven. But the deed concerning the [golden] calf is worst of them all." [Hammer: "I would have overlooked everything that you have done, but the incident of the golden calf is to me worse than all the rest put together.'"]

2. A. R. Judah would say, "There is a parable. To what may the case be compared? To one who made a lot of trouble for his fellow. In the end he added yet another. He said to him, 'Lo, everything you did is forgiven. But this is the worst of them all.'
   B. "So said the Omnipresent to Israel, 'Lo, everything you did is forgiven. But the deed concerning the [golden] calf is worst of them all.'"

The place-name calls to mind the sin of the golden calf. This is made explicit as a generalization at IX.1, and then, IX.2, Judah restates the matter as a story.

I:X

1. A. R. Simeon says, "There is a parable. To what may the case [of Israel's making the calf of gold] be compared? To one who extended hospitality to sages and their disciples, and everyone praised him.

   B. "Gentiles came, and he extended hospitality to them. Muggers came and he extended hospitality to them.

   C. "People said, 'That is So-and-so's nature—to extend hospitality [indiscriminately] to anyone at all.'

   D. "So did Moses say to Israel, '[Di zahab, meaning, enough gold, yields the sense,] There is enough gold for the tabernacle, enough gold also for the calf!'"

2. A. R. Benaiah says, "The Israelites have worshipped idolatry. Lo, they are liable to extermination. Let the gold of the tabernacle come and effect atonement for the gold of the calf."

3. A. R. Yose b. Haninah says, "'And you shall make an ark cover of pure gold' (Exodus 25:17).

   B. "Let the gold of the ark cover come and effect atonement for the gold of the calf."

A common form announces a catalogue of facts. In the example before us, the catalogue is tacked on to our sequence of verses at X.4.A, but then it proceeds in its own direction. It announces that God was made to undergo ten trials in the wilderness. No proposition is announced, but, of course, it is easy enough to state what is implicit.

4. A. R. Judah says, "Lo, Scripture states, 'In the wilderness, in the plain.'

   B. "These are the ten trials that our fathers inflicted upon the Omnipresent in the wilderness.

   C. "And these are they: two at the sea, two involving water, two involving manna, two involving quails, one involving the calf, and one involving the spies in the wilderness."

   D. Said to him R. Yose b. Dormasqit, "Judah, my honored friend, why do you distort verses of Scripture for us? I call to testify against me heaven and earth that we have made the circuit of all of these places, and each of the places is called only on account of an event that took place there [and not, as you say, to call to mind Israel's sin].

E. "And so Scripture says, And the herdsmen of Gerar strove with the herdsmen of Isaac, saying, 'The water is ours.' And he called the name of the well *Esek*, because they contended with him (Genesis 26:29). 'And he called it Shibah' (Genesis 26:33)."

I:X.1–3 carries forward the matter of DiZahab and amplifies the theme, not the proposition at hand. X.4 then presents a striking restatement of the basic proposition, which has been spelled out and restated in so many ways. It turns out that Judah takes the position implicit throughout and made explicit at I.X.4. There is then a contrary position, at X.4.D. We see, therefore, how the framers have drawn upon diverse materials to present a single, cogent syllogism, the one then stated in most succinct form by Judah. The contrary syllogism, that of Yose, of course is not spelled out, since amplification is hardly possible. Once we maintain that each place has meaning only for what happened in that particular spot, the verse no longer bears the deeper meaning announced at the outset—admonition or rebuke, specifically for actions that took place in various settings and that are called to mind by the list of words (no longer placenames) of Deuteronomy 1:1.

I:XI

1. A. Along these same lines [of dispute between Judah and Yose:]
   B. R. Judah expounded, "The burden of the word of the Lord. In the land of Hadrach, and in Damascus, shall be his resting-place, for the Lord's is the eye of man and all the tribes of Israel" (Zechariah 9:1):
   C. "[Hadrach] refers to the Messiah, who is sharp [*had*] toward the nations, but soft [*rakh*] toward Israel."
   D. Said to him R. Yose b. Dormasqit, "Judah, my honored friend, why do you distort verses of Scripture for us? I call to testify against me heaven and earth that I come from Damascus, and there is a place there which is called Hadrach."
   E. He said to him, "How do you interpret the clause, 'and in Damascus, shall be his resting-place'?"
   F. [Yose] said to him, "How do we know that Jerusalem is destined to touch the city limits of Damascus? As it is said, 'and in Damascus, shall be his resting-place.' And 'resting place' refers only to Jerusalem, as it is said, 'This is my resting place forever' (Psalm 132:14)."
   G. [Judah] said to him, "How then do you interpret the verse,

'And the city shall be built upon its own mound' (Jeremiah 30:18)?"

H. [Yose] said to him, "That it is not destined to be moved from its place."

I. [Yose continued,] saying to him, "How do I interpret the verse, 'And the side chambers were broader as they wound about higher and higher; for the winding about of the house went higher and higher round about the house, therefore the breadth of the house continued upward' (Ezekiel 41:7)? It is that the Land of Israel is destined to expand outward on all sides like a fig tree that is narrow below and broad above. So the gates of Jerusalem are destined to reach Damascus.

J. "And so too Scripture says, 'Your nose is like the tower of Lebanon, which looks toward Damascus' (Song of Songs 7:5).

K. "And the exiles will come and encamp in it, as it is said, 'And in Damascus shall be his resting place' (Zechariah 9:1).

L. "'And it shall come to pass in the end of days that the mountain of the Lord's house shall be established at the top of the mountains and shall be exalted above the hills, and all nations shall flow into it, and many peoples shall go and say ...' (Isaiah 2:2-3)."

I:XII

1. A. Along these same lines [of dispute between Judah and Yose]:

B. R. Judah expounded, "And he made him to ride in the second chariot which he had, and they cried before him, 'Abrech'" (Genesis 41:43):

C. "[Abrech] refers to Joseph, who is a father [*ab*] in wisdom, but soft [*rakh*] in years."

D. Said to him R. Yose b. Dormasqit, "Judah, my honored friend, why do you distort verses of Scripture for us? I call to testify against me heaven and earth that the meaning of Abrech pertains to knees and is simply, 'I shall cause them to bend their knees' [appealing to the causative applied to the root for knee].

E. "For everyone came and went under his authority, as Scripture says, 'And they set him over all of Egypt' (Genesis 41:43)."

I:XI–XII simply lay out further instances of the same hermeneutical dispute between Judah and Yose. All three items—I:X–XII—form a single cogent dispute on its own terms. Then the composite establishes a distinct statement, which concerns figurative, as against literal, interpretation. Once worked out, the whole found an appropriate place here, at I:X.4. The whole is tacked on, and, apart from the commonplace dispute form, I see no implications for the formal character or structure of Sifré to Deuteronomy.

These are the forms that, in a theory formed out of a survey of the opening pisqa, comprise the repertoire of Sifré to Deuteronomy.

1. The proposition and its syllogistic argument

A mark of the syllogistic form is that two or more verses will be served, and the proposition by definition will concern more than the base verse at hand. Indeed, the form cannot serve a single verse or rely for evidence on only one verse, assuredly not the base verse.

2. Exegetical form with an implicit proposition

This form is amazingly simple: citation of a clause of a verse followed by a sentence, generally a simple declarative one, that states a point about that clause. This form may be endlessly repeated, but it will not vastly expand in its formal traits. But a sequence of such patterns forms a complex, and that complex may be seen to demonstrate a proposition; it is the proposition, repeated throughout, that shows we have a complex, not a simple repetition, of the "commentary-form." What I call "exegetical form with an implicit proposition" therefore forms a variation of other modes of setting forth and demonstrating, through probative facts, a given proposition.

It follows that identifying the form in this case requires us also to define the logic of cogency that renders complex and developed in a well-crafted composite that which is, in terms of pattern, simply a sequence of clauses or verses of a base text followed by phrases or sentences offered in amplification in one way or another. Distinguishing rhetoric from logic is not only impossible; it misleads. Yet, to do our work step by step, we must pretend to examine one type of data in one chapter, another type in a later chapter. I do not know of any way to overcome the slightly distorting effect of this procedure; merely describing the evidence in some small measure distorts the evidence we describe. But once we know it, we can also control for it.

3. Composite of sayings of sages on a single proposition

This will be made up of sayings—X says, or Said X—followed by diverse ways of saying the same thing or of developing the same point. What joins the whole are (1) shared theme focused upon (2) a single proposition, resting on the authority of not Scripture but (3) named sages. In logical cogency this is a counterpart to the foregoing, in that a number of sayings on a single theme—parallel to the single clause or verse above—make essentially the same point but in different ways.

Let me spell this point out. The form that involves an attributive (X says . . .) plus a statement of a given fact, one after another, is not terribly different, except in details of the arrangements of components of the composite, from the exegetical form that generates a proposition. That is, instead of sequences of clauses of a verse or verses, we have sequences of sages' sayings. But the proposition that is attached to the sequential clauses of a verse, or the proposition that is attached to the attributive (X says . . .) in either case forms part of a chain of propositions that say the same thing and so prove the same point. Once more, the consideration of the logic of cogency intervenes. Just as we may have sequences of clauses of a verse followed by amplifications, in which each entry constitutes a fact unrelated to other facts fore and aft, so we may have sequences of *X says + statement,* in which no component relates to anything fore *or* aft. But, in point of fact, Sifré to Deuteronomy contains many of the former and none of the latter. The two are logically identical, but formally quite unrelated.

4. The particular proposition and the generalizing parable

This is in no way an exegetical composition. Following Sifré to Deuteronomy I:IX as our model, we commence with a proposition particular to a given verse. Then we issue a fairly general comment, though that comment retains relevance solely to the case before us. What serves to turn the case into a proposition is the parable, which generalizes by comparing the case to a more general situation. Now we can see out of the concrete and the specific a far more encompassing condition and we can draw from the case at hand a governing rule. The formal requirement is not difficult to discern. We begin with a generalization pertinent to a cited verse—nothing other than the exegetical form, involving citation of a clause and then some words of explanation of that clause. Here it is "the place name means . . ." with a second statement. The parable then is tacked on and it produces the effect of saying the whole in exceedingly general terms, but it ends with a "thus," that is, in the present case, "So said the Omnipresent to Israel, 'Lo, everything you did is forgiven. But the deed concerning the [golden] calf is worst of them all.'" This reverts to the particular case and ties the whole together in a stunningly united and effective statement of a general point. We note in Sifré to Deuteronomy I:X, that a second parable is then tacked on to make a quite different point. But it is cogent to the original clause of the cited verse, and that proves the power of the form at hand, which can contain a variety of points within a single coherent formal structure.

5. The catalogue of facts that yield a proposition

Here we have a list of parallel items, which all together point to a simple conclusion; the conclusion may or may not be given at the end of the catalogue, but the catalogue—by definition—is pointed and follows a tight form. The catalogue's items ordinarily will be in the same syntactic form, for example, whole sentences, balanced clauses, a set of simple nouns (as in the first instance before us). That this form finds its counterpart in sequences of names of authorities followed by statements of fact, all of them pointing toward a single proposition, or in sequences of clauses of a verse, followed by amplifications or imputations of meaning, all of them pointing toward a single prevailing proposition, is self-evident.

6. Exegetical form with no implicit proposition

The discrete exegetical form, involving a clause of a verse or a whole verse, followed by a phrase or a sentence that imputes to the cited formula a given meaning, never stands all by itself. Very frequently, we will find a sequence of such episodic and ad hoc units of thought—simple sentences, when seen naked. But these sentences, which constitute facts, in the minds of the compositors of Sifré to Deuteronomy, follow in sequence if not in connection of thought, from one to the next. We know it because the compositors have made up some proportion of the whole of such episodic, naked units of thought: sentences that are simple facts. In terms of the analogy just now given, we find in the mass before us atoms that form molecules, but also atoms that do not form molecules (although no protons, no negative charges, no positive charges, all by themselves—to allow this metaphor to peter out).

If I may now organize and summarize the findings, we may distinguish all units of thought in our opening pisqa by a simple criterion. Some units of thought contain generalizations, principles or propositions that bear implications beyond the statement of fact, and others do not. Generalizations or philosophical propositions, for example, may be stated in a variety of ways. These encompass (1) syllogistic argument; (2) lists of classified facts, in the form of exegesis, that point toward a given proposition or generalization; (3) a particularization of a proposition, followed by a narrative (parable) that restates the proposition in highly general terms; and (4) lists of meanings imputed to a single clause or verse, all of them pointing toward a single conclusion of a general or propositional character.

These ways of proving a point have in common an interest in stating not solely a fact but the proposition, or the conclusion the authorship wishes us to draw. That is, then, the proposition, implicit or otherwise, to be drawn from that fact (or a set of facts). Units of thought that bear no proposition, implicit or otherwise, beyond themselves contain a simple statement of fact. All such units of thought adhere to the exegetical form in its primitive state. The fact is deemed to bear its own (self-evident) meaning, and in the context of a sequence of such self-contained facts, the links between one fact and another are deemed equally obvious (or, alternatively, equally inconsequential). These classifications of units of thought admittedly derive from considerations not only of form and rhetoric, but also of logic and the matter of cogency. But they serve, for the moment, to allow us to distinguish among the patterns of speech we may readily identify. Now to generalize this preliminary exposition.

We have seen that determinate rhetorical choices guided our authorship in its composition of whole and completed units of thought involving two or more sentences. What about the connections, as to sense, between one sentence and the next formed into a single pattern, that is, the logic of cogent discourse? Let us proceed to the second indication that we deal with a purposive composition, not merely a collection of this and that. The second indicator derives from ample evidence that a closely defined, highly restricted logical plan guided the authorship of Sifré to Deuteronomy not merely in joining rhetorically well-defined groups of sentences but also in connecting one sentence to the next.

Let me give examples of the four logics as they occur in Sifré to Deuteronomy. To begin with, I refer back to the opening pisqa. Sifré to Deuteronomy I:I offers a fine instance of philosophical proposition, which is proved valid by a survey of evidence, and which begins in the facts of philology but ends in the principles of philosophy. What I present are two examples of modes of philosophical discourse. The first is syllogistic. The second shows us how an implicit proposition may be stated by indirection but powerfully argued through a survey of pertinent, probative facts.

The syllogism and its cogent statement

The mark of the syllogism is that the proposition that is proposed is never particular to a single verse. A proposition will encompass two or more verses, and the upshot will be to make a point that applies in a variety of settings.

The evidence vastly transcends the case, which is what turns the statement into a proposition bearing syllogistic proof and broad application. What holds the whole together and makes the proposition emerge with great clarity is the repeated mode of formal argument, which proceeds by asking the required question, "Did he not write the entire Torah?" A fact is established through a proof: indeed he did write the entire Torah. Then what is the sense of the verse at hand? "Words" refers in particular to words of admonition, and that becomes the syllogism to be demonstrated through a sequence of probative examples, all of them sustained by factual evidence. The sole point at which this mode of stating a proposition differs from our own mode of argument is the failure to propose a null hypothesis and ask whether the word at hand can mean anything other than the meaning already given.

The exegesis and its principle of propositional cogency: The implicit proposition

The exegetical form before us requires only a clause of a base verse followed by an explanation of some fact or detail carried by that clause. But the simplicity should not deceive us into missing the highly formalized character of discourse. What holds the whole together, that is, A, B, is a question that A raises and B presupposes. The really difficult question is not what holds a simple clause and a gloss together. That involves the givenness of the verse and anything that is tied to the verse. What is hard to explain is how a sequence of exegetical statements hangs together, if it does hang together. Let us look at our opening example, treated in Chapter 2.

Sifré to Deuteronomy I:II–III: We have three distinct exegeses of the same clause, "to all Israel," indicating that everybody was there (I:II.1), everyone had a chance to answer back (I:II.2), and everyone was subject to Moses' admonition and could cope with it (I:III.1). Now when we see the three comments individually, of course, they can be read without being joined into a single statement. But when we see them as a sequence of statements, we realize that the exegeses of the same clause in this instance yield a cogent proposition, not proved as a syllogism or even stated as a proposition, but, nonetheless, fully cogent in the tight link between one statement and the next. This is far more than simply a chain of thematically related items, or even a sequence of discrete comments on the same phrase. It is, in fact, a way of accomplishing the statement of an implicit proposition, one that is not stated but that is repeatedly implied and so fully exposed through the repetition of the cases. Note the case of Sifré to Deuteronomy I:IV–VII, which follows the same principle of intelligible discourse and makes a clearly discernible point.

An example of fixed-associative discourse and its cogency

The fixed-associative mode of discourse in our document appeals not to a list of names but to the equivalent of a list of names, namely, a verse of Scripture—indeed, most of the verses of Deuteronomy. Let us rapidly review the criteria for the logic of fixed association. The negative ones are: first, two or more sentences do not together yield a statement that transcends the sum of the parts. Fact 1 and fact 2 will not yield fact 3 (or proposition A). The two facts remain just what they were: unrelated facts. Fixed associative compositions, it follows, do not gain cogency through statements of propositions. The sentences are cogent, but the cogency derives from a source other than shared propositions or participation in an argument yielding a shared proposition. The fixed association derives, it follows, from a "text" outside of the composition at hand, but known to, taken for granted by, the composition at hand. That "text" may be a list of names; it may be a received document or portion of it. But it is the *given,* and its cogency is the single prevailing premise that otherwise unrelated facts belong together in some sort of established sequence and order. Here is a simple instance.

CLXXVIII:III

   1. A. "... the prophet has uttered it presumptuously":
      B. One is liable for acting presumptuously, and one is not liable for acting in error.

   2. A. "... do not stand in dread of him":
      B. Do not hesitate to hold him guilty as charged.

Each numbered unit forms a single declarative sentence. III.1 makes a distinction important only in legal theory, and III.2 simply exhorts people to enforce the law. Nothing joins III.1 to III.2 except that both rest upon clauses of the same verse. The writer of the passage took for granted that this fixed association validated his joining III.1 to III.2. I must admit that my sample contains very few instances of this logic. The fourth logic by contrast is ubiquitous in our document.

An example of the cogent discourse attained through fixed-analytical method

One recurring exercise, which fills up much of the discussion of the legal passages of Deuteronomy in Sifré to Deuteronomy (as in Sifra, as we saw earlier), systematically proposes to generalize the case-discourse of the Book of Deuteronomy and to reframe the case into the example of a law. The "if a person does such and so," or the details of a case as spelled out in Scripture will be subjected to a sustained exercise of generalization. In this exercise we do two things. Either—in the process of generalization—we restrict the rule, or we extend it. If Scripture contains a detail, such as the statement of a case always demands, we ask whether that detail restricts the rule to a kind of case defined by the detail, or whether that detail represents a more general category of cases and is to be subjected, therefore, to generalization. (In the unfortunate term of contemporary philosophy, the fixed analytical method at hand investigates issues of generalizability.) Here is an example of many instances in which the authorship of a sustained discourse proposes to turn a case into a law.

CLXVI:I

1. A. "[You shall also give him] the first fruits of your new grain and wine and oil, [and the first shearing of your sheep. For the Lord your God has chosen him and his descendants, out of all your tribes, to be in attendance for service in the name of the Lord for all time]" (Deuteronomy 18:1-6):

   B. This teaches that offerings are taken up for the priestly rations only from produce of the finest quality.

The point applies to more than the case at hand.

2. A. Just as we find that as to two varieties of produce of fruit-bearing trees, priestly rations are not taken from one variety to provide the requisite gift for the other variety as well,

   B. so in the case of two varieties of produce of grain and vegetables, priestly rations are not taken from the one to provide the requisite gift for the other as well.

I.2 is parachuted down and has no bearing upon anything in the cited verse. But the importance is to derive a general rule, as stated at B, which applies to a broad variety of categories of priestly gifts, just as at I.1.

CLXVI:II

1. A. ". . . the first shearing of your sheep":
   B. not the fleece that falls off when the sheep is dipped.

2. A. ". . . the first shearing of your sheep":
   B. excluding a sheep that suffers from a potentially fatal ailment.

3. A. ". . . the first shearing of your sheep":
   B. whether in the land or abroad.

II.1 is particular to our verse, II.2, 3 are general rules invoked case by case. These items are not coherent, one by one, and the three sentences in no way state a single proposition, explicit or otherwise. And yet the exercise of analysis is uniform—precisely the same distinctions are made in dozens of other cases—and the purpose is clear. It is to impose upon the case a set of generalizing issues, which yield either restrictive or expansive definitions. This is a fine instance of what I mean by attaining cogent discourse—linking one sentence to another—through an established methodical analysis of one sort or another.

CLXVI:IV

1. A. "You shall also give him":
   B. This indicates that there should be sufficient fleece to constitute a gift.
   C. On this basis sages have ruled:
   D. How much does one give to the priest?
   E. Five selas' weight in Judah, equivalent to ten in Galilee, bleached but not spun,
   F. sufficient to make a small garment from it,
   G. as it is said, "You shall also give him":
   H. This indicates that there should be sufficient fleece to constitute a gift.

The same pattern recurs, and the interest is in an autonomous program. This represents a different kind of methodical analysis. The framer wishes to relate a verse of Scripture to a rule in the Mishnah and so asks how C-F are founded on Scripture. G-H go over the ground of

A–B. The work of restriction or expansion of the rule is now implicit, of course.

Do the rhetoric and logic of our document derive from the (supposed) purpose of the authorship of forming a commentary? Not at all. To the contrary, in general, the logic of our document is sustained, propositional, mostly philosophical, and not that of commentary. What holds things together for our authorship does not rely on the verse at hand to impose order and cogency on discourse. To the contrary, the authorship of this document ordinarily appeals to propositions to hold two or more sentences together. If, by definition, a commentary appeals for cogency to the text that the commentators propose to illuminate, then the document is in no essential way a commentary. The logic is not that of a commentary, and the formal repertoire shows strong preference for non-commentary-form.

So far as commentary dictates both its own rhetoric and its own logic, this is no commentary. It is, in fact, a highly argumentative, profoundly well crafted and cogent set of propositions. We may indeed speak of a message, a topical program, such as, in general, a commentary that in form appeals to a clause of a verse and a phrase of a sentence, and in logic holds things together through fixed associations. A commentary makes statements about meanings of verses, but it does not make a set of cogent statements of its own. I have now shown that in rhetoric and in logic, Sifré to Deuteronomy takes shape in such a way as to yield a statement, or a set of cogent statements. A document such as ours indicates that an authorship has found a need for propositions to attain cogency or impart connections to two or more sentences. It calls upon narrative and demands recurrent methodical analyses. The text that is subjected to commentary is asked only occasionally to join sentence to sentence. That brings us to the third analytical inquiry: the one concerning the topical program of our authorship.

The logic of Sifré to Deuteronomy is sustained, propositional, mostly philosophical, and not commentary. That which holds things together for our authorships relies only occasionally on the verses at hand to impose order and cogency upon discourse. The logic is not that of a commentary, and the formal repertoire shows strong preference for something other than commentary-form. The importance of this fact is obvious when we remember the counterpart traits of Mekhilta Attributed to R. Ishmael, which do serve principally as media for the formation of a commentary, and only secondarily as modes of expression of propositions, whether explicit, as in Sifré to Deuteronomy, or implicit, as in Sifra.

BASIC PROPOSITIONS IN SIFRÉ TO DEUTERONOMY

In Sifré to Deuteronomy we find a highly propositional statement. To set forth the propositions paramount in this compilation, I begin with what seem primary, Israel's relationship with God and the responsibilities within that relationship. These encompass, first of all, the theme of Israel and God and the implications of the covenant. The basic proposition is that Israel stands in a special relationship with God, and that relationship is defined by the contract, or covenant, that God made with Israel. The covenant comes to particular expression in Sifré to Deuteronomy in two matters, the land, and the Torah. Each marks Israel as different from all other nations and as selected by God. In these propositions, sages situate Israel in the realm of heaven, finding on earth the stigmata of covenanted election and the concomitant requirement of loyalty and obedience to the covenant. These propositions find a place in the foreground of Sifré to Deuteronomy. When we come to Mekhilta Attributed to R. Ishmael, we shall ask where, and how, these positions make their appearance.

God's merciful character

First comes the definition of those traits of God that our authorship finds pertinent. God sits in judgment of the world, and his judgment is true and righteous. God punishes faithlessness, but His fundamental and definitive trait is mercy. The basic relationship of Israel to God is God's grace for Israel. God's loyalty to Israel endures, even when Israel sins. When Israel forgets God, God is pained. Israel's leaders plead with God only for grace, not for their own merit. Correct attitudes in prayer derive from the need for grace, Israel having slight merit on its own account. Israel should follow only God, carrying out religious deeds as the covenant requires, in accord with the instructions of prophets. Israel should show mercy to others, in the model of God's merciful character.

The basis for the covenant

Second, the contract, or covenant, produces the result that God has acquired Israel, His creation. The reason is that, of all the nations, only Israel accepted the Torah, and that is why God made the covenant with Israel in particular. Why is the covenant made only with Israel? The Gentiles did not accept the Torah; Israel did, and that has made all the difference. Israel recognized God forthwith; the very peace of the world and of nature depends upon God's giving the Torah to Israel. That is why Israel is the sole nation worthy of dwelling in the palace of God and that is the basis for the covenant, too. The covenant secures for Israel an enduring relationship of grace with God. It cannot be revoked and endures forever. The covenant, the terms of which are specified in the Torah, has duplicate terms: if you do well, you will bear a blessing, and if not, you will bear a curse. That is the singular mark of the covenant between God and Israel. A mark of the covenant is the liberation from Egypt and that sufficed to impose upon Israel God's claim for their obedience. An important sign of the covenant is the possession of the land. Part of the covenant is the recognition of merit of the ancestors. God promised, in making the covenant, recognition for the children of the meritorious deeds of the ancestors. The conquest of the land and its inheritance are marks of the covenant, which Israel will find within its power because of God's favor. It is the highest and choicest mark of merit, inherited from the ancestors. All religious duties are important, those that seem trivial as much as those held to be weightier.

God always loves Israel. That is why Israel must carry out the religious duties of the Torah with full assent. Israel must be whole-hearted in its relationship with God. If it is, then its share is with God, and if not, then not. The right attitude toward God is love, and Israel should love God with a whole heart. But Israel may hate God. The reason that Israel rebels against God is their prosperity. Wealthy people become arrogant and believe that their prosperity derives from their own efforts. But that is not so, and God punishes people who rebel to show them that their prosperity depends on Him. When Israel practices idolatry, God punishes them, through exile, for example, through famine, or through drought. Whether or not Israel knows or likes this fact, Israel has no choice but to accept God's will and fulfill the covenant.

The heaven and the earth respond to the condition of Israel and therefore carry out the stipulations of the covenant. If Israel does not carry out religious duties concerning heaven, then heaven bears witness against them. This especially concerns the land of Israel. Possession of the land is conditional, not absolute. It begins with grace, not merit. It is defined by the stipulation that Israel observe the covenant, in which case Israel will retain the land. If Israel violates the covenant, Israel will lose the land. When Israel inherits the land, in obedience to the covenant and as an act of grace bestowed by God, it will build the Temple, where Israel's sins will find atonement. The conquest of the land itself is subject to stipulations, just as possession of the land, as an act of God's grace, is marked by religious obligations. If Israel rebels or rejects the Torah, it will lose the land, just as the Canaanites did because of their idolatry.

The land is not the only, or the most important, mark of the covenant. The most important is Israel's dedication to the Torah which shows that Israel stands in a special relationship to God. The Torah is the source of life for Israel. It belongs to everyone, not only the aristocracy. Children should start studying the Torah at the earliest age possible. The study of the Torah is part of the fulfillment of the covenant. Even the most arid details of the Torah contain lessons, and if one studies the Torah, the reward comes both in this world and in the world to come. The possession of the Torah imposes the requirement on every male Israelite to study the Torah, which involves memorizing each lesson. This is a daily requisite. Study of the Torah should be one's main obligation, before anything else. The correct motive is not for the sake of gain, but for the love of God and the desire for knowledge of God's will. People must direct heart, eyes, and ears, to teachings of the Torah. Study of the Torah transforms human relationships, so that strangers become the children of the master of the Torah whom they serve as disciples. However unimportant the teaching or the teacher, all is as if on the authority of Moses at Sinai. When a person departs from the Torah, that person becomes an idolator. Study of the Torah prevents idolatry. The Torah's verses may be read in such a way that different voices speak discrete clauses of a single verse. One of these will be the Holy Spirit, another, Israel, and so on.

THE HISTORY OF ISRAEL

This brings us to the relationship between Israel and the nations, hence to the meaning of history. The covenant, through the Torah of Sinai, governs not only the ongoing life of Israel but also the state of human affairs universally. The history of Israel forms a single, continuous cycle, in that what happened in the beginning prefigures what will happen at the end of time. Events of Genesis are reenacted both in middle history, between the beginning and the end, and also at the end of time. The personal traits of the tribal founders were passed on and so dictated the history of their families to both the here and now and also the eschatological age. Moses was shown the whole of Israel's history, past, present, and future. The times of the patriarchs are reenacted in the messianic day. This shows how Israel's history runs in cycles, so that events of ancient times prefigure events now. The prophets, beginning with Moses, describe these cycles. What has happened bears close relationship to what is going to happen. The prophetic promises, too, were realized in the times of the Temple, and will be realized at the end of time.

The periods in the history of Israel, marked by the exodus and wandering, the inheritance of the land and the building of the Temple, and the destruction, are all part of a divine plan. In this age—the third century—Rome rules, but in the age to come, marked by the study of the Torah and the offering of sacrifices in the Temple cult, Israel will be in charge. That is the fundamental pattern and meaning of history. The Holy Spirit makes possible actions that bear consequences only much later in time. The prefiguring of history forms the dominant motif in Israel's contemporary life, and the reenacting of what has already been forms a constant. Israel, therefore, should believe, if not in what is coming, then in what has already been. The very names of places in the land attest to the continuity of Israel's history, which follows rules that do not change. The main point is that while Israel will be punished in the worst possible way, Israel will not be wiped out.

But the cyclical character of Israel's history should not mislead. Events follow a pattern, but knowledge of that pattern, which is found in the Torah, permits Israel both to understand and also to affect its own destiny. Specifically, Israel controls its own destiny through its conduct with God. Israel's history is the culmination of Israel's conduct, moderated by the merit of the ancestors. Abraham effected a change in God's relationship to the world. But merit, which makes history, is attained by one's own deeds as well. The effect of merit, in Israel's standing among the other nations, is simple. When Israel enjoys merit, it gives testimony against itself, but when Israel has no merit, then the most despised nation testifies against it. But God is with Israel in time of trouble. When Israel sins, it suffers; when it repents and is forgiven, it is redeemed. For example, Israel's wandering in the wilderness took place because of its failure to attain merit. Sin is what caused the wandering in the wilderness. People rebel against Torah because they are prosperous. The merit of the ancestors works historically to Israel's benefit. What Israel does not merit on its own, at a given time, the merit of the ancestors may secure in any event. The best way to deal with Israel's powerlessness is through Torah study; the vigor of engagement with Torah study compensates for weakness.

It goes without saying that Israel's history follows a prescribed time; at the end of such a period of time, an awaited event will take place. The prophets prophesy concerning the coming of the day of the Lord. Therefore, nothing is haphazard, and all things happen in accord with a plan. That plan encompasses this world, the time of the Messiah, and the world to come, in that order. God will personally exact vengeance at the end of time. God also will raise the dead. Israel has overcome difficult times and can continue to do so. The task ahead is easier than the tasks already accomplished. Israel's punishment is only once, while the punishment to the nations will be unremitting. Peace is worthwhile and everyone needs it. Israel's history ends in the world to come or in the days of the Messiah. The righteous will inherit the Garden of Eden. The righteous in the age to come will be joyful. God acts in history and does so publicly, in full light of day. This is to show the nations who rules. The Torah is what distinguishes Israel from the other nations. The other nations had every opportunity to understand and accept the Torah, and all declined it; that is why Israel was selected. And that demonstrates the importance of both the covenant and the Torah, the medium of the covenant. The nations even had a prophet, comparable to Moses. The nations have no important role in history, except as God assigns them a role in relationship to Israel's conduct. The nations are estranged from God by idolatry. That is what prevents goodness from coming into the world. The name of God rests upon Israel in greatest measure. Idolators do not control heaven. The greatest sin an Israelite can commit is idolatry, and those who entice Israel to idolatry are deprived of the ordinary protections of law. As to the nations' relationships with Israel, they are guided by its condition. When Israel is weak, the nations take advantage; when Israel is strong, they are sycophantic. God did not apportion love to the nations of the world as he did to Israel.

Consider Israel at home, the community and its governance. A mark of God's favor is that Israel has (or, has had and will have) a government of its own. Part of the covenantal relationship requires Israel to follow leaders whom God has chosen and instructed, such as Moses and the prophets. Accordingly, Israel is to establish a government and follow sound public policy. Its leaders are chosen by God. Israel's leaders, the prophets, for example, are God's servants, and that is a mark of the praise that is owing to them. They are to be in the model of Moses, humble, choice, select, well known. Moses was the right one to bestow a blessing, Israel were the right ones to receive the blessing. Yet all leaders are mortal and even Moses died. The saints—holy persons—are leaders ready to give their lives for Israel. The greatest of them enjoy exceptionally long life. But the sins of the people are blamed on their leaders. The leaders depend on the people to keep the Torah, and Moses thanked them in advance for keeping the Torah after he died. The leaders were to be patient, honest, give a full hearing to all sides, and make just decisions in a broad range of matters. To stand before the judge is to stand before God. God makes sure that Israel does not lack for leadership. The basic task of the leader is both to rebuke and also to console the people. The rulers of Israel are servants of God. The prophets exemplify these leaders, in the model of Moses, and Israel's rulers act only on the instruction of prophets. Their authority rests solely on God's favor and grace. At the urging of God, the leaders of Israel speak, particularly words of admonition. These are delivered before the leaders die, when the whole picture is clear. Then people can draw the necessary conclusions. These words, when Moses spoke them, therefore covered the entire history of the community of Israel. But the Israelites can deal with the admonition and draw the correct conclusions. Repentance overcomes sin, as with the sin of the golden calf. The Israelites were contentious, nitpicking, litigious, and, in general, gave Moses a difficult time. Their descendants should learn not to do so. Israel should remain united and obedient to its leaders. When the Israelites are of one opinion on earth, God's name is glorified above. This survey of the propositions set forth in Sifré to Deuteronomy shows us that, were we to have to point to a single document for the representation of the Judaism of the dual Torah, it would have to be this one. That sets the standard for measuring the propositional character of other writings and shows us, by contrast, the ad hoc and episodic character of such propositions, independent of mere textual paraphrase, as may make their way into the pages of Sifra.

IMPLICIT PROPOSITIONS

Sifré to Deuteronomy also presents an account of the structure of the intellect. The explicit propositional program of our document is joined by a set of implicit ones. These comprise the repeated demonstration of a point that is never fully stated. The implicit propositions have to do with the modes of correct analysis and inquiry that pertain to the Torah. For example, one may use reason to discover the meaning and rules of Scripture. Analogy, for example, may provide adequate ground for extending a rule. There are many instances in which that same mode of reasoning can be seen. The upshot is that, while it is not made explicit, the systematic and orderly character of Scripture is repeatedly demonstrated, with the result that from numerous instances, one may independently reach the correct conclusion.

Two implicit propositions predominate. The first, already familiar from Sifré to Numbers as well as Sifra, is that pure reason does not suffice to produce reliable results. Only through linking our conclusions to verses of Scripture may we come to final and fixed conclusions. The implicit proposition, demonstrated many times, may therefore be stated very simply. The Torah (written) is the sole source of reliable information. Reason undisciplined by the Torah yields unreliable results. These items may occur, also, within the rubrics of the specific propositions that they contain. Some of them, moreover, overlap with the later catalogue, but, if so, are not listed twice. Our authorship will have found itself entirely at home in this corner of Sifré to Deuteronomy. And in the following, it will have claimed for itself the position of role model for the other authorship.

The second of the two recurrent modes of thought is the more important. It is the demonstration that many things conform to a single structure and pattern, that is, the propositional formulation of the upshot of methodical-logical thought. We can show this uniformity of the law by addressing the same questions to disparate cases and, in so doing, composing general laws that transcend cases and form a cogent system. What is striking, then, is the power of a single set of questions to reshape and reorganize diverse data into a single cogent set of questions and answers, all things fitting together into a single, remarkably well-composed structure. When we review the numerous passages where we find, in the logical repertoire, what I call methodical-analytical logic, we find a single program. It is an effort to ask whether Scripture imposes a rule that limits or imparts a rule on a case that augments the application of the law at hand. A systematic reading of Scripture permits us to restrict or to extend the applicability of the detail of a case into a rule that governs many cases. A standard repertoire of questions may be addressed to a variety of topics, to yield the picture of how a great many things make essentially a single statement. This seems to me the single most common topical inquiry in Sifré to Deuteronomy. It covers most of the laws of Deuteronomy 12-26. The list of explicit statements of the proposition that the case at hand is subject to either restriction or augmentation, that the law prevailing throughout is limited to the facts at hand or exemplified by those facts, is considerable. The size, the repetitious quality, the obsessive interest in augmentation and restriction, generalization and limitation—these traits of logic and their concomitant propositional results form the centerpiece of the whole.

The basic proposition, spelled out in detail, is that Israel stands in a special relationship with God, and that relationship is defined by the contract, or covenant, that God made with Israel. The covenant comes to particular expression, in our document, in two matters; first, the land, second, the Torah. Each marks Israel as different from all other nations, and as selected by God.

What then is the point? The survey of the topical and propositional program of Sifré to Deuteronomy dictates what is truly particular to that authorship. It is its systematic mode of methodical analysis, in which it does two things. First, our authorship takes the details of cases and carefully reframes them into rules pertaining to all cases. It asks those questions of susceptibility to generalization (*generalizability*) that first class philosophical minds raise. And it answers those questions by showing what details restrict the prevailing law to the conditions of the case, and what details exemplify the encompassing traits of the law overall. These are the two possibilities. The law is either limited to the case and to all cases that replicate this one, or the law derives from the principles exemplified, in detail, in the case at hand. Essentially, as a matter of both logic and topical program, our authorship has reread the legal portions of the Book of Deuteronomy and turned Scripture into what we now know as the orderly and encompassing code supplied by the Mishnah. To state matters simply, this authorship *mishna-izes* Scripture. I find in Sifra, as well as in Sifré to Numbers, little parallel to this dominant and systematic program of Sifré to Deuteronomy. So that is what I think is, if not unique, then at least, distinctive and particular to the authorship of Sifré to Deuteronomy. In this one aspect Sifré to Deuteronomy presents a systemic exercise all its own, and in that one way the document forms a distinctive component of its species of the larger genus, the canonical writings of the Judaism of the dual Torah addressed to the written half of the whole Torah of Moses, our rabbi.

But the secondary consequence of that remarkable exercise of applied logic and practical reason links Sifré to Deuteronomy to all others. And it is here that I find a trait that—as a matter of hypothesis—I should be prepared to impute to that encompassing Judaic system, the "Judaism out there," beyond the texts. In the two Sifrés and Sifra we find a recurrent motif, intense here, episodic there, of how the written component revelation in the Torah, serves as the sole source of final truth. Logic or reason untested against Scripture produces flawed or unreliable results. Reason on its own is subordinate. The reader will recall how commonly that proposition came before us, and a survey of the closely intersecting documents will surely concur.

For their search for the social rules of Israel's society, the priority of the covenant as a reliable account of the workings of reality, and the prevailing laws of Israel's history decreed by the terms of the covenant, the fundamental claim is the same. There are rules and regulations, but reason alone will not show us what they are. A systematic and reasoned reading of the Torah—the written Torah—joined to a sifting of the cases of the Torah in search of the regularities and points of law and order— these are what will tell us the prevailing rule. A rule of the Mishnah and its account of the here and now of everyday life rests upon the Torah, not upon (mere) logic. A rule of Israel's history, past, present, and future, likewise derives from a search for regularities and points of order identi- fied not by logic alone, but by logic addressed to the Torah. So there are these modes of gaining truth that apply equally to Mishnah and Scrip- ture. There is logic, applied reason and practical wisdom, such as sages exhibit; there is the corpus of facts supplied by Scripture, read as sages read it. These two together form God's statement upon the world today.

Part II

THE FOURTH- AND FIFTH-CENTURY COMPILATIONS

The Earlier Rabbah Midrashim

5

Genesis and Genesis Rabbah

In the Book of Genesis, as the sages who composed Genesis *Rabbah* see things, God imparted to Moses the entire scope and meaning of Israel's history among the nations and salvation at the end of days. Genesis drew their attention more than any other book of the Pentateuch—the five Books of Moses—and, as a matter of fact, the opening synagogue lection, or *parashah, Bereshit*, received nearly as much comment as the other eleven weekly synagogue lections of the Book of Genesis put together. Sages, who flourished at the third and fourth centuries in the Land of Israel, read Genesis not as a set of individual verses, but as one coherent statement, whole and complete. In a few words let me restate the conviction of the framers of Genesis *Rabbah* about the message and meaning of the Book of Genesis:

"We now know what will be in the future. How do we know it? Just as Jacob had told his sons what would happen in time to come, just as Moses told the tribes their future, so we may understand the laws of history if we study the Torah. And in the Torah, we turn to beginnings: the rules as they were laid out at the very start of human history. These we find in the Book of Genesis, the story of the origins of the world and of Israel.

"The Torah tells us not only what happened but why. The Torah permits us to discover the laws of history. Once we know those laws, we may also peer into the future and come to an assessment of what is going to happen to us—and, especially, of how we shall be saved from our present existence. Because everything exists under the aspect of God's timeless will, and all things express God's program and plan, in the Torah we uncover the workings of God's will. Our task as Israel is to accept, endure, submit, and celebrate."

What makes this an astonishing reading of Genesis? In general, people nowadays read the Book of Genesis as the story of how Israel saw the past, not the future: the beginning of the world and of Israel, humanity from Adam to Noah, then from Noah to Abraham, and the story of the three patriarchs and four matriarchs of Israel—Abraham, Isaac, Jacob, Sarah, Rebecca, Leah, and Rachel—and finally, Joseph and his brothers—from creation to the descent into Egypt. But to the rabbis who created Genesis *Rabbah*, the Book of Genesis tells the story of Israel, the Jewish people, in the here and now. The principle? What happened to the patriarchs and matriarchs signals what will happen to their descendants: the model of the ancestors sends a message for the children. So the importance of Genesis, as the sages of Genesis *Rabbah* read the book, derives not from its lessons about the past but its message for Israel's present—and, especially, future.

THE PAST AND PRESENT JOINED

Their conviction is that what Abraham, Isaac, and Jacob did in the past shaped the future history of Israel. If, therefore, we want to know the meaning of present events and those in the future, we look back to find out. But the interest is not merely in history as a source of lessons; it is history as the treasury of truths about the here and now and especially about tomorrow. The same rules apply. Why did the sages come to Genesis with the questions of their own day? Because, they maintained, the world reveals not chaos but order, and God's will works itself out not once, but again and again. If we can find out how things got started, we can also find meaning in today and method in where we are heading. So did our sages believe. And that is why they looked to a reliable account of the past and searched out the meanings of their own day. Bringing to the stories of Genesis the conviction that it told not only the story of yesterday but also the tale of tomorrow, the sages whose words are before us in this anthology transformed a picture of the past into a prophecy for a near tomorrow.

Why did Israel's sages look longingly at the beginnings of the world and Israel? Because in their own day they entertained deep and dread forebodings about Israel's prospects. To understand why, we have to ask where and when our book, Genesis *Rabbah*, reached its conclusion. We want also to know who stands behind the work, its authorship and—in particular—how the authorship expressed itself.

Let us begin with the simplest: the literary character of our book. It is a composite of paragraphs, not a sustained essay. Each paragraph takes up a verse of the Book of Genesis in sequence. So the whole of Genesis *Rabbah* is organized around the order of Genesis itself. Who speaks through the book before us? We hear two different voices; (1) the voice of the author of the paragraph, and, (2) the voice of the one who selected the paragraph and put it in the document, so speaking *through* choosing and including the paragraph, but not through writing it. The narrators are named throughout. They are mostly later third and fourth century sages. The organizers and editors are not named, but they do not have to be: we hear from them above all.

What sort of voice is this? It is the voice of the compiler, editor, arranger. As the editor of a newspaper speaks through the selection and arrangement of stories, so the framers of Genesis *Rabbah* talk to us through what they have chosen and how they have laid things out. It is the picture created by a great arrangement of flowers, the tableau deep with meaning. It is as if you undertook to write a book by selecting paragraphs from letters you received. Your book would have two voices, the voice of your correspondents, and your voice as the one who selected and arranged. So Genesis *Rabbah* speaks through selection and arrangement. That is why, when we want to know who we hear in this book, we turn first of all to the people who made the choices and arranged the book's materials as we now have them. We do not know who, where, when, or why the paragraphs before us were written. But we do have the document itself.

This digression into literary questions is important, because it tells us the answer to the question just now raised: *from whom do we hear in this book*? When we know the answer to that question, we also can say why the message proved urgent and immediate; why, in other words, the sages turned to Genesis with the questions they found compelling. Since, in our own day, the Book of Genesis forms the battlefield of theologians, some of whom wish to read it in a very literal way, as a work in geology, we have to assess what brings people to this holy book before we try to understand what they find in it.

Now, all scholars agree, Genesis *Rabbah* came to closure around the year 400 C.E., give or take a half a century. Taking as fact the conclusions of people who have worked hard on the problem, we can place the document in one location. Once we know where and when the document reached its conclusion, we also can see more clearly to whom its message made a difference. And, the answer of the question of where and when, is simple: [1] in the Land of Israel, [2] toward the end of the fourth century of the Common Era.

What made that particular time crucial in the life of Jewish people, in the Land of Israel, is an event that also shaped the entire history of Western civilization. For in the fourth century, the Roman Empire became Christian, and the history of the West as Christian commenced. Judaism in the West from that time to nearly the present had to address a world in which the truths of Christianity were found self-evident, those of Judaism not.

We may, in fact, locate the sages' rereading of the Torah's account of the beginnings, the beginnings of the world and of Israel, the book of Genesis, at exactly that moment at which Western Christian civilization also came to its genesis. That is, the fourth century marked the entrance of Western civilization into present definition. So here, in a way our sages cannot have known, the West really did find its genesis, and the choice of the book of Genesis bore an aptness our sages did not then discern.

What happened at this turning point in time? It was, first, the conversion to Christianity of Constantine, the emperor of Rome, and the legalization of Christianity, then its designation as the state's favored religion, and finally, by the end of the century, the establishment of Christianity as the religion of Rome. To the Christians, it was an age of vindication and validation. Some of the church's leading figures had met persecution and imprisonment in the decades just prior to Constantine's conversion, but took on new lives as high officials of the Roman Empire at his court.

If the great German rabbi, Leo Baeck, released from Theresienstadt in 1945, had become prime minister of Germany in 1947, under the successor of Adolf Hitler, we might begin to imagine the power of events as Christians then experienced them. The triumph of Christianity changed the history of Western civilization because from that point onward, the principal institutions of politics, culture, and social organization found their definition and meaning in the Christian religion—pure and simple. Since Rome encompassed the greater part of that, the fourth century therefore encompassed the re-definition of the West. What happened may be summarized very simply: Rome became Christian, and a formerly despised and illicit religious group took power.

But that event, by itself, need not have greatly confounded Israel and its sages. A second event, at the same critical time, mattered more. To understand it, we have to recall that the Jewish people had hoped, since the destruction of the Temple in 70 C.E., to witness its rebuilding, together with the restoration of Israel's government in its land and the advent of the Messiah, Israel's righteous and rightful ruler. Reason for that hope derived from the destruction of the first Temple, in 586 B.C.E., about a thousand years earlier, when, after the passage of a few generations, Israel returned to its land, the Levites to their platform, and the priests to the altar of God. So hope persisted that the same pattern would find renewal, and the prophets' promises of redemption—which the Christians claimed had already been kept in the restoration after 586— would once more be kept. Then Israel's faith as the ancient prophets had formed it would find the vindication that Christianity (from Israel's viewpoint, momentarily) enjoyed.

As the years passed, after Constantine's conversion in 312 C.E., Israel's thinkers may well have pondered the meaning of events. We know that their counterparts in the Christian world found they had to revise and rewrite the entire history of the world, from creation onward, to provide an explanation of the new age in the continuity of time. It would be speculative to claim that Israel, the Jewish people, as a whole expected the Messiah just then, as the claim so long rejected, that Jesus had been Christ, and that He now triumphed. For Christians claimed, quite plausibly for many, that the conversion of the hated Rome to Christianity validated and vindicated their original conviction about Jesus as the Christ.

Whether or not Israel in its land worried over that matter we do not know. But we do know one stunning fact. In 360 C.E., a generation after Constantine's conversion, an emperor came to the throne who threw off Christianity and reaffirmed paganism. Julian, whom Christians from then to now have called "the apostate," reestablished the overthrown idols, reopened the philosophical schools of pagan tradition, and presented paganism in its elegant and cultured form, to a startled empire. At the same time Julian undertook to embarrass and humiliate the Christians. Since the Christians had by no means gained a majority of the population when Julian revealed his stunning plans, the Christian dream seemed to turn into a nightmare. For those who recalled the miracle of Constantine's conversion and the consequent upward move of Christianity, the movement forebode a miserable end.

The reason all this affected Israel is simple. As part of his program to embarrass Christianity and disprove its claims, Julian announced that the Jews might go back to Jerusalem and rebuild their Temple. The Gospels represent Jesus as predicting that no stone on stone would remain, for the Temple would be destroyed and never rebuilt. Well, no stone did remain, but now, it appeared, Jesus' prediction would be shown to be a lie. Then what would come of the rest of his other claims, as these circulated in the New Testament and in the Church? And how would the Christians disprove the Jews' insistence that the prophets' promises of old would yet be kept? Since the Christians had long pointed to the destruction of the Temple and the loss of Jerusalem as a mark of Israel's punishment for rejecting Jesus' claim to be the Messiah, that is, the Christ, Julian's action seemed to have malicious intent. Here, in Julian's mind, people could find yet another cause to reject Christianity and all its claims. For the Jews, of course, Julian's move stood for something quite the opposite: the vindication of Israel's patience, endurance, and hope. Julian seemed to some as God's agent, as much as Nebuchadnezzar had been—but for a different reason. Now it all seemed to come true—and that on the eve of the 300th anniversary of the destruction. By the Jews' reckoning, the Temple had been destroyed in the year 68. If it took a few years—from 360 onward—by the year 368 Israel would regain the sacred city and its holy altar, God would receive the sacrifices so long suspended, and—by Israel's hopeful reckoning—the world would conclude the sorry history and celebrate the coming of the Messiah.

But it was not to be. Within the year, Julian died on a battlefield in far-off Iran, near the waters of Babylon where so large a portion of Israel then lived. Christians reported that on his lips, as he breathed his last, were the words, "Galilean, thou hast triumphed." Whatever he said—if anything—hardly matters. How people understood the event does matter, and Christians now claimed that the anti-Christ was dead and Christ's rule would endure for millennia, as from their perspective, it did. So the Christian world concluded that Jesus was now finally vindicated as the Christ. Julian's death in his campaign against the Iranian empire under its most brilliant ruler, Shapur II, of the dynasty known as the Sasanian (hence, in the history books, Sasanian Iran), for all time wiped out the last hope of a pagan renaissance in Rome. For Israel in its land, the disappointment proved the least problem.

Over the next generation lay a trial the Jewish people in the Roman Empire had never before known. Judaism in Rome, from the beginnings of Roman rule in the Middle East before the time of the Maccabees, had enjoyed the status of a protected, completely licit religion. They could not, for example, be forced to violate the Sabbath. Buildings for Judaic worship enjoyed the protection of the state. Constantine had done little to limit the Jews' rights, either as citizens or as believers in their faith. But now that freedom for the first time faced abridgement—and worse. What was happening was simple. After Julian, the initial policy of tolerance of both paganism and Judaism shifted. The once again Christian Roman government determined that their grasp on power never again would weaken. So laws against paganism in all its forms went forth from Constantinople to the entire empire, placing severe restraints on all forms of pagan worship and imposing heavy penalties on those who fostered paganism.

When Christian zealots attacked pagan temples, they went after synagogues and Jews as well, just as, in times past, pagan zealots had harassed and murdered Christians. In the counterattack on paganism, the net that was cast caught Israel, too. Before Constantine, of course, Christianity had no politics, and therefore, no policy for Israel, the Jewish people, either. Later, in a matter of a few generations, Christianity had to develop a politics, a view of history, and a governing policy toward Israel, the Jewish people. As a matter of theology, there had been a Christian policy of tolerance for Israel, meant to await the second coming and the last judgment as witness to the truth of Christianity. This, in general, yielded a political policy that Jews were not to be exterminated, as pagans in times to come would be exterminated, and Judaism was not to be extirpated, as, in the future, paganism would be destroyed. But that was to be the general policy for the long haul. What in particular happened now—toward the end of the fourth century, from Julian's death after 360 C.E. to the turn of the fifth century C.E.? A policy, drawn from the program against paganism, limited Israel's right to the security and freedom that the nation had enjoyed, in its land, with only a few (bitter) periods, from the coming of Roman governance and rule in the first century B.C.E. Specifically, synagogues were destroyed, Jews lost the right to convert slaves whom they had purchased, and in various other ways Jews' former privileges and rights were abridged or revoked. Jews who became Christians enjoyed the protection of the state. By the turn of the fifth century, around 410, the Jews' institution of self-government in the land of Israel, the rule by their patriarch, came to an end. In all, it was a very difficult time, not because of trouble alone, not even because of the unprecedented character of the new laws and outrages, but because of the disappointment and despair that followed the high hopes kindled by Julian's abortive scheme.

To revert to our sad analogy, if in 1937 Hitler's regime had given way to a democratic government that restored Jewish rights, and in 1939, a new Nazi government had come back to power and revoked those rights, we might have a relevant comparison to the awful dread that affected despairing Israel. What now? And what of the brief hope of yesterday? In consequence of the restoration of Christian rule and the disappointment attached to the failure of Julian's scheme to rebuild the Temple,

Israel's hope for the Temple and the near-coming of the Messiah turned to ashes. Not only would the Temple not be rebuilt, but the Christian claim that Israel's hope was lost, its land beyond its grasp, its future in doubt, enjoyed renewed self-evidence for those who believed it, and they were now many. Historians tell us that by the end of the fourth century the Land of Israel, now the Holy Land, possessed a Christian, not a Jewish majority. Whether that is so I cannot say, but it does suggest what happened.

So the fourth century, in fact, presented the West and Israel, with its first Christian century. While the Jewish people had managed, on the whole, to ignore the Christians' slow but steady rise to power, they could no longer pretend that Christianity constituted a temporary setback in the journey to the end of time. It was not temporary, it was far more than a setback, and it had to be dealt with. The Land of Israel now found itself in the domain of Christianity, an enormous and historical shift in its status and the status of the Jewish people—therefore also of the Torah. In Genesis *Rabbah* every word is to be read against the background of the world-historical change that had taken place during the formation of the document. The people who compiled the materials we shall now see made a statement through what they selected and arranged. This, then, is their collage, their creation. Genesis *Rabbah*, in its final form, emerges from that momentous first Christian century, the century when the Roman Empire passed from pagan to Christian rule, returned to paganism in 360, and with Julian's death, back again to Christianity. Christianity now adopted a policy of repression that rapidly engulfed Judaism as well.

This is the power of Genesis *Rabbah*. If we listen to its messages, we hear something remarkable. It is how Israel's sages reopened the Book of Genesis and reconsidered its story of beginnings. Why? Because they hoped to find and did find the story of their own day that would indeed form the counterpart and conclusion to the story of beginnings. From creation to conclusion, from the beginnings of salvation in the patriarchs and matriarchs to the ending of salvation and its fulfillment in their own day: this is what our sages sought to discover. And in the Book of Genesis, in the doings of the founders, they found models for deeds of the descendants. That, in a few words, tells us the setting of Genesis *Rabbah*. Born in an age of crisis, the work, which presents comments on successive verses in the Book of Genesis, told Israel the meaning of its day and of many days to come. For Genesis *Rabbah*, the first statement of Judaism on the meaning of the Book of Genesis to be written down, formed the source for centuries to follow.

When, in the coming difficult centuries, Israel would turn to Genesis, the Jewish people would encounter that book through the eyes of the sages who had originally assembled the passages. And when Israel faced disappointment in its messianic hope, when Israel wondered where things were heading, when Jews asked why they should go on and what their duties were, they found answers to their questions in the Book of Genesis. That was because the sages of Genesis *Rabbah* had turned it into a message for Israel's living history. The Book of Genesis explained not a distant past but an immediate moment: today, tomorrow, the near-coming of redemption.

Before proceeding, let me give one concrete example of how sages responded. Their doctrine of Rome must prove critical. Rome now claims to be Israel, that is, Christian and heir to the testament of the founders. How do the sages of Genesis *Rabbah* deal with this new definition of who is Rome? They do not deny it; they affirm it. Rome is Esau, or Moab, or Ishmael. And we? We are Israel. Identifying Rome as Esau is a fresh idea. In the Mishnah, two hundred years earlier, Rome appears as a place, not as a symbol. But in Genesis *Rabbah*, Rome is symbolized by Esau. Why Esau in particular? Because Esau is sibling: relation, competitor, enemy, brother. In acknowledging Rome as the counterpart to Israel, the sages simply opened Genesis and found Israel; that is, Jacob, and his brother, his enemy, in Esau. So why not understand the obvious: Esau stands for Rome, Jacob for Israel, and their relationship represents what Israel and Rome would work out, in the fourth century. So Esau rules now, but Jacob possesses the birthright. Esau/Rome is the last of the four great empires (Persia, Media, Greece, Rome). What happens after Rome? Israel's age of glory. And why is Rome seen as the *brother*? Because, after all, the Christians do claim a common patrimony in the Hebrew Scriptures and do claim to form part of Israel. That claim was not ignored, it was answered: Yes, part of Israel—the rejected part. Jacob carries the blessing and transmits the blessing to humanity; Esau does not. Such a message bore meaning only in the present context. So in a concrete way, Genesis talks the here and now, about *us*, Israel, and about *our sibling*, Rome. That concession represents an implicit recognition of Christianity's claim to share the patrimony of Judaism, to be descended from Abraham and Isaac. So how are we to deal with the glory and the power of our brother, Esau? And what are we to say about the claim of Esau to enthrone Christ? And how are we to assess today the future history of Israel, the salvation of God's first, best love? It is not by denying Rome's claim but by evaluating it, not by turning a back to the critical events of the hour, but by confronting those events forcefully and authoritatively.

Genesis then told about beginnings so as to point to happy endings, and in reading it, Israel could find reason to hope for its future in the certain facts of a long-ago past. That, in a single sentence, states the power of Genesis *Rabbah*, the astonishing achievement of the sages who brought together their chosen paragraphs and formed them into the message at hand. So, to conclude, Genesis *Rabbah* forms part of the great labor of presenting the one whole Torah of Moses, our rabbi, revealed by God to Israel at Mount Sinai. Genesis *Rabbah* forms an important component of the complete Torah worked out by the rabbis of ancient times, from the publication of the Mishnah at c. 200 C.E. to the completion of the Babylonian Talmud at c. 600 C.E. At c. 400 C.E., Genesis *Rabbah* comes midway in the unfolding of the Torah. Sages' reading of Genesis transcends the age in which they did their work. The way in which the great Judaic sages of that time interpreted the stories of Genesis would guide later Judaic exegetes of the same biblical book. So when we follow that work, we gain entry into the way in which Judaism, in its normative and classical form, has understood history. If our sages of blessed memory read the book of Genesis as if it portrayed the history of Israel and Rome, we must ask, why Rome in the form it takes in Genesis *Rabbah*? And how may we understand the obsessive character of the sages' treatment of the theme of Rome? If their picture was merely of Rome as tyrant and destroyer of the Temple, we should have no reason to link the text to the problems of the age of redaction and closure. But now it is Rome as Israel's brother, counterpart, and nemesis, Rome as standing in the way of Israel's, and the world's, ultimate salvation. So the stakes are different and much higher. It is not a political Rome but a messianic Rome that is at issue: Rome as surrogate for Israel, Rome as obstacle to Israel. Why? It is because Rome confronted Israel with a crisis, and, I have argued, Genesis *Rabbah* constitutes a response to that crisis. Sages respond by facing that fact quite squarely and saying, "Indeed, it is as you say, a kind of Israel, an heir of Abraham as your texts explicitly claim. But we remain the sole legitimate Israel, the bearer of the birthright—we and not you. So you are our brother: Esau, Ishmael, Edom." And the rest follows.

Let us begin our survey of our document in this important aspect with a simple example of how ubiquitous is the shadow of Ishmael/ Esau/Edom/Rome. Wherever sages reflect on future history, their minds turn to their own day. They found the hour difficult, because now Christian Rome claimed that very birthright and blessing that they understood to be theirs alone. Christian Rome posed a threat without precedent. Wherever in Scripture they turned, sages found comfort in the iteration that the birthright, the blessing, the Torah, and the hope— all belonged to them and to none other. Here is a striking statement of that constant proposition.

LIII:XII

1. A. "[So she said to Abraham, 'Cast out this slave woman with her son, for the son of this slave woman shall not be heir with my son Isaac.'] And the thing was very displeasing to Abraham on account of his son" (Genesis 21:11):
    B. That is in line with this verse: "And shuts his eyes from looking upon evil" (Isaiah 33:15). [Freedman, *Genesis Rabbah* (London, 1948), p. 471, n. 1: He shut his eyes from Ishmael's evil ways and was reluctant to send him away.]

2. A. "But God said to Abraham, 'Be not displeased because of the lad and because of your slave woman; whatever Sarah says to you, do as she tells you, for through Isaac shall your descendants be named'" (Genesis 21:12):
    B. Said R. Yudan bar Shillum, "What is written is not 'Isaac' but 'through Isaac.' [The matter is limited, not through all of Isaac's descendants but only through some of them, thus excluding Esau.]"

3. A. R. Azariah in the name of Bar Hutah "The use of the B, which stands for two, indicates that he who affirms that there are two worlds will inherit both worlds [this age and the age to come]."
    B. Said R. Yudan bar Shillum, "It is written, 'Remember his marvelous works that he has done, his signs and the judgments of his mouth' (Psalm 105:5). I have given a sign, namely, it is one who gives the appropriate evidence through what he says. Specifically, he who affirms that there are two worlds will be called 'your seed.'
    C. "And he who does not affirm that there are two worlds will not be called 'your seed.'"

XII.1 makes "the matter" refer to Ishmael's misbehavior, not Sarah's proposal, so removing the possibility of disagreement between Abraham and Sarah. XII.2, 3 interpret the limiting particle, "in," that is, *among* the descendants of Isaac will be found Abraham's heirs, but not all the descendants of Isaac will be heirs of Abraham. XII.2 explicitly excludes Esau, that is Rome, and XII.3 makes the matter doctrinal in the context of Israel's inner life.

As the several antagonists of Israel stand for Rome in particular, so the traits of Rome, as sages perceived them, characterized the biblical heroes. Esau provided a favorite target. From the womb, Israel and Rome contended.

LXIII:VI

1. A. "And the children struggled together [within her, and she said, 'If it is thus, why do I live?' So she went to inquire of the Lord. And the Lord said to her, 'Two nations are in your womb, and two peoples, born of you, shall be divided; the one shall be stronger than the other, and the elder shall serve the younger']" (Genesis 25:22–23):
   B. R. Yohanan and R. Simeon b. Laqish:
   C. R. Yohanan said, "[Because the word, 'struggle,' contains the letters for the word, 'run,'] this one was running to kill that one and that one was running to kill this one."
   D. R. Simeon b. Laqish: "This one releases the laws given by that one, and that one releases the laws given by this one."

2. A. R. Berekhiah in the name of R. Levi said, "It is so that you should not say that it was only after he left his mother's womb that [Esau] contended against [Jacob].
   B. "But even while he was yet in his mother's womb, his fist was stretched forth against him: 'The wicked stretch out their fists [see Freedman] from the womb' (Psalm 58:4)."

3. A. "And the children struggled together within her":
   B. [Once more referring to the letters of the word "struggled," with special attention to the ones that mean, "run,"] they wanted to run within her.
   C. When she went by houses of idolatry, Esau would kick, trying to get out: "The wicked are estranged from the womb" (Psalm 58:4).
   D. When she went by synagogues and study-houses, Jacob would kick, trying to get out: "Before I formed you in the womb, I knew you" (Jeremiah 1:5)."

4. A. ". . . and she said, 'If it is thus, why do I live?'"
   B. R. Haggai in the name of R. Isaac: "This teaches that our

mother, Rebecca, went around to the doors of women and said to them, 'Did you ever have this kind of pain in your life?'"

C. "[She said to them,] 'if thus: If this is the pain of having children, would that I had not gotten pregnant.'"

D. Said R. Huna, "If I am going to produce twelve tribes only through this kind of suffering, would that I had not gotten pregnant."

5. A. It was taught on Tannaite authority in the name of R. Nehemiah, "Rebecca was worthy of having the twelve tribes come forth from her. That is in line with the verse:

B. "'Two nations are in your womb, and two peoples, born of you, shall be divided; the one shall be stronger than the other, and the elder shall serve the younger.' When her days to be delivered were fulfilled, behold, there were twins in her womb. The first came forth red, all his body like a hairy mantle, so they called his name Esau. Afterward his brother came forth . . .'" (Genesis 25:23–24).

C. "'Two nations are in your womb': thus two.

D. "'and two peoples': thus two more, hence four.

E. "'. . . the one shall be stronger than the other': two more, so six.

F. "'. . . and the elder shall serve the younger': two more, so eight.

G. "'When her days to be delivered were fulfilled, behold, there were twins in her womb': two more, so ten.

H. "'The first came forth red': now eleven.

I. "'Afterward his brother came forth': now twelve."

J. There are those who say, "Proof derives from this verse: 'If it is thus, why do I live?' Focusing on the word for 'thus,' we note that the two letters of that word bear the numerical value of seven and five respectively, hence, twelve in all."

6. A. "So she went to inquire of the Lord":

B. Now were there synagogues and houses of study in those days [that she could go to inquire of the Lord]?

C. But is it not the fact that she went only to the study of Eber?

D. This serves to teach you that whoever receives an elder is as if he receives the Presence of God.

VI.1–3 take for granted that Esau represents Rome, and Jacob, Israel. Consequently the verse underlines the point that there is natural enmity between Israel and Rome. Esau hated Israel even while he was still in the womb. Jacob, for his part, revealed from the womb those virtues that would characterize him later on, eager to serve God as Esau was eager to worship idols. The text invites just this sort of reading. VI.4 and VI.5 relate Rebecca's suffering to the birth of the twelve tribes. VI.6 makes its own point, independent of the rest and tacked on.

LXIII:VII

2. A. "Two nations are in your womb, [and two peoples, born of you, shall be divided; the one shall be stronger than the other, and the elder shall serve the younger]" (Genesis 25:23):
   B. There are two proud nations in your womb, this one takes pride in his world, and that one takes pride in his world.
   C. This one takes pride in his monarchy, and that one takes pride in his monarchy.
   D. There are two proud nations in your womb.
   E. Hadrian represents the nations, Solomon, Israel.
   F. There are two who are hated by the nations in your womb. All the nations hate Esau, and all the nations hate Israel.
   G. [Following Freedman's reading:] The one whom your creator hates is in your womb: "And Esau I hated" (Malachi 1:3).

3. A. "and two peoples, born of you, shall be divided":
   B. Said R. Berekhiah, "On the basis of this statement we have evidence that [Jacob] was born circumcised."

4. A. ". . . the one shall be stronger than the other, [and the elder shall serve the younger]" (Genesis 25:23):
   B. R. Helbo in the name of the house of R. Shila: "Up to this point there were Sabteca and Raamah, but from you will come Jews and Romans." [Freedman, p. 561, n. 8: "Hitherto even the small nations such as Sabteca and Raamah counted; but henceforth all these will pale into insignificance before the two who will rise from you.]

5. A. ". . . and the elder shall serve the younger" (Genesis 25:23):
   B. Said R. Huna, "If he has merit, he will be served, and if not, he will serve."

The syllogism invokes the base verse as part of its repertoire of cases. VII.2 augments the statement at hand, still more closely linking it to the history of Israel. VII.3, 4, and 5 gloss minor details. The same polemic proceeds in what follows.

LXIII:VIII

3. A. "The first came forth red":

   B. R. Haggai in the name of R. Isaac: "On account of the merit attained by obeying the commandment, 'You will take for yourself on the first day . . .' (Leviticus 23:40),

   C. "I shall reveal myself to you as the First, avenge you on the first, rebuild the first, and bring you the first.

   D. "I shall reveal myself to you the First: 'I am the first and I am the last' (Isaiah 44:6).

   E. ". . . avenge you on the first: Esau, 'The first came forth red.'

   F. ". . . rebuild the first: that is the Temple, of which it is written, 'You throne of glory, on high from the first, you place of our sanctuary' (Jeremiah 17:12).

   G. ". . . and bring you the first: that is, the messiah-king: 'A first unto Zion will I give, behold, behold them, and to Jerusalem' (Isaiah 41:27)."

LXIII:X

1. A. "[When the boys grew up,] Esau was a skillful hunter, [a man of the field, while Jacob was a quiet man, dwelling in tents]" (Genesis 25:27):

   B. He hunted people through snaring them in words [as the Roman prosecutors do:] "Well enough, you did not steal. But who stole with you? You did not kill, but who killed with you?"

2. A. R. Abbahu said, "He was a trapper and a fieldsman, trapping at home and in the field.

   B. "He trapped at home: 'How do you tithe salt?' [which does not, in fact, have to be tithed at all!]

   C. "He trapped in the field: 'How do people give tithe for straw?' [which does not, in fact, have to be tithed at all!]"

3. A. R. Hiyya bar Abba said, "He treated himself as totally without responsibility for himself, like a field [on which anyone tramples].

   B. "Said the Israelites before the Holy One, blessed be He, 'Lord of all ages, is it not enough for us that you have subjugated us to the seventy nations, but even to this one, who is subjected to sexual intercourse just like a woman?'

   C. "Said to them the Holy One, blessed be He, 'I too will exact punishment from him with those same words: "And the heart of the mighty men of Edom at that day shall be as the heart of a woman in her pangs'" (Jeremiah 49:22)."

4. A. "... while Jacob was a quiet man, dwelling in tents" (Genesis 25:27):
   B. There is a reference to two tents, that is, the school house of Shem and the school house of Eber.

5. A. "Now Isaac loved Esau, because he ate of his game":
   B. It was first-rate meat and wine for Isaac's eating.

6. A. "... but Rebecca loved Jacob" (Genesis 25:28):
   B. The more she heard his voice, the more she loved him.

X.1–3 deal with the description of Esau, explaining why he was warlike and aggressive. Nothing Esau did proved sincere. He was a hypocrite, even when he tried to please his parents.

LXV:I

1. A. "When Esau was forty years old, he took to wife Judith, the daughter of Beeri, the Hittite, and Basemath, the daughter of Elon the Hittite; and they made life bitter for Isaac and Rebecca" (Genesis 26:34–35):
   B. "The swine out of the wood ravages it, that which moves in the field feeds on it" (Psalm 80:14).
   C. R. Phineas and R. Hilqiah in the name of R. Simon: "Among all of the prophets, only two of them spelled out in public [the true character of Rome, represented by the swine], Asaf and Moses.
   D. "Asaf: 'The swine out of the wood ravages it.'
   E. "Moses: 'And the swine, because he parts the hoof' (Deuteronomy 14:8).
   F. "Why does Moses compare Rome to the swine? Just as the swine, when it crouches, puts forth its hoofs as if to say, 'I am clean,' so the wicked kingdom steals and grabs, while pretending to be setting up courts of justice.
   G. "So Esau, for all forty years, hunted married women, ravished them, and when he reached the age of forty, he presented himself to his father, saying, 'Just as father got married at the age of forty, so I shall marry a wife at the age of forty.'
   H. "'When Esau was forty years old, he took to wife Judith, the daughter of Beeri, the Hittite, and Basemath, the daughter of Elon the Hittite.'"

The exegesis of course once more identifies Esau with Rome. The roundabout linking with Esau's taking a wife, passes through the territory of Roman duplicity. Whatever the government does, it claims to do in the general interest. But it really has no public interest at all. Esau, for his part, spent forty years pillaging women and then, at the age of forty pretended, to his father, to be upright. That, at any rate, is the parallel clearly intended by this obviously unitary composition. The issue of the selection of the intersecting verse does not present an obvious solution to me; it seems to me that only the identification of Rome with swine accounts for the choice. The contrast between Israel and Esau produced the following anguished observation. But here Rome is not yet Christian, as far as the clear reference is concerned.

LXV:XXI

3. A. Said R. Judah bar Ilai, "Rabbi would give the following exposition:
   B. 'The voice is Jacob's voice,' that is, the voice of Jacob crying out on account of what 'the hands of Esau' have done to him."
   C. Said R. Yohanan, "It is the voice of Hadrian, may his bones be pulverized, killing in Betar 80,000 myriads of people."

The insistence upon reading the history of Israel into the biography of Jacob stands behind XXI.3. The question then arises, why the enmity?

LXVII:VIII

1. A. "Now Esau hated Jacob [because of the blessing with which his father had blessed him, and Esau said to himself, 'The days of mourning for my father are approaching; then I will kill my brother Jacob]'" (Genesis 27:41):
   B. Said R. Eleazar b. R. Yose, "He turned into a vengeful and vindictive enemy of his, just as even today they are called *senators* in Rome [with the word for *senator* bearing the consonants that appear in the words for enemy and vindictive]."

LXXV:I

1. A. "And Jacob sent messengers before him [to Esau his brother in the land of Seir, the country of Edom, instructing them, 'Thus shall you say to my lord Esau, "Thus says your servant Jacob, 'I have sojourned with Laban and stayed until now.

And I have oxen, asses, flocks, menservants and maidservants; and I have sent to tell my lord, in order that I may find favor in your sight']" (Genesis 32:4):

B. R. Phineas in the name of R. Reuben opened discourse by citing the following verse: "Arise, O Lord, confront him" (Psalm 17:13).

C. R. Phineas in the name of R. Reuben said, "There are five passages in the first book of Psalms in which David asks the Holy One, blessed be He, to rise: 'Arise O Lord, save me O my God' (Psalm 3:8); 'Arise, O Lord, in your anger' (Psalm 7:7); 'Arise, O Lord, O God, lift up your hand' (Psalm 10:12); 'Arise, O Lord, let not man prevail' (Psalm 9:20).

D. "'Arise, O Lord, confront him' (Psalm 17:13):

E. "Said the Holy One, blessed be He, to him, 'David, my son, even if you ask me to rise a thousand times, I shall not arise. When shall I arise? When you see the poor oppressed and the needy groaning.'

F. "'For the oppression of the poor, for the sighing of the needy, now I will arise, says the Lord' (Psalm 12:6)."

2. A. ["For the oppression of the poor, for the sighing of the needy, now I will arise, says the Lord":] R. Simeon b. Jonah said, "'Now I will arise.' As long as [Jerusalem] wallows in the dust, as it were. But when that day comes, concerning which it is written, 'Shake yourself from the dust, arise, and sit down, O Jerusalem' (Isaiah 52:2), at that time, 'Be silent, all flesh, before the Lord' (Zechariah 2:17).

B. "Why so? 'For he is aroused out of his holy habitation' (Zechariah 2:17)."

C. Said R. Aha, "Like a chicken that shakes itself out of the dust."

3. A. "[Arise, O Lord,] confront him" (Psalm 17:13):

B. Confront the wicked before he confronts you.

C. "Cast him down" (Psalm 17:13):

D. into the scale of guilt.

E. "Break him," in line with this verse: "They are bowed down and fallen" (Psalm 20:9).

F. "Deliver my soul from the wicked, Your sword" (Psalm 17:13):

G. "From the wicked person who comes with the power of the sword. And by your sword shall you live" (Genesis 27:40).

4. A. Another interpretation of "Your sword":
   B. "[Esau] is Your sword, because with it You punish the world."

5. A. R. Joshua of Sikhnin in the name of R. Levi: "Save my soul from that wicked man who is destined to fall by Your sword: 'For My sword has drunk its fill in heaven, behold, it shall come down upon Edom' (Isaiah 34:5).
   B. "Said the Holy One, blessed be He, to Jacob, 'Esau was walking along his solitary way, and you had to go and send word to him and say to him, 'Thus says your servant Jacob.'" [Freedman, p. 690, n. 1: "You would have had nothing to fear had you not drawn his attention to you, and the same applies to Jacob's descendants in their relations with Rome."]

I.1 makes one point, I.2 a different one. I.1 stresses that God will rouse himself only to aid the poor and oppressed. I.2 then maintains that God rouses himself to save Jerusalem at the end of time. These are distinct motifs. I.3 works on the theme of the sword, in line with Genesis 27:40. I.4 carries forward that same point of intersection. I.5 makes the point articulated by Freedman, and that seems to me the upshot of the entire composition.

LXXV:II

1. A. R. Judah b. R. Simon opened discourse by citing the following verse: "'As a troubled fountain and a corrupted spring, so is a righteous man who gives way before the wicked' (Proverbs 25:26):
   B. "Just as it is impossible for a fountain to be forever muddied and for a spring to be forever spoiled, so it is impossible for a righteous man to be forever humbled before a wicked one.
   C. "And like a fountain that is muddied or a spring that is spoiled, so is a righteous man who is humbled before a wicked man.
   D. "Said the Holy One, blessed be He, to him, 'Esau was walking along his solitary way, and you had to go and send word to him and say to him, "Thus says your servant Jacob."'"

The same message is underlined, now interwoven with a different intersecting verse. Jacob should not have taken an initiative in dealing with Esau. The message of passivity in response to Rome, which Freedman has already underlined, can be seen as the subterranean polemic.

LXXV:IV

2. A. "And Jacob sent messengers before him":
   B. To this one [Esau] whose time to take hold of sovereignty would come before him [namely, before Jacob, since Esau would rule, then Jacob would govern].
   C. R. Joshua b. Levi said, "Jacob took off the purple robe and threw it before Esau, as if to say to him, 'Two flocks of starlings are not going to sleep on a single branch' [so we cannot rule at the same time]."

3. A. "... to Esau his brother":
   B. Even though he was Esau, he was still his brother.

4. A. "... in the land of Seir, the country of Edom":
   B. He was red, his food was red, his land was red, his mighty men were red, their clothing was red, his avenger will be red, and dressed in red. [Red symbolizes war.]
   C. He was red: "And the first came forth ruddy" (Genesis 25:25).
   D. ... his food was red: "Let me swallow some of that red pottage, for I am famished" (Genesis 25:30).
   E. ... his land was red: "To Esau his brother to the land of Seir, the field of red" (Genesis 32:4).
   F. ... his mighty men were red: "The shield of his mighty men is made red" (Nahum 2:4).
   G. ... their clothing was red: "The valiant men are in scarlet" (Nahum 2:4).
   H. ... his avenger will be red: "My beloved is white and ruddy" (Song of Songs 5:10).
   I. ... and dressed in red: "Wherefore is your apparel red" (Isaiah 63:2).

IV.1 pursues a question important to the compositors, namely, the status of the "messenger" wherever such occurs. The point is that if angels served lesser figures, they surely accompanied Jacob. IV.2, 3 make a stunning point. It is that Esau remains Jacob's brother, and that Esau rules before Jacob will. The application to contemporary affairs cannot be missed, both in the recognition of the true character of Esau—a brother!—and in the interpretation of the future of history. IV.4 is familiar and simply works out the meaning of the color red, of the land of Edom, the word meaning red. In what follows Rome is identified with Esau in a less negative context. Rabbi Judah the Patriarch, called simply

Rabbi or *our holy master*, and a Roman emperor called Antoninus are said to have maintained cordial relationships with each other. In that context the following story shows that Esau and Jacob still provided the generative paradigm.

LXXV:V

1. A. "... instructing them, 'Thus shall you say to my lord Esau, "Thus says your servant Jacob, 'I have sojourned with Laban and stayed until now:'"

   B. Our master [Judah the Patriarch] said to R. Efes, "Write a letter in my name to our lord, King Antoninus."

   C. He went and wrote, "From Judah the Patriarch to our lord, King Antoninus."

   D. Rabbi took it, read it, tore it up, and had him write, "To our lord, the king, from Judah your servant."

   E. He said to him, "My lord, why do you treat your own honor with contempt?"

   F. He said to him, "Am I any better than my forefather? Did he not instruct them: 'Thus shall you say to my lord Esau, "Thus says your servant Jacob, 'I have sojourned with Laban and stayed until now'?"

2. A. "I have sojourned with Laban and stayed until now":

   B. "Laban, the master of deceit, did I keep in my sleeve [having got the better of him (Freedman)], and as to you, how much the more so!"

3. A. "And why is it the case that 'I have stayed until now'?"

   B. Because the adversary of Satan had not yet been born.

   C. For R. Phineas in the name of R. Samuel bar Nahman: "It is a tradition that Esau will fall only by the hand of the descendants of the children of Rachel: 'Surely the youngest of the flock shall drag them away' (Jeremiah 49:20).

   D. "[And why does Scripture call them 'the youngest of the flock'? Because they are] the youngest of the tribes."

V.1 cites the base verse for its own purposes, thus showing how the patriarch followed the example of the patriarch, Jacob. V.2 gives Jacob a more ominous message than does the biblical narrative. V.3 goes over familiar ground. Esau, meaning Rome, will fall by the hand of the Messiah.

LXXV:IX

1. A. Someone else commenced discourse by citing this verse: "Do not grant, O Lord, the desires of the wicked, do not advance his evil plan" (Psalm 140:9).

   B. "Lord of all ages, do not give to the wicked Esau what his heart has devised against Jacob."

   C. What is the meaning of, "Do not advance his evil plan"?

   D. He said before him, "Lord of the ages, make a bit for the mouth of the wicked Esau, so that he will not get full pleasure [from anything he does]." [The word for "evil plan" and for "bit" use the same consonants.]

   E. What sort of bit did the Holy One, blessed be He, make for Esau?

   F. Said R. Hama bar Haninah, "These are the barbarian nations, the Germans whom the Edomites fear."

Sages clearly followed the news of the day and drew their own conclusions from the Romans' political problems.

LXXV:XI

1. A. Another explanation of the statement, "And Jacob sent . . ."

   B. Why did he send out messengers to him?

   C. This is what he was thinking, "I shall send messengers to him, perhaps he will return in repentance."

   D. And he said to them, "This is what to say to him: 'Do not suppose that the way that Jacob went forth from the house of his father is the way he is coming back.'"

   E. For it is said, "For with my staff I passed over this Jordan" (Genesis 32:11).

   F. [Reverting to Jacob's message:] "For he did not take anything from his father. But it was for 'my salary [the messengers are to repeat to Esau] that I have acquired all of these properties, through my own strength.'"

   G. For it is said, "And now I have become two camps" (Genesis 32:11).

2. A. At the moment that Jacob referred to Esau as "my lord," the Holy One, blessed be He, said to him, "You have lowered yourself and called Esau 'my Lord' no fewer than eight times.

   B. "I shall produce out of his descendants eight kings before your children [have any]: 'And these are the kings that reigned in the land of Edom before any king ruled the children of Israel' (Genesis 36:31)."

3. A. [In his message to Esau, Jacob said,] "If you are ready for peace, I shall be your counterpart, and if you are ready for war, I shall be your counterpart.

   B. "I have heroic, powerful troops, for if I say something before the Holy One, blessed be He, and He grants what I ask: 'He will fulfill the desire of those who fear Him' (Psalm 145:19)."

   C. Therefore David came to give praise and glory before the Holy One, blessed be He, for He helped him when he fled from Saul, as it is said, "For lo, the wicked bend the bow" (Psalm 11:2), then, "When the foundations are destroyed, what has the righteous done" (Psalm 11:3).

   D. He said to him, "Lord of the age, if you had been angry with Jacob and had forsaken him and not helped him, and he was pillar and foundation of the world, in line with this verse, 'But the righteous is the foundation of the world' (Proverbs 10:25), then 'what has the righteous done' (Psalm 11:3)?"

   E. Concerning that moment it is said: "Some in chariots, some in horses, but we shall call on the name of the Lord our God" (Psalm 20:8). [Freedman, p. 697, n. 4: Jacob discomfitted Esau by mentioning God, and David was saved from Saul by his trust in God.]

XI.1 supplies a message for the messengers in place of that given at Genesis 32:3–4. XI.2 responds to the statement, Genesis 32:3: "Thus you shall say to my lord Esau." The effect is to link Jacob's encounter with Esau to Israel's history with Edom/Rome. There are no surprises here. XI.3 works out a parallel between Jacob and David, as made explicit by Freedman.

LXXV:VII

1. A. "And the messengers returned to Jacob, saying, 'We came to your brother Esau'" (Genesis 32:6):

   B. [They said to him,] "You treat him as a brother, but he treats you as Esau."

2. A. "...and he is coming to meet you, and four hundred men with him" (Genesis 32:6):

   B. R. Simeon b. Laqish said, "'With him' means people equivalent to him.

C. "Just as he has four hundred men with him, so each of them has four hundred men with him."

D. R. Levi said, "He had gone and bought the right to collect duties. He thought to himself, 'If I can overcome him, well and good, and if not, I shall tax him and in doing so I shall kill him.'"

Here again sages refer to contemporary considerations in interpreting the sense of Scripture.

LXXVI:VI

1. A. "Deliver me, I pray you, from the hand of my brother, from the hand of Esau, for I fear him":

B. "From the hand of my brother, who comes against me with the strength of Esau" [which was the sword] (Genesis 27:40).

C. That is in line with this verse: "I considered the horns, and behold, there came up among them another horn, a little one" (Daniel 7:8).

D. This refers to Ben Neser [Odenathus of Palmyra].

E. "Before which three of the first horns were plucked up by the roots" (Daniel 7:8).

F. This refers to Macrinus, Carinus, and Cyriades.

G. "And behold, in this horn were eyes like the eyes of a man and a mouth speaking great things" (Daniel 7:8).

H. This speaks of the wicked realm, which imposes taxes on all the nations of the world.

I. Said R. Yohanan, "It is written, 'And as for the ten horns, out of this kingdom shall ten kings arise' (Daniel 7:24), that is, the ten sons of Esau.

J. "'I considered the horns, and behold, there came up among them another horn, a little one,' meaning, the wicked realm.

K. "'Before which three of the first horns were plucked up by the roots' speaks of the first three monarchies [Babylonia, Media, Greece].

L. "'And behold, in this horn were eyes like the eyes of a man' alludes to the wicked realm, which looks enviously on someone's wealth, saying, 'Since Mr. So-and-so has a lot of money, we shall elect him magistrate,' 'Since Mr. So-and-so has a lot of money, we shall elect him councillor.'"

2. A. "'. . . lest he come and slay us all, the mothers with the children. But you did say, "I will do you good and make your descendants as the sand of the sea, which cannot be numbered for multitude"' (Genesis 32:12):

   B. "But you did say, 'You will not take the dam with the fledglings'" (Deuteronomy 22:6).

   C. Another matter: ". . . lest he come and slay us all, the mothers with the children. But you did say, 'And whether it be cow or ewe, you shall not kill it and its young both in one day'" (Leviticus 22:28).

The explicit allusion at VI.1 to Rome in the time of Odenathus is puzzling, because, of course, Odenathus at Palmyra was an independent chief, not ruler of Rome (!). The reading of Daniel has three Roman generals fall before Palmyra. Now what this has to do with the power of one's brother, the power of the sword, can be understood. Jacob is described as wanting to be saved from someone (from Palmyra) who exercises the sort of power that Esau exercised. The message to Israel is that Palmyra, no less than Rome, exercises a kind of power from which Israel is to be delivered, not wield. Then the sense of Yohanan's statement is that the cited verse speaks of Rome, not Palmyra, and that at issue is Rome as successor to the first three monarchies. So Yohanan reads Daniel in the way in which rabbis generally did, and in his view, there is no point of contact with our base verse. It is a rather interesting construction therefore, in which a dispute on the meaning of Daniel has taken shape, only afterward to be brought into juxtaposition with our base verse. The reason the writer chose the completed statement, of course, is the opening allusion. VI.2 goes over familiar ground, drawing upon the setting of Jacob's address to call to God's attention the requirement of the Torah. The one who gave the Torah must see to it that its rule applies.

LXXVIII:XII

1. A. "Jacob said, 'No, I pray you, if I have found favor in your sight, then accept my present from my hand, for truly to see your face is like seeing the face of God, [with such favor have you received me. Accept, I pray you, my gift that is brought to you, because God has dealt graciously with me, and because I have enough.' Thus he urged him, and he took it]" (Genesis 33:10–11):

B. "Just as the face of God is judgment, so your face is judgment.

C. "Just as the face of God involves this statement: 'You will not see my face empty-handed' (Exodus 23:15), so as to you: I will not see your face empty-handed." [That is the meaning of the comparison Jacob has made.]

2. A. "Accept, I pray you, my gift that is brought to you, because God has dealt graciously with me, and because I have enough":

B. He said to him, "How much I suffered, how hard I worked, before this gift came to me, but to you it comes on its own."

C. What is written is not "which I have brought" but "[on its own] is brought to you."

3. A. "... Thus he urged him, and he took it" (Genesis 33:11):

B. He acted as if to decline, but he put on his hands.

C. R. Judah b. Rabbi said, "'Every one submitting himself with pieces of silver' (Psalm 68:31) means, [Freedman] 'he opens his hand and would be appeased with silver.' [Freedman, p. 723, n. 4: Esau, meaning Rome, demands money for appeasement.]"

4. A. R. Simeon b. Laqish went up to pay his respects to our master [Judah the Patriarch]. He said to him, "Pray for me, because this kingdom is very wicked."

B. He said to him, "Do not take anything from anybody, and you will not have to give anything to anyone. [Stop collecting taxes.]"

C. While they were in session, a woman came along carrying a salver and a knife on it. He took the knife and gave her back the salver.

D. A royal representative came along, saw it, liked it, and took it.

E. In the evening, R. Simeon b. Laqish went up to pay his respects to our master [Judah the Patriarch]. He saw him sitting and laughing.

F. He said to him, "Why are you laughing?"

G. He said to him, "That knife that you saw—a royal representative came along and took it away."

H. He said to him, "Didn't I tell you, 'Do not take anything from anybody, and you will not have to give anything to anyone.'"

5. A. A commoner said to R. Hoshaiah, "If I say something good to you, will you repeat it in my name in public?"

   B. He said to him, "What is it?"

   C. He said to him, "All the gifts that our father, Jacob, gave to Esau are the nations of the world destined to restore to the king-messiah in the age to come.

   D. "What is the verse of Scripture that indicates it? 'The kings of Tarshish and of the isles shall return tribute' (Psalm 72:10).

   E. "What is said is not, 'bring,' but 'return.'"

   F. He said to him, "By your life, that indeed is a good thing that you have said, and in your name I shall repeat it."

XII.1 amplifies Jacob's statement. XII.2 subjects the cited verse to an acute reading, producing the indicated exegesis. XII.3 is important because of its more general comment on Esau's rule, following Freedman, another instance of drawing from Jacob's life a lesson for the life of the people, Israel. XII.4 is probably tacked on because it underlines the judgment of XII.3 about Roman rule. XII.5 reverts to the theme of the gifts of Jacob to Esau, joins the tale to Israel's history, and imparts to it an eschatological dimension.

LXXXIII:I

1. A. "'These are the kings who reigned in the land of Edom before any king reigned over the Israelites: Bela the son of Beor reigned in Edom, the name of his city being Dinhabah'" (Genesis 36:31-32):

   B. R. Isaac commenced discourse by citing this verse: "Of the oaks of Bashan they have made your oars" (Ezekiel 27:6).

   C. Said R. Isaac, "The nations of the world are to be compared to a ship. Just as a ship has its mast made in one place and its anchor somewhere else, so their kings: 'Samlah of Masrekah' (Genesis 36:36), 'Shaul of Rehobot by the river' (Genesis 36:27), and: 'These are the kings who reigned in the land of Edom before any king reigned over the Israelites.'"

2. A. ["An estate may be gotten hastily at the beginning, but the end thereof shall not be blessed" (Proverbs 20:21)]: "An estate may be gotten hastily at the beginning." "These are the kings who reigned in the land of Edom before any king reigned over the Israelites."

B. ". . . but the end thereof shall not be blessed": "And saviors shall come up on Mount Zion to judge the mount of Esau" (Obadiah 1:21).

I.1 contrasts the diverse origin of Roman rulers with the uniform origin of Israel's king in the House of David. I.2 makes the same point still more forcefully. How so? Freedman makes sense of I.2 as follows: Though Esau was the first to have kings, his land will eventually be overthrown (Freedman, p. 766, n. 3). So the point is that Israel will have kings after Esau no longer does, and the verse at hand is made to point to the end of Rome, a striking revision to express the importance of Israel's history to events in the lives of the patriarchs.

LXXXIII:II

1. A. "These are the kings who reigned in the land of Edom before any king reigned over the Israelites: Bela the son of Beor reigned in Edom, the name of his city being Dinhabah" (Genesis 36:31–32).

B. Said R. Aibu, "Before a king arose in Israel, kings existed in Edom: 'These are the kings who reigned in the land of Edom before any king reigned over the Israelites.'" [Freedman, p. 766, n. 4: "1 Kings 22:48 states, 'There was no king in Edom, a deputy was king.' This refers to the reign of Jehoshaphat. Subsequently in Jehoram's reign, Edom revolted and 'made a king over themselves' (2 Kings 8:20). Thus from Saul to Jehoshaphat, in which Israel had eight kings, Edom had no king but was ruled by a governor of Judah. Aibu observes that this was to balance the present period, during which Edom had eight kings while Israel had none. For that reason, Aibu employs the word for deputy when he wishes to say 'existed' thus indicating a reference to the verse in the book of Kings quoted above."]

C. R. Yose bar Haninah said, "[Alluding to a mnemonic, with the first Hebrew letter for the word for kings, judges, chiefs, and princes:] When the one party [Edom] was ruled by kings, the other party [Israel] was ruled by judges, when one side was ruled by chiefs, the other side was ruled by princes."

D. Said R. Joshua b. Levi, "This one set up eight kings and that one set up eight kings. This one set up Bela, Jobab, Husham, Samlah, Shaul, Hadad, Baalhanan, and Hadar. The other side set up Saul, Ishbosheth, David, Solomon, Rehoboam, Abijah, Asa, and Jehoshaphat.

E. "Then Nebuchadnezzar came and overturned both: 'That made the world as a wilderness and destroyed the cities thereof' (Isaiah 14:17).

F. "Evil Merodach came and exalted Jehoiakin, Ahasuerus came and exalted Haman."

The passage once more stresses the correspondence between Israel's and Edom's governments, respectively. The reciprocal character of their histories is then stated in a powerful way, with the further implication that, when the one rules, the other waits. So now Israel waits, but it will rule. The same point is made in what follows, but the expectation proves acute and immediate.

LXXXIII:IV

3. A. "Magdiel and Iram: these are the chiefs of Edom, that is Esau, the father of Edom, according to their dwelling places in the land of their possession" (Genesis 36:42):

B. On the day on which Litrinus came to the throne, there appeared to R. Ammi in a dream this message: "Today Magdiel has come to the throne."

C. He said, "One more king is required for Edom [and then Israel's turn will come]."

4. A. Said R. Hanina of Sepphoris, "Why was he called Iram? For he is destined to amass [a word using the same letters] riches for the king-messiah."

B. Said R. Levi, "There was the case of a ruler in Rome who wasted the treasuries of his father. Elijah of blessed memory appeared to him in a dream. He said to him, 'Your fathers collected treasures and you waste them.'

C. "He did not budge until he filled the treasuries again."

IV.3 presents once more the theme that Rome's rule will extend only for a foreordained and limited time, at which point the Messiah will come. IV.4 explains the meaning of the name Iram. The concluding statement also alleges that Israel's saints even now make possible whatever wise decisions Rome's rulers make. That forms an appropriate conclusion to the matter. Ending in the everyday world of the here and the now, we note that sages atttribute to Israel's influence anything good that happens to Israel's brother, Rome. In our own day, even some of the children of Esau concede that point—but that has come about only after Esau murdered nearly a third of Jacob's sons and daughters.

To reiterate, people generally agree that Genesis *Rabbah* reached closure toward the end of the fourth century. This century marks the beginning of the West as we have known it. Why so? Because in the fourth century, from the conversion of Constantine and over the next hundred years, the Roman Empire became Christian—and with it, the West. So the fourth century marks the first century in which the West would flourish for the rest of time, to our own day. Accordingly, we should not find surprising the sages' recurrent references, in the reading of Genesis, to the struggle of two equal powers, Rome and Israel, Esau and Jacob, Ishmael and Isaac. The world-historical change, marking the confirmation in politics and power of the Christians' claim that Christ was king over all humanity, demanded from the sages an appropriate, and, to Israel, persuasive, response.

By rereading the story of the beginnings, sages discovered the answer and the secret of the end. Rome claimed to be Israel, and sages conceded that Rome shared the patrimony of Israel. That claim took the form of the Christians' appropriation of the Torah as "the Old Testament," so sages acknowledged the notion that, in some way, Rome too formed part of Israel. But it was the rejected part, the Ishmael, the Esau, not the Isaac, not the Jacob. The advent of Christian Rome precipitated the sustained, polemical, and, I think, rigorous and well-argued rereading of beginnings in light of the end. Rome then marked the conclusion of human history as Israel had known it. Beyond? The coming of the true Messiah, the redemption of Israel, the salvation of the world, the end of time. So the issues were not inconsiderable, and when the sages spoke of Esau/Rome, as they did so often, they confronted the life-or-death decision of the day.

Part III

THE SIXTH- AND SEVENTH-CENTURY COMPILATIONS

The Later Rabbah Midrashim

6

Ruth and Ruth Rabbah

Ruth *Rabbah*'s authorship explains not only why people should stay within Israel but also how people gain entry to Israel. In a well-crafted and cogent document, they say one thing in many ways. Endlessly reworked, susceptible to any number of fresh and novel restylings, in the end the message is always uniform; complex in its media of expression, the message is always simple. Discerning how the opposites unite, whether Gentiles and Jews, women and men, or in the Torah of the Judaism of the dual Torah for the outsider and the insider, we know whatever it is that the system at hand wishes to say. In the case of Ruth *Rabbah*, the opposites are Gentile and Israelite, woman and man. It is not sufficient for the system of the dual Torah to show how they are made one—the Gentile into Israelite, the abnormal (woman) into the normal (man). The system must place that union of opposites at the apex and pinnacle of its structure: this shows the power of the Torah to sanctify and normalize what is ordinary and abnormal. When—as in the Book of Ruth—a Moabite woman can be changed into the Israelite Messiah, the system makes its statement with remarkable force, as the complex becomes simple and uniform.

Before proceeding to describe Ruth *Rabbah* and what is important about that document, let us sample first. It is chapter 20, which serves Ruth 1:16:

> But Ruth said, "Entreat me not to leave you or to return from following you; for where you go I will go, and where you lodge I will lodge; your people shall be my people, and your God my God;

XX:i

1. A. "But Ruth said, 'Entreat me not to leave you or to return from following you":
   B. What is the meaning of "entreat me not to leave you"?
   C. This is what she said to her, "Do not sin against me. Do not take your troubles from me." [The words for "entreat" and "troubles" share the same consonants.]

2. A. "to leave you or to return from following you, for where you go I will go, and where you lodge I will lodge; your people shall be my people, and your God my God":
   B. "Under all circumstances I intend to convert, but it is better that it be through your action and not through that of another."

3. A. When Naomi heard her say this, she began enumerating the laws that govern proselytes.
   B. She said to her, "My daughter, it is not the way of Israelite women to go to theaters and circuses put on by idolators."
   C. Ruth said to her, "Where you go I will go."
   D. She said to her, "My daughter, it is not the way of Israelite women to live in a house that lacks a *mezuzah*."
   E. Ruth said to her, "Where you lodge I will lodge."
   F. "your people shall be my people":
   G. This refers to the penalties and admonitions against sinning.
   H. "and your God my God":
   I. This refers to the other religious duties.

4. A. Another interpretation of the statement, "for where you go I will go":
   B. to the tent of meeting, Gilgal, Shiloh, Nob, Gibeon, and the eternal house.
   C. "and where you lodge I will lodge":
   D. "I shall spend the night concerned about the offerings."
   E. "your people shall be my people":
   F. "so nullifying my idol."
   G. "and your God my God":
   H. "to pay a full recompense for my action."

The expansion of story of the conversion of Ruth is accomplished in several ways. First of all, her personal loyalty to Naomi is shown not to be the principal motivation, XX:i.1, 2. XX:i.3 then explains the relevance of each of Ruth's statements to the duties of the Israelite, and XX:i.4 restates matters in terms of the holy life of the cult. One cannot imagine a more profound revision of the tale, or a more authentic one. When we wish to discover how the oral Torah transforms the written one into what *we* now call Judaism, but what our sages called "the one whole Torah—oral and written—of our lord Moses at Sinai," we can point to a no more appropriate passage than this simple and unadorned composition. And, I think it clear, the interests of what we classify as a commentary have generated the whole. This is how theology comes to expression in exegesis.

Now we shall find in Ruth *Rabbah* the whole of what we call *Judaism* in a single verse. It is chapter 56, which serves Ruth 3:7:

> And when Boaz had eaten and drunk, and his heart was merry, he went to lie down at the end of the heap of grain. Then she came softly and uncovered his feet and lay down.

LVI:i

1. A. "And when Boaz had eaten and drunk and his heart was merry":
   B. Why was "his heart merry"?
   C. For he had said a blessing for his food.

2. A. Another explanation of the phrase, "And when Boaz had eaten and drunk and his heart was merry":
   B. for he had eaten various sorts of sweets after the meal, since they make the tongue agreeable to Torah.

3. A. Another explanation of the phrase, "And when Boaz had eaten and drunk and his heart was merry":
   B. For he had occupied himself with teachings of the Torah: "The Torah of your mouth is good to me" (Psalm 119:72).

4. A. Another explanation of the phrase, "And when Boaz had eaten and drunk and his heart was merry":
   B. He was seeking a wife: "Who finds a wife finds a good thing" (Proverbs 18:22).

5. A. "he went to lie down at the end of the heap of grain":
   B. R. Judah the Patriarch raised the question before R. Phineas b. R. Hama: "Boaz was a leading figure in his generation, and you say, 'at the end of the heap of grain'?"
   C. He said to him, "It is because that generation was drunk with

fornication, and they were paying wages of whores from the threshing floors: 'Do not rejoice, O Israel, like the peoples . . . you have loved a harlot's hire on every threshing floor' (Hosea 9:1).

D. "But the righteous do not act in that way.

E. "Not only so, but the righteous are far from thievery, so their capital is valuable to them" [since they do not want it used for immoral purposes, Rabinowitz, p. 72, n. 1: He lay there to prevent the grain from being used for immoral purposes].

The first four glosses surround the tale with the standard concerns for right action in Judaism: grace, Torah study, marriage. The fifth answers an obvious question.

In the case of Ruth *Rabbah*, the issue is the nature of leadership, the leader from the periphery, the Messiah from Moab—in all, Israel on its own terms. All contemporary scholarship reads the Book of Ruth as a powerful statement on that very issue: the Messiah from Moab. Yet Ruth *Rabbah* is hardly a mere reprise, paraphrase, and recapitulation of the received writing. Quite to the contrary. In all its strange and determined program of exegesis and collage, arrangement and collection and restatement, the document bears no literary or rhetorical resemblance to Scripture, even while its propositional program seems to profoundly capture the message of Scripture not only in generalities but acute detail as well. The message of the Book of Ruth, as contemporary scholarship has framed it, condemns ethnocentrism and favors a religious, not an ethnic, definition of who is Israel. For the framers of Ruth *Rabbah* the categories are quite other; they do not understand Ruth as a denial but as an affirmation, and what the document affirmed is their own system. So to conclude that our sages simply restated in their own terms the message of Scripture, paraphrasing and parroting what they found there, is to profoundly misconstrue how they wrote with Scripture. Indeed, among all the Midrash-compilations, I can find none that gives us a better view of what it means to write with Scripture than Ruth *Rabbah*.

Before proceeding, I must address the question raised in the prologue of this book, one that the established (but I think, wrong) reading of Midrash-compilations must provoke: how can I maintain that we should read this document as though it were a document? Ordinarily, people open Midrash-compilations looking for Midrash-exegeses on given verses; they rarely propose to state what the compilers of the whole have wished to state in putting this and that together into a complete book. For commonly, the various Midrash-compilations are read as mere scrapbooks, and the contents are seen as compositions that may float hither and yon, finding a perfectly comfortable place nowhere, because they fit in, somehow, everywhere. Accordingly, my claim that Ruth *Rabbah* addresses a particular problem and makes a systemic statement in its own cogent way, conflicts with the received and established hermeneutic of Midrash-compilations. Before I can set forth what I conceive to be the systemic message as Ruth *Rabbah* casts that common message, I have to validate my approach, which is documentary and not discrete.

The question before us may be phrased in a simple way: which came first, the composition of the document or its conception? What I want to know is whether people decided to make the compilation and then collected whatever they might, or whether they were in process of assembling this and that among the ready-made writings on the Book of Ruth. To frame the question more explicitly: Did our compilers have in hand a sizable corpus of completed writings on the Book of Ruth, which they wished to assemble into a compilation? Or did they determine to make a compilation and only then go in search of whatever might be available concerning the Book of Ruth among materials then in circulation?

The answer to this question derives from a survey of the document as a whole. When we review the proportions and dimensions of the compilation, we see very quickly that the compilers worked out rich materials for some chapters and verses, particularly the earlier ones, but had very little in hand for the later chapters and verses; there are sequences of verses about which our sages had nothing to say. It is not merely that the compilation tends to peter out in the end. These simple facts strongly suggest that the decision to compile Ruth *Rabbah* was not in response to the accumulation of the vast corpus of materials, evenly divided throughout the whole book. Rather, the compilers determined to produce a Midrash-compilation on the Book of Ruth, and then, and only then, did they collect, borrow, and also decide to make up appropriate materials. So the document comes prior to the formation of materials, whether suitable for it or merely useful in accomplishing its framers' goals. And that means the physiognomy of the whole comes prior to the assessment of the parts.

The simple fact that the conception of the document came prior to its execution through the selection and compilation of materials or through the composition of fresh writing points to our task. It is to ask whether the compositors wished to say one thing in response to the one book they have selected for their agglutinative pretext. Or is their interest the book itself: exposition of Ruth wherever it may lead. What we shall now see through results that, when I first reached them, I found amazing, is that there really is a single theme and a single message concerning them. Let us now proceed to consider the categories that, in the abstract and in theory, define the possible themes, then find out which theme is addressed in many ways, and what is said, in dull detail and merciless repetition, about that one theme.

Then precisely, what is the message of the compilation, which I claim constitutes a document with integrity, purpose, plan, and program? To describe the shape and structure of the document viewed all together and all at once ("the physiognomy of the whole"), I now reread every passage with an interest in its topical, and even its propositional, program. For that purpose, my categories no longer derive from inductive sifting of evidence, as evidence, piece by piece coalesces, in accord with a given taxic trait, such as governed the formulation of the studies of the rhetorical and logical traits of Ruth *Rabbah*. I have now to impose my own categories, shaped essentially in the abstract, upon the writing. For what I need to find out is whether, viewed all together, the various components that have been collected coalesce to say some few things, and, in the nature of this kind of inquiry, I have to frame in my own mind the few topics that I think in general must form the program of a compilation through which sages write with Scripture. These concern God and Israel, the nations and Israel, and Israel viewed in its own terms: the three dimensions of the existence of the social entity that defined sages' inquiry and Scripture's frame of reference alike.

Let us now survey the messages they presented in this dialogue with Scripture. In the abstract I see four principal topics on which they present their propositions, of which the first three correspond to the three relationships into which, in the sages' world, that is, Israel, entered: with heaven, on earth, and within its own existence. These yield, for our rubrics, systematic statements that concern the relationships between (1) Israel and God, with special reference to the covenant, the Torah, and the land; (2) Israel and the nations, with interest in Israel's history, past, present, and future, and how that cyclical is to be known; (3) Israel on its own terms, with focus on Israel's distinctive leadership. We shall see that nearly the whole of the propositional substrate of the document deals with the nature of leadership, on the one side, and the definition of Israel, on the other.

The final one addresses (4) the Book of Ruth in particular. This rubric encompasses not specific ad hoc propositions that form aggregates of proofs of large truths, but rather, prevailing modes of thought, demonstrating the inner structure of intellect, in our document yielding the formation, out of the cases of Scripture, of encompassing rules. As I shall point out, this fourth classification of recurrent proposition—predictably, utilizing the logic of fixed association—forms the distinctive contribution of our authorship. There is, further, a body of completed units of thought in which I am able to discern no message subject to classification and generalization, or none particular to our book of the written Torah and its thematic interests; these latter entries ordinarily appear in more than one Midrash-compilation, being suitable anywhere but necessary nowhere. We proceed to catalogue units of completed thought that make the specified points of the systematic statements given at the head of each list.

Israel and God: Israel's relationship with God encompasses the matter of the covenant, the Torah, and the Land of Israel, all of which bring to concrete and material expression the nature and standing of that relationship. This is a topic treated only casually by our compilers. They make a perfectly standard point. It is that Israel suffers because of sin (I:i). The famine in the time of the judges was because of Israel's rebellion: "My children are rebellious. But as to exterminating them, that is not possible, and to bring them back to Egypt is not possible, and to trade them for some other nation is something I cannot do. But this shall I do for them: lo, I shall torment them with suffering and afflict them with famine in the days when the judges judge" (III:i). This was because they became overconfident (III:ii).

Sometimes God saves Israel on account of its merit, sometimes for His own name's sake (X:i). God's punishment of Israel is always proportionate and appropriate, so LXXIV:i: "Just as in the beginning, Israel gave praise for the redemption: 'This is my God and I will glorify him' (Exodus 15:2), now it is for the substitution [of false gods for God]: 'Thus they exchanged their glory for the likeness of an ox that eats grass' (Psalm 106:20). You have nothing so repulsive and disgusting and strange as an ox when it is eating grass. In the beginning they would effect acquisition through the removal of the sandal, as it is said, 'Now this was the custom in former times in Israel concerning redeeming and exchanging: to confirm a transaction, the one drew off his sandal and gave it to the other, and this was the manner of attesting in Israel.' But now it is by means of the rite of cutting off." None of this forms a centerpiece of interest, and all of it complements the principal points of the writing.

Israel and the Nations: Israel's relationship with the nations is treated with interest in Israel's history, past, present, and future, and how that cyclical pattern is to be known. This topic is not addressed at all. Only one nation figures in a consequential way, and that is Moab. Under these circumstances, we can hardly generalize and say that Moab stands for everybody outside of Israel, for that is precisely the opposite of fact. Moab stands for a problem within Israel, the Messiah from the periphery; and the solution to the problem lies within Israel and not in its relationships to the nations.

Israel on Its Own: The Outsider becomes Insider, the Moabite Woman the Israelite Messiah, through the Torah. More to the point (for ours is not an accusatory document), how is the excluded included? And in what way do peripheral figures find their way to the center? Phrased in this way, the question yields the obvious answer, and the answer guides us to the center of the system. Let me state the answer with appropriate emphasis. *It is through the Torah as embodied by the sage, anybody can become Israel, and any Israelite can find his way to the center.*

Moreover—since it is through Ruth that the Moabite becomes the Israelite, and since (for our sages) the mother's status dictates the child's, we may go so far as to say that it is through the Torah that the woman may become a man (at least, in theory). Before proceeding to the account of the whole, let me give one statement of what I conceive to be the stunning systemic message in this document. It involves David, the Messiah-sage, the grandson of the Moabite woman, that is, a Moabite woman is identified as the mother of the Messiah. Only Torah can hold all this together, and it is made explicit. Let me give three concrete statements of the matter. The first concerns Ruth 4:18, "Now these are the descendants of Perez: Perez was the father of Hezron." What is important for my argument is this. Here we see how David, the Messiah-sage, has to confront the fact that he comes from an outsider and derives his personal status from a Moabite woman. The leader from the periphery becomes the Messiah in only one way: through the Torah. This is in two parts. First, knowledge of the Torah allows David to justify himself. Second, mastery of and conformity to the Torah imparts to David the status that he enjoys, just as, in a passage to be cited, Ruth herself is instructed by Boaz on how to transform her status through conformity with the Torah.

LXXXV:i

    1. A. ["Now these are the descendants of Perez: Perez was the father of Hezron":]

B. R. Abba b. Kahana commenced by citing the following verse: "'Rage and do not sin; [commune with your own heart upon your bed and be silent]' (Psalm 4:5).

C. "Said David before the Holy One, blessed be He, 'How long will they rage against me and say, "Is his family not invalid [for marriage into Israel]? Is he not descended from Ruth the Moabitess?"'

D. "'commune with your own heart upon your bed': [David continues,] "Have you too not descended from two sisters?

E. "'You look at your own origins and be silent."

F. "'Tamar who married your ancestor Judah—is she not of an invalid family?

G. "'But she was only a descendant of Shem, son of Noah. And do you come from such impressive genealogy?'"

The form of the intersecting verse/base verse is not fully worked out at i.1, since the intervention of the base verse is only by allusion. But the point is well developed, that the Messiah's family, from Ruth, is not genealogically inferior to the descendants of Judah via Tamar. David solves his problem through his knowledge of the Torah. What about his grandmother, the Moabite woman? She, too, was instructed in the Torah. The base verse is Ruth 2:8:2.

XXXIV:i

1. A. "Then Boaz said to Ruth, 'Now listen, my daughter, do not go to glean in another field'":

B. This is on the strength of the verse, "You shall have no other gods before me" (Exodus 20:3).

C. "'or leave this one'":

D. This is on the strength of the verse, "This is my God and I will glorify him" (Exodus 15:2).

E. "but keep close to my maidens":

F. This speaks of the righteous, who are called maidens: "Will you play with him as with a bird, or will you bind him for your maidens" (Job 40:29).

The glosses invest the statement with a vast tapestry of meaning. Boaz speaks to Ruth as a Jew by choice, and the entire exchange is now typological. But the rich rereading of Ruth by our sages of blessed memory does not deal only with details. Rather, it encompasses vast stretches of Israel's life, treating as metanomic and metaphorical every figure pertinent to that tapestry. Here is how the entire story will be represented in detail through the exposition of Ruth 2:14:

XL:i

1. A. "And at mealtime Boaz said to her, 'Come here and eat some bread, and dip your morsel in the wine.' So she sat beside the reapers, and he passed to her parched grain; and she ate until she was satisfied, and she had some left over":

   B. R. Yohanan interpreted the phrase "come here" in six ways:

   C. "The first speaks of David.

   D. "'Come here' means, to the throne: 'That you have brought me here' (2 Samuel 7:18).

   E. "'and eat some bread': the bread of the throne.

   F. "'and dip your morsel in vinegar': this speaks of his sufferings: 'O Lord, do not rebuke me in your anger' (Psalm 6:2).

   G. "'So she sat beside the reapers': for the throne was taken from him for a time."

   H. As R. Huna said, "The entire six months that David fled from Absalom are not counted in his reign, for he atoned for his sins with a she-goat, like an ordinary person [rather than with a he-goat, as does the king]."

   I. [Resuming from G:] "'and he passed to her parched grain': he was restored to the throne: 'Now I know that the Lord saves his anointed' (Psalm 20:7).

   J. "'and she ate and was satisfied and had some left over': this indicates that he would eat in this world, in the days of the messiah, and in the age to come."

2. A. "The second interpretation refers to Solomon: 'Come here': means, to the throne.

   B. "'and eat some bread': this is the bread of the throne: 'And Solomon's provision for one day was thirty measures of fine flour and three score measures of meal' (1 Kings 5:2).

   C. "'and dip your morsel in vinegar': this refers to the dirty deeds of those [that he did].

   D. "'So she sat beside the reapers': for the throne was taken from him for a time."

   E. For R. Yohai b. R. Hanina said, "An angel came down in the form of Solomon and sat on the throne, but he made the rounds of the doors throughout Israel and said, 'I, Kohelet, have been king over Israel in Jerusalem' (Kohelet 1:12).

F. "What did one of them do? She set before him a plate of pounded beans and hit him on the head with a stick, saying, 'Doesn't Solomon sit on the throne? How can you say, "I am Solomon, king of Israel"?'"

G. [Reverting to D:] "'and he passed to her parched grain': for he was restored to the throne.

H. "'and she ate and was satisfied and left some over': this indicates that he would eat in this world, in the days of the messiah, and in the age to come."

3. A. "The third interpretation speaks of Hezekiah: 'Come here': means, to the throne.

B. "'and eat some bread': this is the bread of the throne.

C. "'and dip your morsel in vinegar': this refers to sufferings [Isaiah 5:1]: 'And Isaiah said, Let them take a cake of figs' (Isaiah 38:21).

D. "'So she sat beside the reapers': for the throne was taken from him for a time: 'Thus says Hezekiah, This day is a day of trouble and rebuke' (Isaiah 37:3).

E. "'and he passed to her parched grain': for he was restored to the throne: 'So that he was exalted in the sight of all nations from then on' (2 Chronicles 32:23).

F. "'and she ate and was satisfied and left some over': this indicates that he would eat in this world, in the days of the messiah, and in the age to come."

4. A. "The fourth interpretation refers to Manasseh: 'Come here': means, to the throne.

B. "'and eat some bread': this is the bread of the throne.

C. "'and dip your morsel in vinegar': for his dirty deeds were like vinegar, on account of wicked actions.

D. "'So she sat beside the reapers': for the throne was taken from him for a time: 'And the Lord spoke to Manasseh and to his people, but they did not listen. So the Lord brought them the captains of the host of the king of Assyria, who took Manasseh with hooks' (2 Chronicles 33:10-11)."

E. R. Abba b. R. Kahana said, "With manacles."

F. Said R. Levi bar Hayyata, "They made him a bronze mule and put him on it and lit a fire underneath it, and he cried out, 'Idol thus-and-so, idol thus-and-so, save me!' When he realized that it did him no good at all, he said, 'I remember that Father would read in Scripture for me, "In your distress, when all

these things have come upon you . . . he will not fail you"
(Deuteronomy 4:30). 'I will call on him. If he answers me, well
and good, and if he does not answer me, then it's all the same.
'"Every face is like every other face.'"

G. "At that moment the ministering angels went and shut all the
windows above. They said before him, 'Lord of the world, a
man who put up an idol in the Holy Temple, will you accept
back in repentance?'

H. "He said to them, 'If I don't take him back, lo, I will be locking
the door against all those who return in repentance.'

I. "What did the Holy One, blessed be He, do? He dug a hole for
him under the throne of his glory, in a place in which no angel
can reach: 'And he prayed to him, and he was entreated by him
and heard his supplication' (2 Chronicles 33:13)."

J. Said R. Levi, "In Arabia they call a hole [by the same letters
as are used in the word 'entreat']."

K. [Reverting to D:] "'and he passed to her parched grain': for he
was restored to the throne: 'And brought him back to Jerusalem to his kingdom'" (2 Chronicles 33:13).

L. How did he restore him?

M. R. Samuel in the name of R. Aha: "He brought him back with
a wind, in line with the usage, 'who causes the wind to blow'
[the letters for the word restore and blowing of the wind being
the same]."

N. "'and she ate and was satisfied and left some over': this indicates that he would eat in this world, in the days of the
messiah, and in the age to come."

5. A. "The fifth interpretation refers to the Messiah: 'Come here':
means, to the throne.

B. "'and eat some bread': this is the bread of the throne.

C. "'and dip your morsel in vinegar': this refers to suffering: 'But
he was wounded because of our transgressions' (Isaiah 53:5).

D. "'So she sat beside the reapers': for the throne is destined to be
taken from him for a time: For I will gather all nations against
Jerusalem to battle and the city shall be taken' (Zechariah
14:2).

E. "'and he passed to her parched grain': for he will be restored to
the throne: 'And he shall smite the land with the rod of his
mouth' (Isaiah 11:4)."

F. R. Berekhiah in the name of R. Levi: "As was the first redeemer, so is the last redeemer:

G. "Just as the first redeemer was revealed and then hidden from them—"

H. And how long was he hidden? Three months: "And they met Moses and Aaron" (Exodus 5:20),

I. [reverting to G:] "so the last redeemer will be revealed to them and then hidden from them."

J. How long will he be hidden?

K. R. Tanhuma in the name of rabbis: "Forty-five days: 'And from the time that the continual burnt offering shall be taken away . . . there shall be a thousand two hundred and ninety days. Happy is the one who waits and comes to the thousand three hundred and thirty-five days' (Daniel 12:11–12)."

L. What are the extra days?

M. R. Isaac b. Kaseratah in the name of R. Jonah: "These are the forty-five days in which the Israelites will harvest [Rabino-witz, p. 65:] saltwort and eat it: 'They pluck saltwort with wormwood' (Job 30:45)."

N. Where will he lead them?

O. From the [holy] land to the wilderness of Judah: "Behold, I will entice her and bring her into the wilderness" (Hosea 2:16).

P. Some say, "To the wilderness of Sihon and Og: 'I will yet again make you dwell in tents as in the days of the appointed season' (Hosea 12:10)."

Q. And whoever believes in him will live.

R. But whoever does not believe in him will go to the nations of idolatry, who will kill him.

S. [Supply: "and she ate and was satisfied and left some over":] Said R. Isaac b. R. Merion, "In the end the Holy One, blessed be He, will be revealed upon them and bring down manna for them: 'And there is nothing new under the sun' (Kohelet 1:9)."

T. "'and she ate and was satisfied and left some over.'"

6. A. "The sixth interpretation refers to Boaz: 'Come here': [supply:] means, to the throne.

B. "'and eat some bread': this refers to the bread of the reapers.

C. "'and dip your morsel in vinegar': it is the practice of reapers to dip their bread in vinegar."

D. Said R. Jonathan, "On this basis we derive the rule that people bring out various kinds of [dishes made with] vinegar to the granaries."

E. [Reverting to C:] "'So she sat beside the reapers': this is meant literally.

F. "'and he passed to her parched grain': a pinch between his two fingers."

G. Said R. Isaac, "One might derive from this passage two rules:

H. "either that a blessing [Rabinowitz, p. 66:] reposed between the fingers of that righteous man,

I. "or that a blessing reposed between the fingers of that righteous woman.

J. "However, since Scripture states, 'and she ate and was satisfied and left some over,' it appears that the blessed reposed in the belly of that righteous woman."

7. A. R. Isaac b. Merion said, "The verse ['and he passed to her parched grain; and she ate until she was satisfied, and she had some left over'] teaches you that if one carries out a religious duty, he should do it with a whole heart.

B. "For had Reuben known that the Holy One, blessed be He, would have written concerning him, 'And Reuben heard it and delivered him out of their hand' (Genesis 37:21), he would have brought him on his shoulder back to his father.

C. "And if Aaron had known that the Holy One, blessed be He, would have written concerning him, 'And also behold, he comes forth to meet you' (Exodus 4:14), he would have gone out to meet him with timbrels and dances.

D. "And if Boaz had known that the Holy One, blessed be He, would have written concerning him, 'and he passed to her parched grain; and she ate until she was satisfied, and she had some left over,' he would have fed her with fatted calves."

8. A. R. Kohen and R. Joshua of Sikhnin in the name of R. Levi: "In the past a person would do a religious duty and a prophet would inscribe it, but now when a person does a religious duty, who writes it down?

B. "It is Elijah who writes it down, and the Messiah and the Holy One, blessed be He, affix their seals with their own hands:

C. "'Then they who feared the Lord spoke with one another, and the Lord listened and heard and a book of remembrance was written before him' (Malachi 3:16)."

XL.i.1-6 form a beautifully crafted and utterly unitary composition, assigned to Yohanan, interpreting the base verse in six ways: David, Solomon, Hezekiah, Manasseh, the Messiah, and Boaz. The last, of course, is quite out of phase in the exegetical side, but fits beautifully in the redactional framework; Boaz, of course, produced the Messiah. His passage comes last solely for redactional reasons. In an autonomous setting, the Messiah would come at the end. But then Boaz is the only one whose reading of the verse is literal, and that marks the i.6 as independent of the foregoing. While i.1-6 then focus upon our base verse, for the framer of i.7 it is simply one fact among a variety of facts that proves his main proposition. It is that if people knew the full value assigned to their deeds by Heaven, they would carry out those deeds with greater enthusiasm than they do ("a whole heart"). XL.i.8 is tacked on to XL.i.7 prior to insertion here; it makes no contribution to the interpretation of our base verse and is out of place except as a complement to i.7. That of course is a commonplace component of the history of a composition: (1) composition joined to (2) a matched or pertinent or somehow intersecting composition, and (3) the whole then inserted where one or another of the parts makes a place for it, now without revision for the purposes of the larger composite in which it is included. We should not lose the main point in the quite natural engagement with this wonderful composition. It is that through the Torah, the Moabite woman has become an Israelite, originally a stranger and a woman and now the center and heart of the life of holy Israel, the Messiah—all through mastery of the Torah. The plethora of details should not obscure the simple and repeated message of the Judaism of the dual Torah: it is Torah alone that matters; here Torah unites opposites, makes the outsider an insider, allows the insider to retain the status of a woman—David's grandmother—but places him at the center of the system. Have I represented the document's message, or merely given some examples of a commonplace message that happens to come up in this document too? The answer derives from the following survey of the way in which the same statement is repeated in one detail after another.

Israel on Its Own: The Documentary Message Viewed Whole: Israel on its own concerns the holy nation's understanding of itself: who is Israel, who is not? Within the same rubric we find consideration of Israel's capacity to naturalize the outsider, so to define itself as to extend its own limits, and other questions of self-definition. And, finally, when Israel considers itself, a principal concern is the nature of leadership, for the leader stands for and embodies the people. Therein lies the paradox of the base-document and the Midrash-compilation alike: how can the leader most wanted, the Messiah, come, as a matter of fact, from the excluded people and not from the holy people? Let us review it from the beginning to the end.

The sin of Israel, which caused the famine, was that it was judging its own judges. "He further said to the Israelites, 'So God says to Israel, I have given a share of glory to the judges and I have called them gods, and they humiliate them. Woe to a generation that judges its judges'" (I:i). The Israelites were slothful in burying Joshua, and that showed disrespect to their leader (II:i). They were slothful about repentance in the time of the judges, and that is what caused the famine; excess of commitment to one's own affairs leads to sin. The Israelites did not honor the prophets (III:iii). The old have to bear with the young, and the young with the old, or Israel will go into exile (IV:i). The generation that judges its leadership ("judges") will be penalized (V:i). Arrogance toward the authority of the Torah is penalized (V:i). Elimelech was punished because he broke the people's heart; everyone depended upon him, and he proved undependable (V:iii); so bad leadership will destroy Israel. Why was Elimelech punished? It was because he broke the Israelites' heart. When the years of drought came, his maid went into the marketplace with her basket in her hand. So the people of the town said, "Is this the one on whom we depended, that he can provide for the whole town with ten years of food? Lo, his maid is standing in the marketplace with her basket in her hand!" So Elimelech was one of the great men of the town and one of those who sustained the generation. But when the years of famine came, he said, "Now all the Israelites are going to come knocking on my door, each with his basket." The leadership of a community is its glory: "The great man of a town—he is its splendor, he is its glory, he is its praise."

A distinct but fundamental component of the theory of Israel in its own terms concerns who is Israel and how one becomes a part of Israel. That theme, of course, proves fundamental to our document, so much of which is preoccupied with how Ruth can be the progenitor of the Messiah, deriving as she does not only from Gentiles but from Moabite stock. Israel's history follows rules that are to be learned in Scripture; nothing is random and all things are connected (IV:ii). The fact that the king of Moab honored God explains why God raised up from Moab "a son who will sit on the throne of the Lord" (VIII:i.3). The proselyte is discouraged but then accepted. Thus XVI:i.2.B: "People are to turn a proselyte away. But if he is insistent beyond that point, he is accepted. A person should always push away with the left hand, while offering encouragement with the right." Orpah, who left Naomi, was rewarded for the little that she did for her, but she was raped when she left her (XVIII:i.1–3). When Orpah went back to her people, she went back to her gods (XIX:i).

Ruth's intention to convert was absolutely firm, and Naomi laid out all the problems for her, but she acceded to every condition (XX:i). Thus she said, "Under all circumstances I intend to convert, but it is better that it be through your action and not through that of another."

Proselytes are respected by God, so XXII:i: "And when Naomi saw that she was determined to go with her, [she said no more]": Said R. Judah b. R. Simon, "Notice how precious are proselytes before the Omnipresent. Once she had decided to convert, the Scripture treats her as equivalent to Naomi." Boaz, for his part, was equally virtuous and free of sins (XXVI:i). The law provided for the conversion of Ammonite and Moabite women, but not Ammonite and Moabite men, so the acceptance of Ruth the Moabite was fully in accord with the law, and anyone who did not know that fact was an ignoramus (XXVI:i.4, among many passages). An Israelite hero who came from Ruth and Boaz was David, who was a great master of the Torah, thus he was "Skillful in playing, and a mighty man of war, prudent in affairs, good-looking, and the Lord is with him" (1 Samuel 16:18):" "Skillful in playing": in Scripture. "And a mighty man of valor": in Mishnah. "A man of war": who knows the give and take of the war of the Torah. "Prudent in affairs": in good deeds. "Good-looking": in Talmud. "Prudent in affairs": able to reason deductively. "Good-looking": enlightened in law. "And the Lord is with him": the law accords with his opinions.

Taking shelter under the wings of the Presence of God, which is what the convert does, is the greatest merit accorded to all who do deeds of grace, thus: So notice the power of the righteous and the power of those who do deeds of grace. For they take shelter not in the shadow of the dawn, nor in the shadow of the wings of the earth, not in the shadow of the wings of the sun, nor in the shadow of the wings of the *hayyot*, nor in the shadow of the wings of the cherubim or the seraphim. But under whose wings do they take shelter? "They take shelter under the shadow of the One at whose word the world was created: 'How precious is your lovingkindness O God, and the children of men take refuge in the shadow of your wings' (Psalm 36:8)." The language that Boaz used to Ruth, "Come here"—as we saw above—bore with it deeper reference to six: David, Solomon, the throne as held by the Davidic monarchy, and ultimately, the Messiah, for example, in the following instance: "The fifth interpretation refers to the Messiah: 'Come here': means, to the throne. 'And eat some bread': this is the bread of the throne. 'And dip your morsel in vinegar': this refers to suffering: 'But he was wounded because of our transgressions' (Isaiah 53:5). 'So she sat beside the reapers': for the throne is destined to be taken from him for a time: 'For I will gather all nations against Jerusalem to battle and the city shall be taken' (Zechariah 14:2). 'And he passed to her parched grain': for he will be restored to the throne: 'And he shall smite the land with the rod of his mouth' (Isaiah 11:4)." R. Berekhiah in the name of R. Levi: "As was the first redeemer, so is the last redeemer: 'Just as the first redeemer was revealed and then hidden from them, so the last redeemer will be revealed to them and then hidden from them'" (XL:i.1ff.).

Boaz instructed Ruth on how to be a proper Israelite woman, so LIII:i: "Wash yourself": from the filth of idolatry that is yours. "And anoint yourself": this refers to the religious deeds and acts of righteousness [that are required of an Israelite]. "And put on your best clothes": this refers to her Sabbath clothing. So did Naomi encompass Ruth within Israel: "and go down to the threshing floor": She said to her, "My merit will go down there with you." Moab, whence Ruth came, was conceived not for the sake of fornication but for the sake of Heaven (LV:i.1.B). Boaz, for his part, was a master of the Torah and when he ate and drank, that formed a typology for his study of the Torah (LVI:i). His was a life of grace, Torah study, and marriage for holy purposes. Whoever trusts in God is exalted, and that refers to Ruth and Boaz; God put it in his heart to bless her (LVII:i).

The role of the grandmother, the Moabite Ruth, is underlined, emphasized, celebrated. For example, David sang psalms to thank God for his grandmother, Ruth, so LIX:i.5, "[At midnight I will rise to give thanks to you] because of your righteous judgments" (Psalm 119:62): [David speaks,] "The acts of judgment that you brought upon the Ammonites and Moabites. And the righteous deeds that you carried out for my grandfather and my grandmother [Boaz, Ruth, of whom David speaks here]. For had he hastily cursed her but once, where should I have come from? But you put in his heart the will to bless her: 'And he said, "May you be blessed by the Lord."'" Because of the merit of the six measures that Boaz gave Ruth, six righteous persons came forth from him, each with six virtues: David, Hezekiah, Josiah, Hananiah, Mishael, Azariah, Daniel, and the royal Messiah.

God facilitated the union of Ruth and Boaz (LXVIII:i). Boaz's relative was ignorant in not knowing that while a male Moabite was excluded, a female one was acceptable for marriage. The blessing of Boaz was, "May all the children you have come from this righteous woman" (LXXIX:i), and that is precisely the blessing accorded to Isaac and to Elkanah. God made Ruth an ovary, which she had lacked (LXXX:i). Naomi was blessed with Messianic blessings (LXXXI:i), thus: "Then the women said to Naomi, 'Blessed be the Lord, who has not left you this day without next of kin, and may his name be renowned in Israel'": Just as "this day" rules dominion in the firmament, so will your descendants rule and govern Israel forever. On account of the blessings of the women, the line of David was not wholly exterminated in the time of Athaliah.

David was ridiculed because he was descended from Ruth, the Moabitess, as LXXXV:i. But many other distinguished families derived from humble origins, so, "Said David before the Holy One, blessed be He, 'How long will they rage against me and say, "Is his family not invalid [for marriage into Israel]? Is he not descended from Ruth the Moabitess?"' 'Commune with your own heart upon your bed': [David continues,] 'You, too, have you not descended from two sisters? You look at your own origins and shut up.'" 'So Tamar who married your ancestor Judah—is she not of an invalid family? But she was only a descendant of Shem, son of Noah. So do you come from such impressive genealogy?'" David referred to and defended his Moabite origins, so LXXXIX:i: "Then I said, 'Lo, I have come [in the roll of the book it is written of me]' (Psalm 40:8)." "[David says,] 'Then I had to recite a song when I came, for the word "then" refers only to a song, as it is said, "Then sang Moses" (Exodus 15:1).' 'I was covered by the verse, "An Ammonite and a Moabite shall not come into the assembly of the Lord" (Deuteronomy 23:4), but I have come "in the roll of the book it is written of me" (Psalm 40:8). "In the roll": this refers to the verse, [David continues], 'concerning whom you commanded that they should not enter into your congregation' (Lamentations 1:10). "'Of the book it is written of me: An Ammonite and a Moabite shall not enter into the assembly of the Lord" (Deuteronomy 23:4). 'It is not enough that I have come, but in the roll and the book it is written concerning me: "'In the roll": Perez, Hezron, Ram, Amminadab, Nahshon, Salmon, Boaz, Obed, Jesse, David. "'In the book": "And the Lord said, Arise, anoint him, for this is he"' (1 Samuel 16:12)."

Various other passages also have either no clear proposition, or none pertinent to our book in particular. In the following I catalogue the philological-propositional and the sustained exegetical passages not pertinent to the Book of Ruth. These too do not form a large proportion of the whole.[1]

IV:ii The meaning of the word "and it came to pass."

V:ii There were ten famines that affected the world. One will take place in the world to come.

VI:i The purpose of the Book of Chronicles is only for interpretation and not for a literal reading.

VII:i People die in cohorts; happy is the person who leaves this world with a good name.

IX:i God injures property, then persons, so as to give people a chance to repent. This proposition has no bearing upon the theme of the Book of Ruth in particular.

XVIII:i.4 Every act of kissing is frivolous except for three: meeting, departing, and inauguration.

XXI:i.4 After death, one cannot repent. It is best to live well in this life, because later on there is no rewriting the record. A long series of stories illustrates this point.

XXVII:i.5 The name of the wicked is given before Scripture gives the name, and the name of the righteous is given afterward.

XXX:i There were three decrees that the earthly court issued, and the heavenly court concurred in their decision. And these are: [1] to give greetings using the name of God; [2] the scroll of Esther; and [3] tithing.

XXXI:i.2-3 A virtuous person always signals virtue through his deeds.

XXXVI:i The interpretation of 1 Chronicles 11:13-14 occupies the entire composition, reading the biblical story typologically as an account of Torah study.

---

[1] It is noteworthy that these items commonly occur in more than a single document, which is quite natural, since they belong nowhere in particular. One of the marks of the itinerant compositions is that they ordinarily stand autonomous of every document in which they occur. In my *Making the Classics in Judaism: The Three Stages of Literary Formation*. Atlanta: Scholars Press for Brown Judaic Studies, 1990, I have explained what is at stake in these remarks.

XXXIX:i The peculiarity of spelling is interpreted.

XLV:i More than the householder does for the poor, the poor does for the householder. How people treat the poor determines the destiny of the nation. There are various propositions on poverty and on helping the poor.

LIX:i David would story the Torah.

LXII:iii There were three who were tempted by their inclination to do evil, but who strengthened themselves against it by taking an oath: Joseph, David, and Boaz.

LXVI:i "In every place in which the Israelites came, they did not go forth empty-handed. From the spoil of Egypt they did not go forth empty-handed. From the spoil of Sihon and Og they did not go forth empty-handed. From the spoil of the thirty-one kings they did not go forth empty-handed."

LXVII:i "The yes said by a righteous person is yes, their no is a no."

LXIX:i An unimportant person has not the right to take his seat before the more important person invites him to do so. This ruling house [David's, hence the patriarch's at this time] appoints elders [to the governing body, even] in their banquet halls! The blessing of the bridegroom requires a quorum of ten.

LXXV:i.1–4 The mode of solving the problem of an obscure antecedent of a pronoun.

What is the message of Ruth *Rabbah*? To speak of *messages* in the Midrash-compilation, Ruth *Rabbah*, is simply misleading. Our document has only one message, which is expressed in a variety of components, but is single and cogent. It concerns the outsider who becomes the principal, the Messiah out of Moab, and this miracle is accomplished through mastery of the Torah. I find these points:

1. Israel's fate depends upon proper conduct toward its leaders.
2. The leaders must not be arrogant.
3. The admission of the outsider depends upon the rules of Torah. These differentiate among outsiders. Those who know the rules are able to apply them accurately and mercifully.

4. The proselyte is accepted because the Torah makes it possible to do so, and the condition of acceptance is complete and total submission to the Torah. Boaz taught Ruth the rules of the Torah, and she obeyed them carefully.

5. Those proselytes who are accepted are respected by God and are completely equal to all other Israelites. Those who marry them are masters of the Torah, and their descendants are masters of the Torah, typified by David. Boaz in his day and David in his day were the same in this regard.

6. What the proselyte therefore accomplishes is to take shelter under the wings of God's presence, and the proselyte who does so stands in the royal line of David, Solomon, and the Messiah. Over and over again, we see, the point is made that Ruth the Moabitess, perceived by the ignorant as an outsider, enjoyed complete equality with all other Israelites, because she had accepted the yoke of the Torah, married a great sage, and produced the Messiah-sage, David.

Scripture has provided everything but the main point—the story, the irritant—the Moabite Messiah. But our sages impose upon the whole their distinctive message, which is the priority of the Torah, the extraordinary power of the Torah to join the opposites—Messiah, utter outsider—into a single figure, and, as I said, to accomplish this union of opposites through a woman. The femininity of Ruth seems to me as critical to the whole, therefore, as the Moabite origin: the two modes of the abnormal (from the Israelite perspective), outsider versus Israelite, woman versus man, are therefore invoked, and both for the same purpose; to show how, through the Torah, all things become one. That is the message of the document, and, I think, the principal message, to which all other messages prove peripheral.

We began with the observation that through Scripture the sages accomplished their writing, and we have further noted throughout that it is not so much by writing fresh discourses as by compiling and arranging materials that the framers of the document accomplished this. It would be difficult to find a less promising mode of writing than merely collecting and arranging available pieces into a composite. But that is the predominant trait of this writing. It is clear that our compilers were as interested in the exposition of the Book of Ruth as in the execution of their paramount proposition through such a compilation. For we have a large number of entries that contain no more elaborate proposition than the exposition through paraphrase of the sense of a given clause or verse.

Indeed, Ruth *Rabbah* proves nearly as much a commentary in the narrowest sense—verse by verse amplification, paraphrase, exposition—as it is a compilation in the working definition of this inquiry. What holds the document together and gives it, if not coherence, then at least flow and movement, after all, are the successive passages of exposition.

As a matter of fact, Lamentations *Rabbah* likewise deals with one topic, which is God's unique relationship with Israel. It makes a single statement about that topic, which is that the relationship of God to Israel is unique among the nations, that relationship works itself out even now, in a time of despair and disappointment. The resentment of the present condition, recapitulating the calamity of the destruction of the Temple, finds its resolution and remission in the redemption that will follow Israel's regeneration through the Torah—that is the program, that is the proposition, and in this compilation, there is no other. And, I also have been able to identify the single topic and message of Esther *Rabbah I*. It concerns Israel among the nations. It is that the nations are swine, their rulers fools, and Israel is subjugated to them, though it should not be, because of its own sins. But just as God saved Israel in the past, so the salvation that Israel can attain will recapitulate the former ones. The theme, then, is Israel among the nations; on that theme, the sages put forth a proposition entirely familiar from the books of Deuteronomy through Kings, on the one side, and much of prophetic literature, on the other.

The proposition is familiar, and so is the theme; but since the book of Esther can hardly be characterized as *deuteronomic*, lacking all interest in the covenant, the land, and issues of atonement (beyond the conventional sackcloth, ashes, and fasting, hardly the fodder for prophetic regeneration and renewal!), the sages' distinctive viewpoint in the document must be deemed an original and interesting contribution of their own. The compilers of Esther *Rabbah I*, who, like the compilers of Ruth *Rabbah*, really constituted an authorship, a single-minded and determined group (whether of one or ten or 200 workers hardly matters) set forth their variation on a very old and profoundly rooted theology. If I had to identify one recurrent motif that captures that theology, it is the critical role of Esther and Mordecai, particularly Mordecai, who, as sage, emerges in the position of Messiah. Here again the theme of the sage-Messiah proves paramount, now through the figure of Mordecai alongside Esther, as much as, in Ruth *Rabbah*, the theme is worked out through David alongside Ruth.

What this fact of description of the compilation means is simple. Our authorship decided to compose a document concerning the Book of

Ruth in order to make a single point. Everything else was subordinated to that definitive intention. Once the work got underway, the task was one of not exposition so much as repetition, not unpacking and exploring a complex conception, but restating the point and eliciting or evoking the proper attitude that was congruent with that point. The decision, viewed after the fact, was to make one statement in an enormous number of ways. This highly restricted program of thought resorted to a singularly varied vocabulary. Indeed, some might call it a symbolic vocabulary, in that messages are conveyed not through propositions but through images, whether visual or verbal.

Since, as they responded to it, Scripture supplied a highly restricted vocabulary, the message was singular, the meanings were few and to be repeated, not many and to be cast aside promiscuously. When we find the "another interpretation" sequences, we see how this works: a great many ways are found to say one thing. That is why we do not find endless multiple meanings[2] but a highly limited repertoire of a few cogent and wholly coherent meanings, to be replayed again and again. It is the repetitious character of discourse, in which people say the same thing in a great many different ways, that characterizes this document. The reason for the repetition is simple: it is through a representation of the simple symbolic vocabulary that the messages emerge.

It was one thing to write with Scripture; that had been done before. It was quite another to write by collecting and arranging verses of Scripture in such a way that many things were made to say one thing. In Ruth *Rabbah*, many things do say one thing, and here, we see, God lives not only in the details, but in the repetition of details, always in the same way, always with the same message. Everything says one thing, and that one thing is, the Torah dictates Israel's fate. If you want to know what that fate will be, study the Torah, and if you want to control that fate, follow the model of the sage-Messiah, in whom are formed the perfect unions of outsider, woman, Moabite and insider, man, Israelite, all one in the Torah of Moses our rabbi.

---

[2]Cf. William Scott Green, "Romancing the Tome: Rabbinic Hermeneutics and the Theory of Literature," *Semeia* 1987, 40:147–169, *Text and Textuality*, ed. Charles Winquist, with special reference to p. 163: "If it is doubtful that rabbis ascribed 'endless multiple meanings' to Scripture, it is no less so that rabbinic hermeneutics encouraged and routinely tolerated the metonymical coexistence of different meanings of Scripture that did not, and could not, annul one another."

7

Song of Songs and Song of Songs Rabbah

Song of Songs *Rabbah* is the greatest intellectual achievement of our sages,[1] because it surmounts the most formidable challenge of all of Scripture: understanding the Song of Songs as a metaphor. Reading the sensual love poetry as a metaphor for God's love for Israel and Israel's love for God, the authorship of Song of Songs *Rabbah* explain how each detail expresses in metaphorical language a palpable fact of that relationship. So far as our sages work out the meanings of the *is* in response to the messages of the *as-if*, in Song of Songs *Rabbah* we see with great clarity the outer limits of their labor. For here the *is* is the love of man for woman and woman for man, and the *as-if* is the love of God for Israel and Israel for God. But that is leaping from metaphor to metaphor, and that is precisely what our sages have done, like a hart, like a gazelle. In my

---

[1]Admittedly, I have reached the same judgment of every rabbinic document I have studied, falling in love with each in its day, then finding the next still more engaging. Still, now that I have completed my translation of all or large parts of every document produced by the Judaism of the dual Torah—that is, the entire canon, from the Mishnah through the Bavli—I see this last one in many ways as the climax of the whole. From the laconic philosophy of the Mishnah through the erotic sensibility of Song of Songs *Rabbah*, a single path moves always upward, from the concrete to the most abstract. And the road from the Mishnah to Song of Songs *Rabbah* surely is from this world and the everyday to the transcendent height attained in the document before us. So my profession of admiration for those compilers and authors is not merely the enthusiasm of the committed moment.

language, they attain here the level of abstraction that fully exposes the deepest layers of sensibility within.

So real and concrete is that poetry, that understanding its implicit meanings, identifying its hidden messages as an account of the lovers, God and Israel, and the urgency of their love for one another represent a triumph of the *as-if* mentality over the mentality of the merely *is*. But, we rapidly realize, the poem is the metaphor, the reality, the tangible and physical and material love of Israel for God and of God for Israel: the urgent, the never-fully-satisfied desire. Given the character of the Song of Songs, our sages' power to grasp its wholly other meanings and plausibly to state them attests to the fullness of their affirmations of God and Israel as the principal figures in contention—as the lover and the beloved must always contend—in this world.

The sages who compiled Song of Songs *Rabbah* read the Song of Songs as a sequence of statements of urgent love between God and Israel, the holy people. Their remarkable document provides the single best entry in all canonical literature of Judaism into the symbolic system and structure of the Judaism of the Dual Torah. The reason is that, over and over again, the compilers of the document as a whole and also the authors of the components they have chosen, appeal to a highly restricted list of implicit meanings, calling upon some very few events or persons, repeatedly identifying these as the expressions of God's profound affection for Israel, and Israel's deep love for God. The message of the document comes not so much from stories of what happened or did not happen, assertions of truth or denials of error, but rather from the repetitious rehearsal of sets of symbols.

The implicit meanings are always few and invariably self-evident; no serious effort goes into demonstrating the fact that God speaks, or Israel speaks; the point of departure is the message and meaning the One or the other means to convey. To take one instance, time and again we shall be told that a certain expression of love is God speaking to Israel about (1) the Sea, (2) Sinai, and (3) the world to come; or (1) the first redemption (from Egypt); (2) the second redemption (from Babylonia); and (3) the third redemption (at the end of days). The repertoire of symbols covers Temple and schoolhouse, personal piety and public worship, and other matched pairs and sequences of coherent matters, all of them seen as embedded within the poetry. Here is poetry read as metaphor, and the task of the reader is to know what each image represents. So Israel's holy life is metaphorized through the poetry of love and beloved, Lover and Israel.

We do find a highly limited repertoire of a few cogent and wholly coherent meanings, to be replayed again and again. It is the repetitious character of discourse, in which people say the same thing in a great many different ways, that characterizes this document. The treatment of the Song of Songs by our sages of blessed memory shows over and over again that long lists of alternative meanings or interpretations end up saying just one thing, but in different ways. The implicit meanings prove very few indeed. Let us see how the document presents many things to make one point.

SONG OF SONGS RABBAH TO SONG OF SONGS 1:2

II:I

1. A. "O that you would kiss me with the kisses of your mouth! [For your love is better than wine]":
   B. In what connection was this statement made?
   C. R. Hinena b. R. Pappa said, "It was stated at the sea: '[I compare you, my love,] to a mare of Pharaoh's chariots' (Song of Songs 1:9)."
   D. R. Yuda b. R. Simon said, "It was stated at Sinai: 'The song of songs' (Song of Songs 1:1)—the song that was sung by the singers: 'The singers go before, the minstrels follow after' (Psalm 68:26)."

2. A. It was taught on Tannaite authority in the name of R. Nathan, "The Holy One, blessed be He, in the glory of His greatness said it: 'The song of songs that is Solomon's' (Song of Songs 1:1),
   B. "[meaning,] that belongs to the King to whom peace belongs."

3. A. Rabban Gamaliel says, "The ministering angels said it: 'the song of songs' (Song of Songs 1:1)—
   B. "the song that the princes on high said."

4. A. R. Yohanan said, "It was said at Sinai: 'O that you would kiss me with the kisses of your mouth!' (Song of Songs 1:2)."

5. A. R. Meir says, "It was said in connection with the tent of meeting."
   B. And he brings evidence from the following verse: "Awake, O north wind, and come, O south wind! Blow upon my garden, let its fragrance be wafted abroad. Let my beloved come to his garden, and eat its choicest fruits" (Song of Songs 4:16).
   C. "Awake, O north wind": this refers to the burnt offerings, slaughtered at the north side of the altar.

D. "and come, O south wind": this refers to the peace offerings, which were slaughtered at the south side of the altar.

E. "Blow upon my garden": this refers to the tent of meeting.

F. "let its fragrance be wafted abroad": this refers to the incense offering.

G. "Let my beloved come to his garden": this refers to the Presence of God.

H. "and eat its choicest fruits": this refers to the offerings.

6. A. Rabbis say, "It was said in connection with the house of the ages [the Temple itself]."

B. And they bring evidence from the same verse: "Awake, O north wind, and come, O south wind! Blow upon my garden, let its fragrance be wafted abroad. Let my beloved come to his garden, and eat its choicest fruits" (Song of Songs 4:16).

C. "Awake, O north wind": this refers to the burnt offerings, slaughtered at the north side of the altar.

D. "and come, O south wind": this refers to the peace offerings, which were slaughtered at the south side of the altar.

E. "Blow upon my garden": this refers to the house of the ages.

F. "let its fragrance be wafted abroad": this refers to the incense offering.

G. "Let my beloved come to his garden": this refers to the Presence of God.

H. "and eat its choicest fruits": this refers to the offerings.

I. The rabbis furthermore maintain that all the other verses also refer to the house of the ages.

J. Said R. Aha, "The verse that refers to the Temple is the following: 'King Solomon made himself a palanquin, from the wood of Lebanon. He made its posts of silver, its back of gold, its seat of purple; it was lovingly wrought within by the daughters of Jerusalem' (Song of Songs 3:9-10)."

K. Rabbis treat these as the intersecting verses for the verse, "And it came to pass on the day that Moses had made an end of setting up the tabernacle" (Numbers 7:1).

7. A. In the opinion of R. Hinena [1.C], who said that the verse was stated on the occasion of the Sea, [the sense of the verse, "O that you would kiss me with the kisses of your mouth"] is, "may he bring to rest upon us the Holy Spirit, so that we may say before him many songs."

B. In the opinion of Rabban Gamaliel, who said that the verse was stated by the ministering angels, [the sense of the verse, "O that you would kiss me with the kisses of your mouth"] is, "may he give us the kisses that he gave to his sons."

C. In the opinion of R. Meir, who said that the verse was stated in connection with the tent of meeting, [the sense of the verse, "O that you would kiss me with the kisses of your mouth"] is, "May he send fire down to us and so accept his offerings."

D. In the opinion of R. Yohanan, who said that the verse was stated in connection with Sinai, [the sense of the verse, "O that you would kiss me with the kisses of your mouth"] is, "May he cause kisses to issue for us from his mouth.

E. "That is why it is written, 'O that you would kiss me with the kisses of your mouth.'"

Our fixed list encompasses [1] Israel at the sea; [2] the ministering angels; [3] the tent of meeting; [4] the eternal house (the Temple); [5] Sinai. This is somewhat curious, mixing as it does occasions in time, locations, the place of the cult, and the Torah. But if we hold them together, we are given the theological repertoire of suitable verbal symbols or reference points: the redemption from Egypt, the Temple and its cult, and the revealed Torah of Sinai. This composite then is not only complementary in a general sense, it also is explicit in a very particular sense, specifying as it does the range of suitable assignees for the authorship and occasion of the poem, and that range then encompasses the acceptable theological vocabulary of—shall we say, Judaism? the Torah? the Midrash-exegesis of our verse? I am not sure of which, but it is clear to me that we may now expect a variety of such lists, a repertoire of those topics or points that all together add up to the relationship between God and Israel that the document portrays. Indeed, even now we may wish to propose that when we seek the theology of the Judaism of the dual Torah, we may do worse than to look at the way in which the Song of Songs is made into a metaphor for everything evocative of the relationship of God and Israel.

Let us attend to the specifics of the passage, if briefly. I.7 once again shows us that our compilers are first-class editors, since they have assembled quite disparate materials and drawn them together into a cogent statement. But the subject is not our base verse, and hence the compilers cannot have had in mind the need of a commentary of a verse-by-verse principle of compilation and organization. The passage as a whole refers in much more general terms to the Song of Songs, and hardly to Song of Songs 1:2 in particular. This is shown by the simple fact that various opinions invoke other verses than the one to which the whole is ultimately assigned. I.1 serves Song of Songs 1:1, and so does I.2. Indeed, I.2 could have been placed in the prior assembly without any damage to its use and meaning. The same is to be said for I.3. In fact, only Yohanan requires the verse to stand where it now does. I.5 and I.6 of course invoke Song of Songs 4:16 and do a fine job of reading that verse in light of the tent of meeting in the wilderness or the Temple in Jerusalem. Song of Songs 3:9-10 serves as an appropriate locus as well. Then the conclusion draws a variety of senses for Song of Songs 1:2 alone, and that conclusion points to the compilers of the whole for its authorship. This is once more a highly sophisticated work of compilation, involving rich editorial intervention indeed.

SONG OF SONGS RABBAH TO SONG OF SONGS 1:5

V:i

1. A. "I am very dark, but comely, [O daughters of Jerusalem, like the tents of Kedar, like the curtains of Solomon]" (Song of Songs 1:5):
   B. "I am dark" in my deeds.
   C. "But comely" in the deeds of my forebears.

2. A. "I am very dark, but comely:"
   B. Said the community of Israel, "'I am dark' in my view, 'but comely' before my Creator."
   C. For it is written, "Are you not as the children of the Ethiopians to Me, O children of Israel, says the Lord" (Amos 9:7):
   D. "as the children of the Ethiopians"—in your sight.
   E. But "to Me, O children of Israel, says the Lord."

3. A. Another interpretation of the verse, "I am very dark": in Egypt.
   B. "but comely": in Egypt.
   C. "I am very dark" in Egypt: "But they rebelled against me and would not hearken to me" (Ezekiel 20:8).
   D. "but comely" in Egypt: with the blood of the Passover offering and circumcision, "And when I passed by you and saw you wallowing in your blood, I said to you, In your blood live" (Ezekiel 16:6)—in the blood of the Passover.
   E. "I said to you, In your blood live" (Ezekiel 16:6)—in the blood of the circumcision.

4. A. Another interpretation of the verse, "I am very dark": at the sea, "They were rebellious at the sea, even the Red Sea" (Psalm 106:7).

B. "but comely": at the sea, "This is my God and I will be comely for him" (Exodus 15:2) [following Simon's rendering of the verse].

5. A. "I am very dark": at Marah, "And the people murmured against Moses, saying, What shall we drink" (Exodus 15:24).

B. "but comely": at Marah, "And he cried to the Lord and the Lord showed him a tree, and he cast it into the waters and the waters were made sweet" (Exodus 15:25).

6. A. "I am very dark": at Rephidim, "And the name of the place was called Massah and Meribah" (Exodus 17:7).

B. "but comely": at Rephidim, "And Moses built an altar and called it by the name 'the Lord is my banner' (Exodus 17:15)."

7. A. "I am very dark": at Horeb, "And they made a calf at Horeb" (Psalm 106:19).

B. "but comely": at Horeb, "And they said, All that the Lord has spoken we will do and obey" (Exodus 24:7).

8. A. "I am very dark": in the wilderness, "How often did they rebel against him in the wilderness" (Psalm 78:40).

B. "but comely": in the wilderness at the setting up of the tabernacle, "And on the day that the tabernacle was set up" (Numbers 9:15).

9. A. "I am very dark": in the deed of the spies, "And they spread an evil report of the land" (Numbers 13:32).

B. "but comely": in the deed of Joshua and Caleb, "Save for Caleb, the son of Jephunneh the Kenizzite" (Numbers 32:12).

10. A. "I am very dark": at Shittim, "And Israel abode at Shittim and the people began to commit harlotry with the daughters of Moab" (Numbers 25:1).

B. "but comely": at Shittim, "Then arose Phinehas and wrought judgment" (Psalm 106:30).

11. A. "I am very dark": through Achan, "But the children of Israel committed a trespass concerning the devoted thing" (Joshua 7:1).

B. "but comely": through Joshua, "And Joshua said to Achan, My son, give I pray you glory" (Joshua 7:19).

12. A. "I am very dark": through the kings of Israel.
    B. "but comely": through the kings of Judah.
    C. If with my dark ones that I had, it was such that "I am comely," all the more so with my prophets.

The contrast of dark and comely yields a variety of applications; in all of them the same situation that is the one also is the other, and the rest follows in a wonderfully well-crafted composition. What is the repertoire of items? Dark in deeds but comely in ancestry; dark in my view but comely before God; dark when rebellious, comely when obedient, a point made at V.i.3, for Egypt, V:i.4, for the sea, and V:i.5 for Marah, V:i.6, for Massah and Meribah, V:i.7 for Horeb, V:i.8 for the wilderness, V:i.9 for the spies in the Land, V:i.10 for Shittim, V:I.11 for Achan/Joshua and the conquest of the Land, V:i.12 for Israel and Judah. We therefore have worked through the repertoire of events that contained the mixture of rebellion and obedience; the theological substrate of this catalogue is hardly difficult to articulate. At VII:ii.5 we have the articulation:

V:ii.

5. A. [As to the verse, "I am very dark, but comely," R. Levi b. R. Haita gave three interpretations:
   B. "'I am very dark': all the days of the week.
   C. "'but comely': on the Sabbath.
   D. "'I am very dark': all the days of the year.
   E. "'but comely': on the Day of Atonement.
   F. "'I am very dark': among the Ten Tribes.
   G. "'but comely': in the tribe of Judah and Benjamin.
   H. "'I am very dark': in this world.
   I. "'but comely': in the world to come."

SONG OF SONGS RABBAH TO SONG OF SONGS 2:6

XXIII:i

1. A. "O that his left hand were under my head":
   B. this refers to the first tablets.
   C. "and that his right hand embraced me":
   D. this refers to the second tablets.

2. A. Another interpretation of the verse, "O that his left hand were under my head":
   B. this refers to the show-fringes.
   C. "and that his right hand embraced me":
   D. this refers to the phylacteries.

3. A. Another interpretation of the verse, "O that his left hand were under my head":
   B. this refers to the recitation of the *Shema.*
   C. "and that his right hand embraced me":
   D. this refers to the Prayer.

4. A. Another interpretation of the verse, "O that his left hand were under my head":
   B. this refers to the tabernacle.
   C. "and that his right hand embraced me":
   D. this refers to the cloud of the Presence of God in the world to come: "The sun shall no longer be your light by day nor for brightness will the moon give light to you" (Isaiah 60:19). Then what gives light to you? "The Lord shall be your everlasting light" (Isaiah 60:20).

Now our repertoire of reference points is [1] the Ten Commandments; [2] the show-fringes and phylacteries; [3] the *Shema* and the Prayer; [4] the tabernacle and the cloud of the Presence of God in the world to come. Why we invoke these as our candidates for the metaphor at hand and the *mezuzah*, seems to me clear from the very catalogue. These reach their climax in the analogy between the home and the tabernacle, the embrace of God and the Presence of God. So the whole is meant to list those things that draw the Israelite near God and make him cleave to God, as the base verse says, hence the right hand and the left stand for the most intimate components of the life of the individual and the home with God.

SONG OF SONGS RABBAH TO SONG OF SONGS 3:8

XXV:i
1. A. "The voice of my beloved! Behold he comes [leaping upon the mountains, bounding over the hills]":
   B. R. Judah and R. Nehemiah and Rabbis:
   C. R. Judah says, "'The voice of my beloved! Behold he comes': this refers to Moses.

D. "When he came and said to the Israelites, 'In this month you will be redeemed,' they said to him, 'Our lord, Moses, how are we going to be redeemed? And did not the Holy One, blessed be He, say to Abraham, "And they shall work them and torment them for four hundred years" (Genesis 15:13), and now we have in hand only two hundred and ten years!'

E. "He said to them, 'Since he wants to redeem you, he is not going to pay attention to these reckonings of yours.

F. "'But: "leaping upon the mountains, bounding over the hills." The reference here to mountains and hills in fact alludes to calculations and specified times. "He leaps" over reckonings, calculations, and specified times.

G. "'And in this month you are to be redeemed: "This month is the beginning of months" (Exodus 12:1).'"

2. A. R. Nehemiah says, "'The voice of my beloved! Behold he comes': this refers to Moses.

B. "When he came and said to the Israelites, 'In this month you will be redeemed,' they said to him, 'Our lord, Moses, how are we going to be redeemed? We have no good deeds to our credit.'

C. "He said to them, 'Since he wants to redeem you, he is not going to pay attention to bad deeds.'

D. "'And to what does he pay attention? To the righteous people among you and to their deeds,

E. "'for example, Amram and his court.

F. "'leaping upon the mountains, bounding over the hills:' mountains refers only to courts, in line with this usage: "I will depart and go down upon the mountains" (Judges 11:37).

G. "'And in this month you are to be redeemed: "This month is the beginning of months" (Exodus 12:1).'"

3. A. Rabbis say, "'The voice of my beloved! Behold he comes': this refers to Moses.

B. "When he came and said to the Israelites, 'In this month you will be redeemed,' they said to him, 'Our lord, Moses, how are we going to be redeemed? And the whole of Egypt is made filthy by our own worship of idols!'

C. "He said to them, 'Since he wants to redeem you, he is not going to pay attention to your worship of idols.

D. "'Rather, "leaping upon the mountains, bounding over the hills:" mountains and hills refer only to idolatry, in line with this usage: "They sacrifice on the tops of the mountains and offer upon the hills" (Hosea 4:13).

E. "'And in this month you are to be redeemed: "This month is the beginning of months" (Exodus 12:1).'"

4. A. R. Yudan and R. Hunia:

B. R. Yudan in the name of R. Eliezer son of R. José the Galilean, and R. Hunia in the name of R. Eliezer b. Jacob say, "'The voice of my beloved! Behold he comes': this refers to the royal Messiah.

C. "When he says to the Israelites, 'In this month you are to be redeemed, they will say to him, 'How are we going to be redeemed? And has not the Holy One, blessed be He, taken an oath that He would subjugate us among the seventy nations.'

D. "Now he will reply to them in two ways.

E. "He will say to them, 'If one of you is taken into exile to Barbary and one to Sarmatia, it is as though all of you had gone into exile.

F. "'And not only so, but this state conscripts troops from all of the world and from every nation, so that if one Samaritan or one Barbarian comes and subjugates you, it is as though his entire nation had ruled over you and as if you were subjugated by all the seventy nations.

G. "'In this month you are to be redeemed: "This month is the beginning of months" (Exodus 12:1).'"

XXV:i.1–3 form a perfectly matched set; remove one and you lose the whole. A fixed catalogue emerges, which can be used in any number of ways to exploit available metaphors. The items go over the trilogy of the timing of redemption, the moral condition of those to be redeemed, and the past religious misdeeds of those to be redeemed. Against these three arguments Moses argues that God will redeem at God's own time, as an act of grace and forgiveness. The theological message emerges with enormous power through invoking the love of God for Israel, God "leaping upon the mountains." One cannot point to a better or more telling example of the rewards accruing to the framers of the document from their decision to work on just this part of Scripture. The obvious necessity of XXV:i.4 to complete the message requires no comment. Any conception that the individual units come first, then the completed composition, seems to me to take second place before the notion that the plan of the whole—as a theological statement, I mean—came prior to the formation of the parts. Then it hardly matters whose names are tacked on to the formally matched and perfect components. The examples suffice to show what I think is in play in this mode of holding together a large mass of discrete and completed material. The logical method of the *davar-aher* construction derives from learning within the intellectual discipline of *Listenwissenschaft* and refers us directly to the method of the framers of the Mishnah. Sequences of comments on the same verse, joined by "another matter," mean to establish compositions of taxically joined facts, that is to say, lists. And as soon as we recognize that obvious fact, we are drawn back to the Mishnah's method, which is that of list-making as well. But learning accomplished through list-making, that is, *Listenwissenschaft*, in the philosophical setting of the Mishnah, differs vastly from the same method of learning worked out in the theological setting of Song of Songs *Rabbah*. The difference, as we shall soon see, is the propositional character of the former, in which lists make points, contrasted with the merely presentational character of the latter, in which lists portray different things that evoke the same attitude without proving how different things prove the same point.

The reason for the difference in the methods of the two list-making documents is blatant. In the Mishnah, philosophy sets forth a system, dynamic and dialectical in character, while in Song of Songs, the theology sets forth a structure, static and unchanging in its display of fixed truth about God and God's relationship with Israel. Were we to catalogue the propositions of our document, stated in the language of philosophical discourse, they would repeatedly set forth the same point: God loves Israel, Israel loves God, and the Torah is the medium of that reciprocal love. However diverse the language and however original the arrangement of the theological "things" that convey that message, the message is uniform throughout, and the articulation is essentially through the repetition in marginally different theological *things* of the same thing: *davar-aher* really does stand for *another matter* that is, in fact, the same matter. So the same method of learning is used for different purposes, the one philosophical, systematizing the evidence of nature, the other theological, recapitulating the evidence of supernature revealed by God in the Torah.

The Mishnah's method, its logic of cogent discourse establishes propositions that rest upon philosophical bases, for example, through the proposal of a thesis and the composition of a list of facts that (through shared traits of a taxonomic order) prove the thesis. The Mishnah presents rules and treats stories (inclusive of history) as incidental and of merely taxonomic interest. Its logic is propositional, and its intellect does its work through a vast labor of classification, comparison, and contrast generating governing rules and generalizations. So, stated very simply, a document such as Song of Songs *Rabbah*, that consists mainly of lists, requires us to compare its method, the *davar-aher* construction, with the method of the Mishnah. The two documents have in common the method of list-making, but they differ very profoundly on the respective uses of their lists.

List-making, which places on display the data of the like and the unlike, implicitly (ordinarily, not explicitly) conveys the rule. Once a series is established, the authorship assumes, the governing rule will be perceived. That explains why, in exposing the interior logic of its authorship's intellect, the Mishnah had to be a book of lists, with the implicit order, the nomothetic traits of a monothetic order, dictating the ordinarily unstated general and encompassing rule. The purpose of list-making in the Mishnah is to repeat a single statement endlessly, and to endlessly repeat in a mass of tangled detail precisely the same fundamental judgment. To form their lists, the framers of the Mishnah appeal solely to the traits of things. The logical basis of coherent speech and discourse in the Mishnah then derives from *Listenwissenschaft*. That mode of thought defines a way of proving propositions through classification, so establishing a set of shared traits that form a rule which compels us to reach a given conclusion. Probative facts derive from the classification of data, all of which point in one direction and not in another.

When in Song of Songs *Rabbah* we have a sequence of items alleged to form taxon, that is, a set of things that share a common taxic indicator, of course what we have is a list. The list presents diverse matters that all together share, and therefore also set forth, a single fact or rule or phenomenon. That is why we can list them, in all their distinctive character and specificity, in a common catalogue of "other things" that pertain all together to one thing. And this draws us to the difference between the Mishnah's *Listenwissenschaft* and that of Song of Songs *Rabbah*. In the document before us the *purpose* is the list. For while we can point to a conclusion for which the Mishnah's authorship uses its list, we can rarely point to a similar conclusion—a proposition important to the components of the list but transcending them—that forms the centerpiece of the discourse. Rather, what we find is a list made up of this and that, combined in one way rather than another, connected to this item, rather than that. Absent a propositional goal closely tied to the items on the list in the way in which the proposition about the hierarchical superiority of the monarch transcends the items on the list we examined in the Mishnah, the display of an arrangement of the items forms the goal of the intellectual enterprise.

What is set on display justifies the display: putting this familiar fact together with that familiar fact in an unfamiliar combination constitutes what is new and important in the list; the consequent conclusion one is supposed to draw, the proposition or rule that emerges—these are rarely articulated (my list of propositional composites shows the possibility) and never important.

True, the list in Song of Songs *Rabbah* may comprise a rule, or it may substantiate a proposition or validate a claim; but more often than not, the effect of making the list is to show how various items share a single taxic indicator. What I find engaging in *davar-aher* constructions is the very variety of things that, on one list or another, can be joined together—a list for its own sake. What we have is a kind of subtle restatement, through an infinite range of possibilities, of the combinations and recombinations of a few essentially simple facts (data). It is as though a magician tossed a set of sticks this way and that, interpreting the diverse combinations of a fixed set of objects. The propositions that emerge are not the main point; the combinations are.

The *davar-aher* constructions we have reviewed provide a fine case in point. I could identify among them no fixed list of items, though some recurred, for example, first redemption (the sea), second redemption (the return to Zion), third redemption (the end of time or the Messiah); Abraham, Isaac, Jacob; Moses, Aaron, Miriam; Moses, David, Messiah, and so on. But if we were to set side-by-side and then catalogue all of the exegetical repertoire encompassed by *davar-aher* constructions, we should have a very long list of candidates for inclusion in any list, and nearly as long a list of groups of candidates that are included in some lists. What are listed are not data of nature but of theology: God's relationship with Israel, expressed in such facts as the three redemptions, the three patriarchs, and holy persons, actions, events, what-have-you. These are facts that are assembled and grouped, just as in the Mishnah, traits of persons, places, things, actions, are assembled and grouped. In the Mishnah the result is propositions, rules; in Song of Songs *Rabbah* the result is not propositional at all, or, if propositional, then essentially the repetition of familiar propositions through unfamiliar data.

That seems to me an important fact, for it tells me that a repertoire of persons and events and conceptions (Torah-study), holy persons, holy deeds, holy institutions, presented candidates for inclusion in *davar-aher* constructions, and the repertoire, while restricted and not terribly long, made possible a scarcely limited variety of lists of things with like taxic indicators. That is to say, the same items occur over and over again, but there is no pattern to how they recur. By pattern I mean that items of the repertoire may appear in numerous *davar-aher* constructions or not; they may keep company with only a fixed number of other items, or they may not. A fixed unit is formed by Abraham, Isaac, and Jacob. But a fixed unit is not formed by Jacob, Moses, and Hananiah, Mishael, and Azariah. We have a fixed unit in the three redemptions but not in the holy way of life sequences, the destruction of the Temple sequences, and the patriarch sequences. Where we have fixed companions, such as the patriarchs or the three redemptions, these rarely form the generative structure of the *davar-aher* construction in which they occur, and ordinarily they do not. But when we ask, is there a counterpart definition of items drawn from the fixed repertoire that ordinarily occur together, the answer is, not at all. Most things can appear in a *davar-aher* composition with most other things. No clear pattern has as yet struck me very forcefully. What that means is that the list-making is accomplished within a restricted repertoire of items that can serve on lists; the list-making then presents interesting combinations of an essentially small number of candidates for the exercise. But then, when making lists, one can do pretty much anything with the items that are combined; the taxic indicators are unlimited, but the data studied, severely limited. And that fact brings us to the question of the theological substrate and structure of our document.

The *davar-aher* construction constitutes a play on what I have now repeatedly called, for lack of more suitable language at this point, theological *things*,[2]—names, places, events, actions deemed to bear theological weight and to affect attitude and action. The play is worked out by a reprise of available materials, composed in some fresh and interesting combination. When three or more such theological *things* are combined in a given document, they constitute the components of the *entire* theological structure that the document affords. The propositions por-

---

[2] I find myself at a loss for a better word choice and must at this stage resort to the hopelessly inelegant, *theological things*, to avoid having to repeat the formula that seems to me to fit the data, namely, names, places, events, actions deemed to bear theological weight and to affect attitude and action. Still, better a simple Anglo-Saxon formulation than a fancy German or Greek or Latin one. And Hebrew, should anyone be interested, whether Mishnaic or modern, simply does not serve for analytical work except when thought conceived in some other language is translated into Hebrew.

trayed visually, through metaphors of sight, or dramatically, through metaphors of action and relationship, or in attitude and emotion, through metaphors that convey or provoke feeling and sentiment, when translated into language prove familiar and commonplace. The work of the theologian in this context is not to say something new or even persuasive, for the former is unthinkable by definition, the latter unnecessary in context. It is, rather, to display theological *things* in a fresh and interesting way, to accomplish a fresh exegesis of the canon of theological *things*.

Let me begin my account of how the *davar-aher* construction of Song of Songs *Rabbah* affords access to theology as the list of comparison and contrast of the Mishnah affords access to philosophy by a simple statement of the theological structure I find expressed in Song of Songs *Rabbah*. It derives from the uses of the metaphor of the nut-tree, but it could as well have come from any number of other metaphors in our document—or drawn upon all of them together. What do the compilers say through their readings of the metaphor of the nut-tree for Israel? First, Israel prospers when it gives up scarce resources for the study of the Torah or for carrying out religious duties; second, Israel sins but atones, and Torah is the medium of atonement; third, Israel is identified through carrying out its religious duties, circumcision, for example; fourth, Israel's leaders had best watch their step; fifth, Israel may be nothing now but will be in glory in the coming age; sixth, Israel has plenty of room for outsiders, but cannot afford to lose a single insider. What we have is a repertoire of fundamentals, dealing with Torah and Torah-study, the moral life and atonement, Israel and its holy way of life, Israel and its coming salvation. Nothing is left out, so far as one can see.

Do these propositions correspond in their way to any of the composites of figures, events, actions, and the like, of which our *davar-aher* composites are made up? A sustained survey of these composites shows the contradictory facts that the several composites are heterogeneous, but the components of the composites derive from a rather limited list, essentially scriptural events and personalities, on the one side, and virtues of the Torah's holy way of life, on the other. Here is a survey of the bulk of the sequences of components drawn from Scripture and the repertoire of virtues of the Torah.

Joseph, righteous men, Moses, and Solomon
Patriarchs as against princes, offerings as against merit, and Israel
 as against the nations
Those who love the king, proselytes, martyrs, penitents
Israel at Sinai

Israel's loss of God's presence because of the golden calf

God's favoring Israel by treating Israel, not with justice, but with mercy

Dathan and Abiram, the spies, Jeroboam, Solomon's marriage to Pharaoh's daughter, Ahab, Jezebel, Zedekiah

Israel is feminine, the enemy (Egypt) masculine, but God the father saves Israel the daughter

Moses and Aaron, the Sanhedrin, the teachers of Scripture and Mishnah, the rabbis

The disciples

The relationship among disciples, public recitation of teachings of the Torah in the right order

Lections of the Torah

The spoil at the sea = the Exodus, the Torah, the Tabernacle, the ark

The patriarchs, Abraham, Isaac, Jacob, then Israel in Egypt, Israel's atonement and God's forgiveness

The Temple where God and Israel are joined, the Temple as God's resting place, the Temple as the source of Israel's fecundity

Israel in Egypt, at the Sea, at Sinai, and subjugated by the Gentile kingdoms, and how the redemption will come

Rebecca, those who came forth from Egypt, Israel at Sinai, acts of lovingkindness, the kingdoms who now rule Israel, the coming redemption

Fire above, fire below, (heavenly and altar fires)

Torah in writing, Torah in memory

Fire of Abraham, Moriah, bush, Elijah, Hananiah, Mishael, and Azariah

The Ten Commandments, *tallit* and phylacteries, recitation of the *Shema* and the Prayer, the tabernacle and the cloud of the Presence of God, the *mezuzah*

The timing of redemption, the moral condition of those to be redeemed, and the past religious misdeeds of those to be redeemed

Israel at the sea, Sinai, the Ten Commandments

The synagogues and school houses

The redeemer

The Exodus, the conquest of the Land, the redemption and restoration of Israel to Zion after the destruction of the first Temple, the final and ultimate salvation

The Egyptians, Esau and his generals, and, finally, the four kingdoms

Moses's redemption, the first to the second redemption in the time of the Babylonians and Daniel

The litter of Solomon, the priestly blessing, the priestly watches, the
   Sanhedrin, and the Israelites coming out of Egypt
Israel at the sea and forgiveness for sins effected by their passing
   through the sea
Israel at Sinai
The war with Midian
The crossing of the Jordan and entry into the Land
The house of the sanctuary
The priestly watches
The offerings in the Temple
The Sanhedrin
The Day of Atonement
God redeemed Israel without preparation
The nations of the world will be punished, after Israel is punished
The nations of the world will present Israel as a gift to the royal
   Messiah, and here the base verse refers to Abraham, Isaac, Jacob,
   Sihon, Og, Canaanites
The return to Zion in the time of Ezra, the Exodus from Egypt in
   the time of Moses
The patriarchs, and with Israel in Egypt, at the sea, and then before
   Sinai
Abraham, Jacob, Moses
Isaac, Jacob, Esau, Jacob, Joseph, the brothers, Jonathan, David,
   Saul, man, wife, paramour
Abraham in the fiery furnace, and Shadrach, Meshach, and Abednego,
   the Exile in Babylonia, now with reference to the return to Zion
—and so forth.

These components form not a theological system, made up of well-
joined propositions and harmonious positions, nor can one discern in the
several lists propositions that can be specified and are demonstrated
syllogistically through comparison and contrast. The point is just the
opposite; it is to show that many different things really do belong on the
same list. The list yields only itself, but, to be sure, invites exegesis,
which can then constitute a canon of selected items. So the list here is the
opposite of the syllogistic and propositional list of the Mishnah; it is a
canon of items, canonical because selected, and the connections among
these items require exegesis (or eisegesis). What this adds up to, then, is
not argument for proposition, hence comparison and contrast and rule-
making of a philosophical order, but rather a theological structure comprising well-defined attitudes.

While, as previously stated, the listed items can have yielded propositions, what is important in the *davar-aher* constructions is not the proposition but the interesting array and arrangement of the components of the *davar-aher* constructions themselves. That is why I have shown that the *davar-aher* construction serves without consequential propositional result, even though it frequently yields some sort of commonplace affirmation. But the details, where the framers have put their best work, serve to repeat in many ways that one point. In the Mishnah's counterpart, the details serve to demonstrate a proposition. The difference then seems to be that the Mishnah's list contributes toward a system, while Song of Songs *Rabbah's* list portrays a structure. The theological purpose therefore is to arrange and rearrange a few simple propositions, represented by a limited vocabulary of symbols. In such a structure we organize set-piece tableaux, rather than putting forth and demonstrating propositions. Philosophy's syllogistic argument in behalf of well-tested propositions contrasts with theology's evocation through well-arrayed symbols of correct attitudes.

In a word, we find in the *davar-aher* construction a selection, that is, a canon, of things that pertain to theology, chosen out of a larger but still highly restricted canon of candidates, all serving, each in itself, all in various combinations and recombinations, a single purpose: to portray in many ways, but in a systematic and orderly manner, the representation of God's relationship to Israel. The relationship is one of love, and that is always the same. However, it is a relationship of many splendors, captured, in all those aspects and objects that contain and express and convey the love: whether the Torah and its study, whether Moses and David, whether the "event"[3] at the sea and at Sinai. To identify that canon—the theological *things* on the list, the source of those *things*, the way in which those *things* combine and recombine to form a cogent portrait—we consult the combinations and recombinations defined for us by our document. Then the *davar-aher* construction forms a theological structure within a larger theological structure, a reworking of canonical materials.

It follows that *another matter* is the same matter said in different words. *Another matter* really is the same thing twice. Is there then a

---

[3] I put "event" into quotation marks, because in this context, it cannot possibly mean what it means in ordinary and secular contexts. This event is neither a singular happening nor a paradigm; it is something else. A "symbol" would be equally misleading.

fixed symbolic vocabulary to which our authorships repeatedly appeal, and which we can discover and define? If we can, then we shall have taken a long step toward the identification, through correct method, of the theology of the Judaism of the dual Torah. For then we shall know precisely how to identify those theological *things*, those symbols, whether expressed visually or conveyed in words, that for this Judaism constitute the theological language and therefore define the theological structure—the syntax of intellect, if not the grammar of speech—of this Judaism.

At stake in this analysis of the Midrash is a basic question, namely, the description of the theological structure and system of the Judaism of the dual Torah, for until now, in my judgment, we have had no method both coherent with the character of the documents and also coherent with the tasks of theological description. By theological description I mean the account of the principles and ideas concerning God's relationship with Israel (for we speak of a Judaism) that form the foundation and substrate of the thought that comes to expression in a variety of canonical writings. The problem has been the character of the documents and its mode of theological discourse. It is not that the writers speak only in concrete terms; we could readily move from their detail to our abstraction and speak in general terms about the coherence of prevailing principles of a theological order. The problem has been much more profound. We face a set of writings that clearly mean to tell us about God and God's relationship to Israel and Israel's relationship to God. The authorships a priori exhibit the conviction that the thoughts of the whole are cogent and coherent, since they prove deeply concerned to identify contradiction, disharmony, and incoherence, and remove it. But we have not known how to find the connections between what they have written and the structure or system of thought that leads them to say, in detail, the things that they say.

When we propose to describe the theological system to which a piece of well-crafted writing testifies, our task is simplified when the piece, at the outset, discusses in syllogistic logic and within an appropriate program of propositions what we conceive to be theological themes or problems. Hence—it is generally conceded—we may legitimately translate the topically theological writings of Paul, Augustine, or Luther into the systematic and coherent theologies of those three figures, respectively, finding order and structure in materials of a cogent theological character. But how to deal with a literature that does not set forth theological propositions in philosophical form, even while using profoundly religious language for self-evidently religious purposes? Surely that literature testifies to an orderly structure or system of thought, for the alternative would be to impute to those writings the status of mere episodic and unsystematic observations about this and that. True, profound expressions of piety may exhibit the traits of intellectual chaos and disorder, and holy simplicity may mask confusion. But, as I have already stressed, such a description of the rabbinic literature of late antiquity, which I call the canon of the Judaism of the dual Torah, defines the most definitive and indicative traits of the writings. These are order, system, cogency, coherence, proportion, fine and well-crafted thought.

The Mishnah, with which the writing begins, is a profoundly philosophical statement; the two Talmuds presuppose the harmony and unity of the conceptions of the Mishnah and their own conceptions; the various Midrash-compilations make statements that exhibit intellectual integrity; they do not show the marks of confusion and contradiction, only of variety and richness, and they assuredly do not merely compile ad hoc and episodic observations. The results of this survey, showing that the compilers of each of these documents proposed to say one thing in a great many ways, hardly sustain the (wrong-headed) thesis that the Midrash-compilations cannot be read as expressions of orderly minds. So, by their own character, these writings point toward some sort of logic and order and structure that as a matter of fact find attestation in the writings themselves. And when we seek to articulate the principles of order and structure as these pertain to the fundamental characteristics of God, the Torah, and Israel, we set forth the theology of the canon of the Judaism of the dual Torah.

Now the simple and well-acknowledged fact of the yearning for order and structure characteristic of that Judaism leads us to the question of these essays: How to move from literature to the description of a theological system that gives sense, structure, and cogency to the literature's fundamental convictions? What is the theology, or what are the theologies, that make the literature what it is: coherent in sense and in meaning? That is the question that faces anyone who wants to know whether the canonical literature of the Judaism of the dual Torah constitutes a mass of discrete observations about this and that or a well-crafted structure and system. For the canonical writings, appealing to God's revelation to Moses at Sinai, everywhere calling upon God and spelling out what God wants of Israel in quest of God and God's service, form one of the great religious writings of humanity. But do these writings yield theology, in addition to religion? That is to say, can we see them as system, structure, order, or merely as a vast and confusing mass of half-coherent thoughts? And how are we to test the perception of order amid the appearance of chaos, such as these writings, this literature, creates?

To begin with, we have to justify the theological inquiry into literature that self-evidently does not conform to the conventions of theological discourse to which Western civilization with its Greco-Roman heritage, and Christian (as well as Muslim) civilization, in its philosophical
formulation has accustomed us. The Muslim and Christian theological
heritage, formulated within the conventions of philosophical argument,
joined by a much smaller Judaic theological corpus, to be sure, does not
allow us to read as a theological statement a single canonical writing of
the Judaism of the dual Torah of late antiquity. So if the literary canons
of Western theology are to govern, then the literature of Judaism, in its
formative age by definition, can present no theological order and system
at all.

But that proposition on the face of it hardly proves compelling. For it
is difficult for us to imagine a mental universe so lacking in structure,
form, and order as to permit everything and its opposite to be said about
God, to imagine a God so confused and self-contradictory as to yield a
revelation lacking all cogency and truly unintelligible.[4] The very premises of all theology—that there is order, structure, and composition,
proportion, and form in God's mind, which in fact is intelligible to us
through the medium of revelation properly construed—a priori render

---

[4]As a matter of fact, the great Zoroastrian theologians of the ninth century
criticized Judaism (and other religions) on just this point; see my "Zoroastrian
Critique of Judaism," reprinted in my *History of the Jews in Babylonia* (Leiden:
E. J. Brill, 1969) 4:403-423. But not a single Judaic thinker, whether a philosopher or a theologian, whether in the Islamic philosophical tradition or the
Western theological and philosophical tradition, has ever entertained the proposition that the God who gave the Torah is confused and arbitrary; and why
should anyone have thought so, when, after all, the entire dynamic of Judaic
thought embodied within the great halakhic tradition from the Yerushalmi and
Bavli on has aimed at the systematization, harmonization, and ordering of
confusing, but never confused, facts of the Torah. There is, therefore, no possibility of finding in the Judaism of the dual Torah the slightest hint of an unsystematic system, an atheological corpus of thought. True, a fixed truth of the
theological system known as *die Wissenschaft des Judenthums* has maintained
that "Judaism has no theology," but that system knew precisely what it meant by
Judaism, even while never explaining what it might mean by *theology* that that
Judaism did not have. But that is a problem of description, analysis, and interpretation for those who take an interest in the system of thought that underpins
Jewish scholarship (and Reform Judaism in particular) those specialists in the
history of ideas in the nineteenth century, and of the nineteenth century in the
twentieth century. These are not statements of fact that must be taken into
account in describing, analyzing, and interpreting documents of the Judaism of
the dual Torah.

improbable the hypothesis that the canonical writings of the Judaism of the dual Torah violate every rule of intelligible discourse concerning the principle and foundation of all being. If, after all, we really cannot speak intelligibly about God, the Torah, holy Israel, and what God wants of us, then why write all those books to begin with?

The character of the Midrash-literature, its rather hermetic modes of discourse, arcane language of thought, insistence on speaking only about detail and rarely about the main point—these traits stand in the way of the description of theology because of their very unsyllogistic character. And yet, if we consider not the received modes of discourse of theology in our civilization but rather the problem and topic of theology—systematic and orderly thinking about God through the medium of revelation—we can hardly find a more substantial or suitable corpus of writing for theological analysis than the literature of the Judaism of the dual Torah.

For while theology may comprise propositions well crafted into a cogent structure, about fundamental questions of God and revelation, the social entity that realizes that revelation, the attitudes and deeds that God, through revelation, requires of humanity, there is another way entirely. Theology—the structure and system, the perception of order and meaning of God, in God, through God—these may make themselves known in ways other than through the media of thought and expression that yield belief that, theology can deliver its message to and through sentiment and emotion, heart as much as mind; it can be conviction as much as position, and conviction for its part also is orderly, proportioned, compelling of mind and intellect by reason of right attitude, rather than right proposition or position. That is to say, theology may set forth a system of thought in syllogistic arguments concerning the normative truths of the world view, social entity, and way of life of a religious system. But theology may speak in other than dynamic and compelling argument, and theologians may accomplish their goal of speaking truth about God through other than the statements made by language and in conformity with the syntax of reasoned thought.

Theology may also address vision and speak in tactile ways; it may utilize a vocabulary of, not proposition, but opaque symbol (whether conveyed in visual or verbal media). And through portraying symbol, theology may affect attitude and emotion, speak its truth through media other than those of philosophy and proposition. From the time of Martin Buber's *Two Types of Faith* (nearly four decades ago), people have understood that this other type of theology, the one that lives in attitude and sentiment and that evokes and demands trust, may coexist, or even compete with the philosophical type to the discourse of which, in general, we are accustomed.

᛭Ruth *Rabbah*, and Song of Songs *Rabbah* make theological statements. These statements are not episodic but systematically presented; they are repeated over and over again. That justifies my claim to know the difference between a document that falls into the category of theological discourse and one that does not but is, rather, of philosophical genre, purpose, and character. These four compilations, all of them generally regarded as belonging in the same age as the Talmud of Babylonia, as a matter of simple fact make theological, only theological, and only a few theological statements. That is the upshot of these four volumes of introduction to the Midrash-compilations of the sixth and seventh centuries, at the conclusion and—with the Bavli—the triumphant climax of the age of the formation of the Judaism of the dual Torah.

Bibliography of Midrash Studies

BIBLIOGRAPHY OF THE RABBINIC LITERATURE

The Study of Ancient Judaism. New York: Ktav, 1981: I–II.

I.   *The Study of Ancient Judaism: Mishnah, Midrash, Siddur.*
II. *The Study of Ancient Judaism: The Palestinian and Baby-lonian Talmuds.* Second printing: 1988.

TRANSLATIONS AND STUDIES OF MIDRASH COMPILATIONS AND THEIR CONTENTS

Aphrahat and Judaism. The Christian Jewish Argument in Fourth Century Iran. Leiden: Brill, 1971.

Development of a Legend. Studies on the Traditions Concerning Yohanan ben Zakkai. Leiden: Brill, 1970.

The Rabbinic Traditions about the Pharisees before 70. Leiden: Brill, 1971: I–III.

I.   *The Rabbinic Traditions about the Pharisees before 70. The Masters.*
II. *The Rabbinic Traditions about the Pharisees before 70. The Houses.*

221

III.   *The Rabbinic Traditions about the Pharisees before 70. Conclusions.*

Eliezer ben Hyrcanus. The Tradition and the Man. Leiden: Brill, 1973: I–II.

    I.   *Eliezer ben Hyrcanus. The Tradition and the Man. The Tradition.*

    II.   *Eliezer ben Hyrcanus. The Tradition and the Man. The Man.*

Torah from Our Sages: Pirke Avot. A New American Translation and Explanation. Chappaqua: Rossel, 1983. Paperback edition: 1987.

For Leviticus *Rabbah*, see *Judaism and Scripture: The Evidence of Leviticus Rabbah.*

Genesis Rabbah. The Judaic Commentary on Genesis. A New American Translation. Atlanta: Scholars Press for Brown Judaic Studies, 1985: I–III.

    I.   *Genesis Rabbah. The Judaic Commentary on Genesis. A New American Translation. Parashiyyot One through Thirty-Three. Genesis 1:1–8:14.*

    II.   *Genesis Rabbah. The Judaic Commentary on Genesis. A New American Translation. Parashiyyot Thirty-Four through Sixty-Seven. Genesis 8:15–28:9.*

    III.   *Genesis Rabbah. The Judaic Commentary on Genesis. A New American Translation. Parashiyyot Sixty-Eight through One Hundred. Genesis 28:10–50:26.*

Sifra. The Judaic Commentary on Leviticus. A New Translation. The Leper. Leviticus 13:1–14:57. Chico: Scholars Press for Brown Judaic Studies, 1985. With a section by Roger Brooks. Based on *A History of the Mishnaic Law of Purities. VI. Negaim. Sifra.*

Sifré to Numbers. An American Translation. I. 1–58. Atlanta: Scholars Press for Brown Judaic Studies, 1986.

Sifré to Numbers. An American Translation. II. 59–115. Atlanta: Scholars Press for Brown Judaic Studies, 1986. III. *116–161*: William Scott Green.

The Fathers According to Rabbi Nathan. An Analytical Translation and Explanation. Atlanta: Scholars Press for Brown Judaic Studies, 1986.

Pesiqta deRab Kahana. An Analytical Translation and Explanation. I. *1-14.* Atlanta: Scholars Press for Brown Judaic Studies, 1987.

Pesiqta deRab Kahana. An Analytical Translation and Explanation. II. *15-28. With an Introduction to Pesiqta deRab Kahana.* Atlanta: Scholars Press for Brown Judaic Studies, 1987.

For Pesiqta Rabbati, see *From Tradition to Imitation. The Plan and Program of Pesiqta deRab Kahana and Pesiqta Rabbati.*

Sifré to Deuteronomy. An Analytical Translation. Atlanta: Scholars Press for Brown Judaic Studies, 1987. I. *Pisqaot One through One Hundred Forty-Three. Debarim, Waethanan, Eqeb, Re'eh.*

Sifré to Deuteronomy. An Analytical Translation. Atlanta: Scholars Press for Brown Judaic Studies, 1987. II. *Pisqaot One Hundred Forty-Four through Three Hundred Fifty-Seven. Shofetim, Ki Tese, Ki Tabo, Nesabim, Ha'azinu, Zot Habberakhah.*

Sifré to Deuteronomy. An Introduction to the Rhetorical, Logical, and Topical Program. Atlanta: Scholars Press for Brown Judaic Studies, 1987.

Sifra. An Analytical Translation. Atlanta: Scholars Press for Brown Judaic Studies, 1988: I-III.

    I.   *Introduction* and *Vayyiqra Dibura Denedabah* and *Vayiqra Dibura Dehobah.*
    II. *Sav, Shemini, Tazria, Negaim, Mesora,* and *Zabim.*
    III. *Aharé Mot, Qedoshim, Emor, Behar,* and *Behuqotai.*

Uniting the Dual Torah: Sifra and the Problem of the Mishnah. Cambridge and New York: Cambridge University Press, 1989.

Sifra in Perspective: The Documentary Comparison of the Midrashim of Ancient Judaism. Atlanta: Scholars Press for Brown Judaic Studies, 1988.

Mekhilta Attributed to R. Ishmael. An Analytical Translation. Atlanta: Scholars Press for Brown Judaic Studies, 1988. I. *Pisha, Beshallah, Shirata, and Vayassa.*

Mekhilta Attributed to R. Ishmael. An Analytical Translation. Atlanta: Scholars Press for Brown Judaic Studies, 1988. II. *Amalek, Bahodesh, Neziqin, Kaspa and Shabbata.*

Mekhilta Attributed to R. Ishmael. An Introduction to Judaism's First Scriptural Encyclopaedia. Atlanta: Scholars Press for Brown Judaic Studies, 1988.

Translating the Classics of Judaism. In Theory and in Practice. Atlanta: Scholars Press for Brown Judaic Studies, 1989.

Lamentations Rabbah. An Analytical Translation. Atlanta: Scholars Press for Brown Judaic Studies, 1989.

Esther Rabbah I. An Analytical Translation. Atlanta: Scholars Press for Brown Judaic Studies, 1989.

Ruth Rabbah. An Analytical Translation. Atlanta: Scholars Press for Brown Judaic Studies, 1989.

Song of Songs Rabbah. An Analytical Translation. Volume One. *Song of Songs Rabbah to Song Chapters One through Three.* Atlanta: Scholars Press for Brown Judaic Studies, 1990.

Song of Songs Rabbah. An Analytical Translation. Volume Two. *Song of Songs Rabbah to Song Chapters Four through Eight.* Atlanta: Scholars Press for Brown Judaic Studies, 1990.

The Midrash Compilations of the Sixth and Seventh Centuries. An Introduction to the Rhetorical Logical, and Topical Program. Atlanta: Scholars Press for Brown Judaic Studies, 1990: I-IV.

  I.   *Lamentations Rabbah.*
  II.   *Esther Rabbah I.*
  III. *Ruth Rabbah.*
  IV.   *Song of Songs Rabbah.*

The Integrity of Leviticus Rabbah. The Problem of the Autonomy of a Rabbinic Document. Chico: Scholars Press for Brown Judaic Studies, 1985.

Comparative Midrash: The Plan and Program of Genesis Rabbah and Leviticus Rabbah. Atlanta: Scholars Press for Brown Judaic Studies, 1986.

From Tradition to Imitation. The Plan and Program of Pesiqta deRab Kahana and Pesiqta Rabbati. Atlanta: Scholars Press for Brown Judaic Studies, 1987. With a fresh translation of *Pesiqta Rabbati Pisqaot* 1-5, 15.

Canon and Connection: Intertextuality in Judaism. Lanham: University Press of America, 1986. *Studies in Judaism* series.

Midrash as Literature: The Primacy of Documentary Discourse. Lanham: University Press of America, 1987. *Studies in Judaism* series.

Invitation to Midrash: The Working of Rabbinic Bible Interpretation. A Teaching Book. San Francisco: Harper & Row, 1988.

What Is Midrash? Philadelphia: Fortress Press, 1987.
    Dutch translation: Hilversum: Gooi & Sticht, 1989.
    Japanese translation: Tokyo: Kyo Bun Kwan, 1990.

A Midrash Reader. Minneapolis: Augsburg-Fortress, 1990.

Making the Classics in Judaism: The Three Stages of Literary Formation. Atlanta: Scholars Press for Brown Judaic Studies, 1990.

Judaism and Scripture: The Evidence of Leviticus Rabbah. Chicago: The University of Chicago Press, 1986. Fresh translation of Margulies' text and systematic analysis of problems of composition and redaction. Jewish Book Club selection, 1986.

Judaism and Story: The Evidence of the Fathers According to Rabbi Nathan. Chicago: University of Chicago Press, 1990.

The Foundations of Judaism. Method, Teleology, Doctrine. Philadelphia: Fortress Press, 1983-1985: I-III.

I. *Midrash in Context. Exegesis in Formative Judaism.* Atlanta: Scholars Press for Brown Judaic Studies, 1988. Second printing.

II. *Messiah in Context. Israel's History and Destiny in Formative Judaism.* Lanham: University Press of America, 1988. *Studies in Judaism* series. Second printing.

III. *Torah: From Scroll to Symbol in Formative Judaism.* Atlanta: Scholars Press for Brown Judaic Studies, 1988. Second printing.

The Foundations of Judaism. Philadelphia: Fortress, 1988. Abridged edition of the foregoing trilogy.

Dutch translation: Katholieke Bijbelstichting (in press).

The Oral Torah. The Sacred Books of Judaism. An Introduction. San Francisco: Harper & Row, 1985. Paperback: 1987. B'nai B'rith Jewish Book Club Selection, 1986.

Scriptures of the Old Torah. Sanctification and Salvation in the Sacred Books of Judaism. San Francisco: Harper & Row, 1987. Jewish Book Club Selection, 1988.

Vanquished Nation, Broken Spirit. The Virtues of the Heart in Formative Judaism. New York: Cambridge University Press, 1987. Jewish Book Club selection, 1987.

Judaism and Christianity in the Age of Constantine. Issues of the Initial Confrontation. Chicago: University of Chicago Press, 1987.

Judaism and Its Social Metaphors. Israel in the History of Jewish Thought. New York: Cambridge University Press, 1988.

The Incarnation of God: The Character of Divinity in Formative Judaism. Philadelphia: Fortress Press, 1988.

Writing with Scripture: The Authority and Uses of the Hebrew Bible in the Torah of Formative Judaism. Philadelphia: Fortress Press, 1989.

The Making of the Mind of Judaism. Atlanta: Scholars Press for Brown Judaic Studies, 1987.

The Formation of the Jewish Intellect. Making Connections and Drawing Conclusions in the Traditional System of Judaism. Atlanta: Scholars Press for Brown Judaic Studies, 1988.

The Christian and Judaic Invention of History. Atlanta: Scholars Press for American Academy of Religion, 1989. *Studies in Religion* series. Edited with William Scott Green.

Torah through the Ages. A Short History of Judaism. New York and London: Trinity Press International and SCM, 1990.

From Literature to Theology in Formative Judaism. Three Preliminary Studies. Atlanta: Scholars Press for Brown Judaic Studies, 1989.

From Mishnah to Scripture. The Problem of the Unattributed Saying. Chico: Scholars Press for Brown Judaic Studies, 1984. Reprise and reworking of materials in *A History of the Mishnaic Law of Purities.*

Oral Tradition in Judaism: The Case of the Mishnah. New York: Garland Publishing Co., 1987. *Albert Bates Lord Monograph Series* of the journal, *Oral Tradition.* Restatement of results in various works on the Mishnah together with a fresh account of the problem.

Ancient Judaism and Modern Category-Formation. "Judaism," "Midrash," "Messianism," and Canon in the Past Quarter-Century. Lanham: University Press of America, 1986. *Studies in Judaism* series.

From Description to Conviction. Essays on the History and Theology of Judaism. Atlanta: Scholars Press for Brown Judaic Studies, 1987.

Why No Gospels in Talmudic Judaism? Atlanta: Scholars Press for Brown Judaic Studies, 1988.

Formative Judaism. Religious, Historical, and Literary Studies. First Series. Chico: Scholars Press for Brown Judaic Studies, 1982.

Formative Judaism. Religious, Historical, and Literary Studies. Second Series. Chico: Scholars Press for Brown Judaic Studies, 1983.

Formative Judaism. Religious, Historical, and Literary Studies. Third Series. Torah, Pharisees, and Rabbis. Chico: Scholars Press for Brown Judaic Studies, 1983.

Formative Judaism. Religious, Historical, and Literary Studies. Fourth Series. Problems of Classification and Composition. Chico: Scholars Press for Brown Judaic Studies, 1984.

Formative Judaism. Religious, Historical, and Literary Studies. Fifth Series. Revisioning the Written Records of a Nascent Religion. Chico: Scholars Press for Brown Judaic Studies, 1985.

Formative Judaism. Religious, Historical, and Literary Studies. Sixth Series. Atlanta: Scholars Press for Brown Judaic Studies, 1989.

Major Trends in Formative Judaism. First Series. Society and Symbol in Political Crisis. Chico: Scholars Press for Brown Judaic Studies, 1983.

Major Trends in Formative Judaism. Second Series. Texts, Contents, and Contexts. Chico: Scholars Press for Brown Judaic Studies, 1984.

Major Trends in Formative Judaism. Third Series. The Three Stages in the Formation of Judaism. Chico: Scholars Press for Brown Judaic Studies, 1985.
    Italian translation: Casale Monferrato: Editrice Marietti, 1989.

The Religious Study of Judaism. Description, Analysis, Interpretation. Volumes I–IV. Lanham: University Press of America, 1986. *Studies in Judaism* series.

    Volume II. *The Centrality of Context*, 1986.
    Volume III. *Context, Text, and Circumstance*, 1987.
    Volume IV. *Ideas of History, Ethics, Ontology, and Religion in Formative Judaism*, 1988.

Understanding Seeking Faith. Essays on the Case of Judaism. Volumes I–III. Atlanta: Scholars Press for Brown Judaic Studies.

    Volume I. *Debates on Method, Reports of Results*, 1986.
    Volume II. *Literature, Religion, and the Social Study of Judaism*, 1987.
    Volume III. *Society, History, and the Political and Philosophical Uses of Judaism*, 1989.

Medium and Message in Judaism. First Series. Atlanta: Scholars Press for Brown Judaic Studies, 1989.

History and Torah. Essays on Jewish Learning. London: Vallentine, Mitchell, 1965. New York: Schocken Books, 1964, 1967.

Our Sages, God, and Israel. An Anthology of the Yerushalmi. Chappaqua: Rossel, 1984. 1985 selection, Jewish Book Club.

The Jewish War against the Jews. Reflections on Golah, Shoah, and Torah. New York: Ktav, 1984.

Genesis and Judaism: The Perspective of Genesis Rabbah. An Analytical Anthology. Atlanta: Scholars Press for Brown Judaic Studies, 1986.

Christian Faith and the Bible of Judaism. Grand Rapids, MI: Wm. B. Eerdmans Publishing Co., 1987.

Reading Scriptures: An Introduction to Rabbinic Midrash. With Special Reference to Genesis Rabbah. New York: Rossel/Behrman House, 1987.

From Testament to Torah: An Introduction to Judaism in Its Formative Age. Englewood Cliffs, NJ: Prentice Hall, 1987.

Index

231